CREATING A THIRD WORLD

Betsy, thank you in
I can not your support with
enough for my years with
my research during Latin American studies
the Center at at Latin friendship and
at KU. I truly value our researcher and
all I learned from you as a to see you soon
professor. Take care and hope

Your Rhode

CREATING A THIRD WORLD

MEXICO, CUBA, AND THE UNITED STATES

DURING THE CASTRO ERA

▼▼▼

CHRISTOPHER M. WHITE

UNIVERSITY OF NEW MEXICO PRESS

ALBUQUERQUE

© 2007 by the University of New Mexico Press
All rights reserved. Published in 2007
Printed in the United States of America

13 12 11 10 09 08 07   1 2 3 4 5 6 7

LIBRARY OF CONGRESS CATALOGING-IN-PUBLICATION DATA

White, Christopher M., 1974–
Creating a third world : Mexico, Cuba, and the
    United States during the Castro era / Christopher M. White.
    p. cm.
Includes bibliographical references and index.
ISBN 978-0-8263-4238-6 (pbk. : alk. paper)
1. Cuba—Relations—Mexico.
2. Mexico—Relations—Cuba.
3. United States—Relations—Mexico.
4. Mexico—Relations—United States.
I. Title.
    F1228.5.C9W55 2007
    327.720729109′045—dc22

2007015445

DESIGN AND COMPOSITION: *Mina Yamashita*

For Queta, Anita, Alejandro, Miguel, and Rosita,

who hosted an American student seventeen years ago,

and have semiannually since then.

I hope they know the impact they continue to have.

CONTENTS

▼▼▼

PREFACE

THE RELATIONSHIP BETWEEN MEXICO and Cuba grabbed international headlines in 2002 and 2004 owing to a rift in their relations resulting from a shift in Mexican foreign policy toward Cuba that had dated back to the first days of the triumph of the Cuban Revolution in 1959. The Mexican presidency under Vicente Fox Quesada (2000–2006) diverged from the policies followed by the Institutional Revolutionary Party (PRI) that dominated Mexico from 1929–2000. The National Action Party (PAN) finds Cuba less attractive as a friend than the former PRI foreign policy makers, which partly explains the divergence today, but much larger issues are also at play: the struggle for identity and political legitimacy in Third World countries and ultimately the alleviation of the ills of underdeveloped societies. This book locates the Mexican-Cuban relationship within this greater context.

The headlines themselves reflect a general understanding among educated and interested parties that Mexican-Cuban relations have been unique, special, and friendly since Castro's rise to power in joint opposition to U.S. policy over Cuba primarily as well as other foreign policy issues during the Cold War. A form of "transnationalism" has at times developed among Mexicans and Cubans both in official and unofficial circles from this relationship, and observers propagate the idea that their friendship is strong, noting especially the uniqueness of Mexico's stance as the only Latin American nation not to sever relations with Castro's Cuba during the 1960s. While the relationship is unique to a degree, in many ways it is too complex to characterize in such simple terms. Understanding the relationship requires, rather, a broad-based history that looks at the role of the United States as both the closest and most powerful nation geographically and politically to Cuba and Mexico as well, and this is what I attempt to provide herein. The relationship between Cuba and Mexico

▼▼▼

has not only been affected by direct U.S. intervention in the region, but also by its mere presence as a superpower in the hemisphere. The common experience of living in the shadow of U.S. power has consistently shaped relations between the two countries, pushing them together and reinforcing nationalistic feelings that transcend both time and space.

In light of this, I believe the foundation of the official bilateral relationship between the two countries is largely imaginary despite the very real transnationalist sentiments expressed by unofficial and official agents. The purpose of this fictitious aspect is obviously important, for it provides legitimacy to U.S., Mexican, and Cuban interests. The Mexican-Cuban relationship played a role in shaping international relations during the Cold War precisely because the Cold War was both a global war of survival and a struggle over ideologies.

Marxist thought and policies did not solve the problems of the developing world during the post-WWII era but neither did capitalism or Western notions of democracy. As Mexico and Cuba sought to find their way in the midst of the Cold War struggle over these competing ideals, albeit in different forms, in response to one another's influence and that of the United States in the Third World, they became transnational leaders in their own right. In particular, they helped lead the Non-Aligned movement and promoted *tercermundismo*, an idea advanced largely by Mexican president Luis Echeverría Alvarez (1970–76). Mexico and Cuba valued their relationship because it enabled them to enhance their role on the world scene and legitimize their leftist credentials at home. The Cold War made their bilateral relationship more visible, and because during the Cold War the issues of the developing world were treated more globally than they ever had been before, Mexico and Cuba became true actors on the international relations world stage.

In other words, the Cold War saw the rise of a bipolar world order led by the United States and the Soviet Union but simultaneously and unwittingly provided a platform for developing world actors to become integral participants in shaping the nature of the international relations arena. The extent to which this presented an opportunity for Third World nations can be determined by the level of attention superpowers paid to Third World events during the Cold War as well as by the high level of participation in international relations on the part of Third World nations, many of which had been deemed rather insignificant in this regard before the Cold War. For example, consider the global level of concern over conflict in Nicaragua in the 1920s compared to that of the 1980s or over Cuba in the 1890s versus the 1960s. There are dozens of examples that further illustrate this pattern and demonstrate the agency of Third World nations during the Cold War.

The Global Cold War, a recent comprehensive study by Odd Arne Westad, views the Cold War in terms of superpower interventions in the Third World. That is, the Cold War was far from merely a strategic military and nuclear buildup that led both superpowers to the brink of nuclear annihilation without ever firing a shot against each other. Instead, the Cold War was in many ways the longest running world war in human history, as we see conflicts once isolated to the regions in which they erupted taking on global strategic significance to the United States and the Soviet Union. I agree with Westad's assessment that Third World nations had their own Cold War agendas; that is, they weren't merely passively impacted by Moscow or Washington but actively sought to protect their interests. Mexico and Cuba, for example, were led by officials who were *not controlled* by their superpower friends, even if they often operated under their influence. The relationship between Mexico and Cuba was significant for other reasons, too. Extremist groups, particularly in Mexico and the United States, with both marginal and high-level influence took the Mexican-Cuban relationship very seriously as a result of the Cold War pressures. Communists, anti-Communists, nationalists, and transnationalists all used the Cold War to their advantage whenever possible.

Mexican-Cuban relations have rarely been examined in a tri-lateral context to the extent that they are in my study, which draws attention to the role played by various nongovernmental groups as well as governmental. The Cold War atmosphere in particular helped shape the relations among all three countries considerably. Mexico and the United States found themselves combating Cuban Communism in cooperation with

▼▼▼

one another, while Mexico maintained relations with Communist Cuba. Anti-Communist Cuban exiles and Mexicans produced extensive literature condemning Mexico's relationship with Cuba as well as denouncing as Communist any participant who either punished anti-Communist initiatives or supported dialogue with Cuba. Furthermore, leftists in Cuba and Mexico have been steady promoters of the story of friendly Mexican-Cuban relations, and the Mexican governments under the PRI leadership as well as the Revolutionary Democratic Party (PRD) and the Workers' Party (PT) echoed these sentiments toward Cuba, making this relationship rhetorically and pragmatically significant despite the fictitious nature of its foundation.

Like all other authors, I have incurred many debts over the years that deserve more gratitude than can be conveyed here. The scholarly and personal relationships that have helped make this work special to me and hopefully to the reader are what make in-depth analysis of complex topics worth undertaking. The friends and colleagues who listen to our research ideas as we flesh them out ask the scholar the deep questions and offer us the penetrating comments necessary to round out our projects.

My first acknowledgment goes to the people of Mexico, Cuba, and the United States, for their interest in one another and for my encounters with them that have made me a more complete scholar and person, even as I sit here thinking of all of the misunderstandings in our mutual history. Next I want to thank Sterling Evans for his confidence in my work and for the feedback he has given me on various panels over the years. Sterling also inspired me to carry out my graduate work at the University of Kansas. There I met Charles L. Stansifer, his former advisor, who became my advisor. Charley has always been there for me, motivating me and challenging me to dig deeper into the complexities of Mexican-Cuban relations. He contributed greatly to my academic training, which was also supplemented by difficult courses on Mexican and Cuban history as well as on Latin American foreign relations. Elizabeth Kuznesof also deserves considerable mention here for her support through the Center of Latin American Studies and for her high standards as a professor. It is to her leadership, as well as to that of Charley Stansifer and too many others to be named at the Center of Latin American Studies, that KU owes its stellar reputation in this multidisciplinary field.

Jana Krentz and Gregory Cushman have also influenced my work in unique ways. I thank Jana for her help in tracking down an array of sources, from Latin American newspapers to dissertations, secret cables, declassified documents, speech databases, scholarly articles, rare books, and various other ephemera that have broadened the implications of this book. I cannot thank you enough, honestly. I also hold a special place here for Greg Cushman for challenging me to rethink the theoretical underpinnings of my dissertation. The idea of autonomy exertion as a function of the Mexican-Cuban relationship came from his detailed rereading of my dissertation. Even though I had already successfully defended it, his thought-provoking remarks prompted me to read more of the secondary literature on this topic, leading me to better understand the true context of the relationship between the two countries.

There are also many who helped me find materials when I was in Cuba and Mexico. First and foremost among them is Kate Doyle of the National Security Archive. Her discoveries of Mexican and American documents helped to pave the way for this book. Kate also advised me when I was in Mexico on how to search for materials at the Secretaría de Relaciones Exteriores. I cannot thank her enough. The staff at the archives there also deserve thanks for their efforts down the years.

To my interviewees and friends in Mexico and Cuba, such as Enrique Camacho Navarro and Tomas Fernández Robaina, who challenged me to look beyond diplomatic relations to the nonstate actors involved in cultivating the Mexican-Cuban connection, I thank you for your honesty and interest in my research; thank you Tomas, too, for helping me find a place to stay while I was in Havana. To the members of my dissertation committee, Charles L. Stansifer, Gregory Cushman, Ted Wilson, William Tuttle, and Charles Epp, I am deeply grateful for and appreciative of your integrity in helping me to ask the larger questions associated with my research topic. My Indigenous Nations Studies advisor, Peter Herlihy, also deserves a special thanks, for his example of activist-based academic research in Honduras and other places. His concern for the survival of indigenous peoples in an ever-globalizing world drives his work, and he is an example for others to follow.

Likewise, I thank my good friend and colleague Brent Metz, whose feedback over the years has helped me to fine-tune my main ideas and conceptualize the transnational nature of my work. Thanks also to my father, mother, stepmother, stepfather, and two brothers for their encouragement and support down the years. I must also thank my wife, Kimberly, whose patience in dealing with my trips to archives across the continent, the countless hours I spent away from home writing, and the general frustration of living with an academic, has shown me the meaning of true dedication to another person. And to my twin boys, Vincent and Mason, may you always search for meaning through in-depth analysis and may a strong sense of humanity especially guide you.

INTRODUCTION

MEXICO AND CUBA: A CAPSULE HISTORY OF RELATIONS

I must begin by saying that Cuba and Mexico
are living through the worst moment of diplomatic
relations in more than one hundred years.

—Cuban foreign minister Felipe Perez Rogue
during a press conference, May 5, 2004

THE MEXICAN-CUBAN RELATIONSHIP finds its initial roots in the conquest of Mexico by Cuba-based Hernán Cortez in 1521, the conquistador whose initiative resulted in the Spanish crown's centralization of North American control in Mexico City, the seat of power for the viceroyalty of New Spain. New Spain encompassed both Mexico and Cuba throughout the three-hundred-year span of colonial history, which fully entrenched both the commonalities and differences between the two. This colonial regime implemented the rule of the Catholic Church and centralized authority and cultural connections through shipping and regular sea travel. Significant differences also developed between the two. For example, there was a higher level of slavery in Cuba, which produced a monoculture dependency on sugar, whereas Mexico had a predominantly mestizo and indigenous population accompanied by a much more diversified economy compared to Cuba.

Colonialism brought the two nations together through a mutual identification of problems associated with it and with the underdevelopment it caused, and it also inherently atomized them in several respects. Most

▼▼▼

notably they were geographically divided by the Gulf of Mexico, although the gulf was in fact easily bridged owing to the proximity (two hundred kilometers) between the Yucatán peninsula and the western tip of Cuba as well as through the two major port cities of Veracruz in Mexico and Havana in Cuba. That these two cities bear considerable structural resemblance while being officially connected to different countries today is merely representative of the problem inherent in Third World solidarity as a whole. The resemblance/separation can be viewed as an example of both the natural mutual identification among poor countries with a history of centralized foreign oppression, exploitation, and control as well as their natural desire to be independent as individually nationalistic peoples, a desire that brings its own problems in the form of racial and class divisions within their countries. Hence the difficulties Third World nations have in fomenting solidarity movements to combat problems of underdevelopment in a development-oriented world.

The relationship between Mexico and Cuba later developed when they cooperated in anticolonial struggle against Spain in the 1800s and then through Cuban support for Mexican revolutionaries during the Mexican Revolution (1910–20). The following decades saw further deterioration of Cuban democratic aspirations, which caused prominent Cuban leftists such as Julio Antonio Mella to flee in exile to Mexico, where the vibrant revolutionary governments of the 1920s and 1930s inspired Cuban radicals to stand up for their own rights in Cuba. Mexican president Lázaro Cárdenas (1934–40) began to stand out during his presidency, as his redistribution of wealth and land to the marginalized Mexican populace raised the specter of revolution in other Latin American countries. Cárdenas in fact went on to assist Fidel Castro and his followers in their release from Mexican prison in 1956, after which the Cuban revolutionaries mounted their attack on Batista's forces from Mexico in November of that year. Cárdenas later led the MLN (National Liberation Movement), a pro-Castro political organization in Mexico that used the successes of the Cuban Revolution to revive the ideals of the Mexican Revolution, the basic tenets of which had been subordinated to state-based industrialization goals.

While Cárdenas helped to tie Mexico to Cuba, Fidel Castro's actions tied Cuba to Mexico. Castro represented a newfound energy among Third World leaders that challenged the influence of the "Colossus to the North." These leaders sought an image of self-reliance for the Third World, so long seen as dependent on the First World. We see a similar dynamic in the rise of pro–Hugo Chavez leaders in Latin America today. I argue that the Castro-Cárdenas connection represents the dawn of strong Cuban-Mexican relations and that their relationship symbolized the strength, validity, independence, and agency of both countries during the Cold War. The power of this relationship rested on the idea that through mutual solidarity, the two nations could work to reverse the colonially entrenched systems of domination and dependency that had plagued these nations and the rest of the Third World. It is important to note the overarching postcolonialist aims as central to this bilateral relationship, through which like-minded participants in both countries found meaning for the mutual "struggle."

This "struggle" became more relevant to the Cuban situation by 1964, when all Latin American nations except Mexico had severed relations with the Communist island. Mexico's lone stance has signified to generations of Cubans and Mexicans the everlasting brotherhood between these two countries. However, the more conservative forces operating for the anti-Communist cause in the United States and Mexico have also found meaning in this relationship. Mexican officials seeking a stronger economic relationship with the United States in the wake of the beginnings of the Border Industrialization Project of 1965 and those concerned with Cuban-inspired Communism in Mexico worked ever closer with American officials in their leadership against Communism.

New evidence also suggests Mexico cooperated with U.S. officials to gather sensitive information on official Cuban activities through the Mexican embassy in Havana in the 1960s and 1970s. Moreover, the documents do not indicate that the United States put any pressure on Mexico to carry this out. In fact, the correspondence from the Mexican ambassadors' gathering indicates that the Mexicans were as concerned to defuse Communism as were the Americans. This further demonstrates the level of agency Mexican officials had in Cold War international policies. That

▼▼▼

is, the Cold War was just as much Mexico's war as it was America's, and it was Cuba's war as much as it was the Soviets'. The Mexican political establishment valued its relationship with Castro as long as it did not hurt the stranglehold of the PRI (Institutional Revolutionary Party) on power within Mexico, and it feared the spread of Castro's influence there much more than it feared U.S. influence.

In 1968, the Mexican government dealt with the internal leftist problem head-on, which ended in mass murder on October 2 in Tlatelolco. The Mexican government came down on the students with its full force, proving that its direction was not with the left or anything resembling a revolution and that the pro-Castro students hoping for a change would have to wait. Of course, the 1970s saw a leftward shift in Mexican politics with the initiative of President Luis Echeverría Alvarez (1970–76) in which he was joined by revolutionary Peru to reintegrate Cuba into the international system under the Organization of American States (OAS). Echeverría's relationship with Castro developed on a personal level as well, which helped both of their images at home, and soon each leader took the lead in parallel but different movements of Third World empowerment. José López Portillo (1976–82) enhanced relations between the two countries over the course of his presidency through mutual aid projects in education and industry and through cultural celebrations and state visits as well as by providing joint assistance with Cuba to Central American revolutionaries working in opposition to U.S.-backed forces.

The 1982–88 era was marked by structural adjustment austerity programs in Mexico in the wake of the 1982 debt crisis and the continuation of the Central American conflicts. President Miguel de la Madrid (1982–88) played a leadership role in attempting to end the conflicts in Nicaragua and El Salvador during this period, which Castro also supported. The following president, Carlos Salinas de Gortari (1988–94), persevered in this process with two slight changes: the Mexican president spoke with Cuban exile groups opposed to Castro in Miami and played a decisive role in enacting the North American Free Trade Agreement (NAFTA), which brought Canada, Mexico, and the United States under one large free-trade zone beginning in 1994.

These two moves on the part of the Mexican president could have created a rift with the Cuban leader, but Mexico and Cuba only developed their relationship further. Trade grew across the board between Mexico and Cuba in the 1990s, particularly after the exit of the Soviets from Cuba. Relations were steady under the first six years of NAFTA, as the U.S. government under the administrations of George Bush (1989–93) and Bill Clinton (1993–2001) attempted to use the free-trade agreement to isolate Cuba. Both Mexico and Canada objected outright to this stratagem, calling on international arbitrating authorities on several occasions.

By 2000, the PRI's absolute hold over Mexican politics came to an end with the election of Vicente Fox Quesada (2000–2006), the strong PAN (National Action Party) candidate whose party had spent the past six decades opposing the PRI and its policy of support for Cuba. The following six years proved challenging for all Mexican parties from left to right because they all believed the Mexican-Cuban relationship was important and, at times, too complex to understand entirely.

The Big Picture: Mexico and Cuba as Cold War Actors

The Cold War tension between East and West forced the Third World onto the international stage like no other era. In this conflict, Western Cold War strategy hinged on Eastern Hemisphere security, with the Middle East, Asia, and Europe being of utmost concern, and on U.S. hegemony in the Western Hemisphere. Cold War historians have concentrated on almost entirely the role the Unites States played in controlling the Western Hemisphere. These accounts inevitably devote much attention to the Cuban Missile Crisis and some even mention the Central American conflicts of the 1980s when referring to Latin America, and yet, the Third World, where central actors played a role in shaping international relations, in general receives scant attention. Ho Chi Minh, Fidel Castro, Che Guevara, and Patrice Lumumba are often mentioned, but their roles are considered problematic to the aims of the United States, who thought they were all being manipulated by Moscow, and so they are not typically treated as actors with agency who made the Cold War their war, too. Relatively weaker nations in the Third World indeed found themselves forced to choose paths in this game of the great powers: would they hop on the bandwagon and join forces with a superpower or would they develop their own vision? Some, like Mexico and Cuba, became allied to enemy superpowers, but at the same time, they used their "revolutionary" credentials to advance agendas of their own with each other's assistance.

Given their central role in the Cold War as proxy war sites, the image portrayed by Cold War historians concentrating on superpower activity during this period of Third World countries as either expedients or mere victims in the struggle is not accurate. A different picture of the Cold War emerges in the Third World itself, where postcolonialist movements became Cold War struggles characterized by resistance and widespread conflict in Vietnam, Angola, South Africa, Zaire, Nicaragua, Argentina, Brazil, Chile, El Salvador, Guatemala, the Dominican Republic, Haiti, Cuba, and Mexico. These struggles led to the deaths of millions of people and suffering from displacement, disease, and famine, not to mention the brutality of Communist and right-wing dictators from Cuba to China to Guatemala, which led to the deaths of millions more. When the Third World experience is center stage, Third World actors can be viewed as "cold warriors," with the proviso that they were fighting a war defined by themselves as well as the superpowers.

Unfortunately, the big questions most Cold War historians ask often ignore Third World agency and autonomy and focus instead on what are considered the central issues, namely superpower strategies and their impact on matters such as the "success" of U.S. policies or the failures of Soviet policies, and so on. Leading Cold War historian John Lewis Gaddis examines issues such as the U.S. justification in creating the Manhattan Project and the initiation of the nuclear arms race, for example. His 1997 book, *We Now Know*, uses previously classified documentation indicating Stalin's efforts to obtain nuclear technology before the United States developed the atomic bomb. Diane Kunz's study of American Cold War economic policy, *Butter and Guns*, also sheds light on U.S. influence, arguing that the U.S. government's policy of outspending the Russians in the areas of the military and financial assistance helped the United States to win the Cold War. Likewise, Aaron L. Friedberg's book, *In the Shadow of the Garrison State*, examines the role U.S. governmental respect for domestic American freedoms played in U.S. Cold War victory.

These books explain a considerable amount about this era, but in focusing on the extent to which the Cold War was controlled by the superpowers, they place those who suffered the most from the Cold War on the wings. Odd Arne Westad's *The Global Cold War* (Bancroft Prize winner) goes further than any other text in this regard and has helped me to more precisely place the Mexican-Cuban relationship within the Cold War struggle. We now need to put the regions where most of the battles took place center stage. In asking how, for example, inter–Latin American relations (this book's example being the relationship between Mexico and Cuba) fit into the Cold War, we may learn about yet another dimension of this not-so "cold" war.

A few recent studies have addressed Third World agency in the realm of inter–Latin American relations during this era. Cuban foreign relations specialists such as Jorge I. Dominguez, Louis A. Perez, H. Michael Erisman, and Michael D. and Donna Rich Kaplowitz explain Communist Cuba's foreign policy as a tool to preserve the revolution, detailing involvement in Africa, Asia, Latin America, and the Soviet Union. These studies elaborate on the direction and intention of Cuban foreign policy in the greatest possible geographic context. My approach, on the other hand, focuses on Mexico and the United States.

Political scientists have been able to shed considerable light on the role of the Third World in the Cold War. Peter H. Smith, G. Pope Atkins, Jorge Castañeda, Bruce Cumings, and Robert C. Young have made contributions on this subject by complementing the debates raised by Cold War historians. These scholars see primary actors in the Third World during the Cold War, actors who often operate in a separate realm of influence entirely from that of the superpowers. For example, Smith's perspective derives from a vision of U.S.–Latin American relations operating within the context of greater world events as opposed to resulting merely from U.S. policy. He expands the analysis of the role of the United States in Latin America by exploring factors beyond any of the participants' control. Atkins's multiple studies of the part Latin America has played in the

▼▼▼

world locate Latin America within the global political, economic, and cultural system, demonstrating that Latin America is full of important agents of continuity and change. Castañeda has the unique perspective of a Latin American scholar with access to many politicians and archives. This access has given him greater insight than perhaps any other scholar of Latin America into the interplay of civil and official society in the realm of international relations.

Specialists focusing on the Third World who are personally sympathetic to the region shed more light on Third World agency during the Cold War. For example, Korea specialist Bruce Cumings illustrates the gap between U.S. policy and Third World reality by stating that the Third World demonstrated "a human agency the Achesons and the Kennans never imagined: the fierce energy of aroused peoples in the 1940s, collectives for whom imperialism and a recent past were hated realities, and the promises of the American vision an utter chimera."[1] Robert Young's wide-reaching study, *Postcolonialism: An Introduction*, approaches the Third World movements of the twentieth century as oriented toward reversing centuries of European exploitation. His concern for uncovering the genuine complexities of the reasons and circumstances behind these struggles forms the foundation of his research, yielding a plethora of data and allowing for a more complete comprehension of the role of the Third World in the Cold War.

My study demonstrates how Mexican-Cuban relations were an example of Third World agency in shaping international relations during the Cold War. Inquiries such as this lead to the discovery of lost voices and effects emanating from a sector of the world where the vast majority of the planet's population lives (the Third World) and, indeed, where millions died during this era as a result of war. While Mexico and Cuba only represent a small portion of the Third World, their problems as developing nations in the midst of the Cold War struggle between East and West make them relevant and representative of the Third World.

The Mexican-Cuban relationship serves as a fruitful lens through which to view this history for several reasons. First, although other Latin American nations resumed relations with Cuba in the years after 1970,

▼▼▼

starting with Salvador Allende's Chile, the fact that Mexico never broke them off in the first place has been represented by international observers, Mexican and Cuban officials, and the public as proof of the powerful, "revolutionary" bond between the two countries. Second, during the Cold War these countries were arguably the two most important Latin American nations to the United States and were quite important to the USSR, too, situated as they were as "imaginary" friends between the bitter superpower enemies. The "imaginary" nature of the friendship stems from the fact that they simultaneously proclaimed their solidarity and undertook initiatives to thwart each other's government.

THE INTERNATIONAL PERSPECTIVE

The news media recognized the Mexican-Cuban relationship as "special" in 2002 and 2004 after several rifts between the leadership of the two countries. In March 2002, there appeared headlines such as "Fox Outfoxed: Cuba-Mexico Relations Hit New Low" (*World Press Review*, March 25) to stories that told of Castro's alleged recording of a telephone conversation between Castro and Mexican president Vicente Fox, in which Fox asked Castro to leave early from the UN International Conference on Financing for Development, held in Monterrey, Mexico, earlier that month, in order to avoid crossing paths with US president George W. Bush.[2] The next month, Mexico voted for the first time in favor of a UN resolution censuring Cuba's human rights standards. Before this, Mexico's Cuba policy rested on self-determination and nonintervention, which the PRI had effected by abstaining from, or voting against, resolutions censuring Cuba.[3] Castro's response to Mexico's UN vote came the following week when he aired the eighteen-minute conversation with Fox for over one hundred journalists.[4]

Two years later, the Mexican-Cuban relationship hit its lowest point. The dispute began after the Mexican government accused Cuba of interfering in an internal matter and after Castro accused Mexico of subservience to the United States in his May Day speech. The following day, Mexico pulled its ambassador to Cuba and expelled the Cuban ambassador to Mexico, a first in this longtime relationship.[5] However, the ambassadors were restored

▼▼▼

on July 26, the fifty-first anniversary of the Cuban Revolution.[6] The symbolic significance of restoring relations on July 26 reflected a deep-rooted history of "special" relations throughout the Castro era. That this rift drew widespread international attention speaks of the general interest in the Mexican-Cuban relationship, which is founded on the assumption of the strength of Mexican-Cuban historically rooted connections. It is also an example of the sphere of influence Third World actors carved in response to the Cold War atmosphere, leverage that continues to this day in Latin America. Just witness the rise of leftist nationalist leadership in Venezuela, Brazil, Mexico, Chile, Uruguay, Bolivia, Peru, and Argentina, whose leftist parties all claim strong ties to Cuba.

The Mexican-Cuban "Friendship"

In Tuxpan, Veracruz, Mexico, on December 5, 1988, thirty-two years after eighty-two revolutionaries led by Castro left that same port, Mexican interior secretary Fernando Gutierrez Barrios introduced Fidel Castro at a celebration by saying "Mexican and Cuban companions. Let's walk through this painful and long process of our history."[7]

This is only one of many utterances that has given expression to the solidarity experienced between Mexicans and Cubans since 1959.[8] Speeches, poems, and articles with titles such as "Cuba in a Mexican," "Nothing Exists between Us without Old Roots," "Mexico Will Triumph with Cuba," "Yankees, Don't Touch Cuba," and "Mexico Is with Cuba" all come from Mexican and Cuban authors proclaiming unity against U.S. policy toward Castro's Cuba. They demonstrate how transnational solidarity among Mexicans and Cubans finds its roots in demonstrations of historical mutuality, a mutuality that ignores the complexities inherent in general in international relations as a result of their own specialized interests.

The relationship between Mexico and Cuba is deemed unique today by international political observers for several reasons. At the top of the list is Mexico's allegiance to Cuba between 1964 and 1970.[9] Mexico's position toward Cuba especially stands out because Mexico's most powerful ally, the United States, has been Cuba's staunchest official enemy for over four decades. Nevertheless, the U.S. government has placed virtually no pressure on Mexico to alter its position toward Cuba. In fact, the United States has encouraged the relationship at times, expressing only slight concern for brief periods.

Mexican foreign policy has defended Cuban sovereignty, especially at the OAS and the United Nations, when other nations, primarily the United States, have attempted to censure Cuba. The tenets of respect for self-determination and nonintervention in foreign affairs have been central to Mexican foreign policy dating back to the early years of the Mexican Revolution. Mexico's foreign policy may not be unique, but its leadership in espousing these principles has prevailed as a standard in Latin America.

In the late 1910s, the Mexican constitutional revolutionary government under Venustiano Carranza implemented the Carranza Doctrine, which became the foundation for Mexican foreign policy in the twentieth century. It explicitly stated that no nation had the right to intervene in the internal affairs of another. Subsequently, the Carranza Doctrine was espoused by Mexican representatives at inter-American conferences, in particular at the sixth conference in 1928, where the Estrada Doctrine was adopted. This doctrine originated in a proclamation by Mexican foreign minister Genaro Estrada in 1928 and stated that international pressure could not be exerted through international recognition. In 1936, nonintervention was added as inter-American policy, and in 1947, the OAS membership signed the Río Treaty, which provided for the right of the American nations to unite when under attack.[10] The PRI used this policy to defend its support for Cuba in the OAS.

Castro has demonstrated a high level of gratitude for Mexico's stance toward Cuba. For example, in a 1980 speech in Havana during the Mexico-Cuba Friendship Rally, Castro awarded Mexican president José López Portillo with the José Martí Order and stated the following:

> . . . during the shameful times when cowardly and treacherous cliques that could never represent the true feeling of the Latin American peoples backed down and let themselves be used in the

▼▼▼

infamous plan initiated in Washington to isolate the emerging Cuban revolution and try to cut off Cuba from Latin America, Mexico alone maintained the worthy and courageous position of not breaking its relations with Cuba. [Mexico] set an example of international conduct which we Cubans will never forget. For this reason, Mr. President and esteemed friend, when the Council of State, in awarding you the José Martí Order, emphasizes the friendship and solidarity which you have shown toward our country, it recognizes that you are continuing in an eminent manner what in your Mexican nation has been an uninterrupted norm of solidarity conduct.[11]

The invocation of the space of time between 1964 and 1970 as proof of Mexico's "worthy and courageous position" in the OAS speaks to the foundations of the Mexican-Cuban friendship, developed in the vein of revolutionary legitimization via historically bounded roots of mutuality between two sibling nations, "united in history."

It must be recognized that the year 1959 changed international relations in the Western Hemisphere on many levels, most notably geostrategically, considering Cuba's proximity to the United States. On the one hand, the Cuban Revolution's road to Communism and allegiance to the Eastern bloc angered the United States and many of its Latin American allies. On the other, it set an example for Latin American (as well as non–Latin American) leftists. On another level, the Communist island nation's friendship with Mexico factored into U.S. policy, and the relationship between the two countries was transformed by the United States' status as the most powerful force in the hemisphere. The dominant political party of Mexico, the PRI, often found itself in the middle of its two allies.

Public and official interest in this relationship developed within months of Castro's 1959 victory. This interest has been documented in numerous sources, including U.S. Congress papers, presidential archives, anti-Communist and leftist magazines, mainstream dailies, scholarly literature, poetry, personal letters, speeches, joint communiqués, and resolutions, each revealing how passionate different groups felt about the Cold

War implications of the Mexican-Cuban connection within the geopolitical hegemonic orbit of the United States.

The events surrounding the Cuban Revolution brought Cubans and Mexicans closer together, while the United States and Cuba simultaneously drove wedges between one another. Mexico's official decision to maintain its ties to Cuba during Cuba's ostracism of the 1960s reinforced the concept that Mexico was Cuba's only true friend in the Americas. The decision manifested itself in expressions of brotherhood and appreciation on the part of Mexican and Cuban leftist officials, academics, artists, labor leaders, and common folk at the same time that it elicited negative reaction from anti-Communist sectors within the United States and Mexico, who wanted the Mexican government to take a hard-line stance against Cuba. However, the U.S. government, as of 1964, allowed and sometimes encouraged Mexico's independent stance on Cuba in order to facilitate Mexican cooperation in gathering intelligence on Cuban activities.

While genuine signs of friendship have been witnessed between the two Latin American nations, my research demonstrates that the friendship was founded on "realist-idealist" political behavior.[12] The "realist-idealist" argument maintains that although friendly relations most certainly occurred in given sectors and despite leftists in both countries having consistently demonstrated a closeness to one another, political ideologies in each country were so different that interstate solidarity inevitably flagged. The PRI's party line, although revolutionary in rhetoric, has been quite the opposite since the 1940s, with minor exceptions in the 1970s, and certainly did not declare the United States an enemy during the Cold War. Yet, Castro's Cuba has been an enemy of the United States throughout.

This fact separates Cuba and Mexico in the realm of "realist" politics and played a part in the foundation of friendship and cooperation between Mexico and the United States. Recently unearthed information reveals that Cuba supported antistate Mexican guerrilla movements during the 1960s and 1970s, which is a violation of an unwritten understanding between Mexico and Cuba that as long as Mexico defended Cuba's right to self-determination, Cuba would never support resistance movements within Mexico's borders (as it had done in countries all over Latin America as

▼▼▼

well as in Africa and Asia).[13] Along with evidence of Mexican complicity in gathering secretive information on Cuba, this challenges the idea that there was an unwritten understanding between both nations and the notion of friendly relations in general.

Furthermore, although the notion of Mexican-Cuban solidarity is based on several real events, such as Mexican-Cuban cooperation against Spain in the nineteenth century and Mexico's Castro-era position, those promoting the construct of friendly relations between Mexico and Cuba (e.g., PRI, PRD [Revolutionary Democratic Party], MLN, and Castro) have had an interest in establishing their revolutionary credentials. These groups center their discourse on Cuban-Mexican relations around the events that represent this connection as if it were purely revolutionary.

Interests

In light of the complexities, evaluation of the Mexican-Cuban relationship has proven difficult for political observers and scholars. The difficulty is rooted in motivation. What interests motivate this relationship? Cuba, the centerpiece of this triangle as a result of its ability to fuse the interests of the United States, Mexico, and Cuba especially since Castro's rise to power, seeks to maintain the illusion of its "special relationship" with Mexico in order to promote its own "revolutionary" legitimacy, thus strengthening its Third World leadership stance. Cuba's Cold War foreign policy was based on an imperative "to make a world safer for Cuba's brand of socialism"; it defended its revolution by supporting revolutionary movements and increasing the number of "friendly governments" such as Mexico.[14]

Mexico's interests parallel Cuba's. The political party in charge of Mexico from 1929 to 2000 was the PRI, which based its legitimacy on claims to defend the ideals of the Mexican Revolution. Thus, it sought to promote its friendship with Cuba in order to illustrate its "revolutionary" credentials. At the same time, the PRI sought to benefit economically from its growing friendship with the United States, beginning especially in the 1960s, which in turn strengthened its *tercermundismo* stance and enhanced Mexican leadership in the Third World as a counter to Cuban and U.S. influence. Instead of only playing the role of pawns for the superpowers, the governments of Cuba and Mexico exerted their independence or "counterdependence" in the face of pressure from the superpowers and even each other.[15]

One can better comprehend these interests by invoking Eric Hobsbawn's theory of the "invention of tradition." For Hobsbawn, the "invented tradition" signifies "a set of practices, normally governed by overtly or tacitly accepted rules and of a ritual or symbolic nature, which seek to inculcate certain values and norms of behaviour by repetition, which automatically implies continuity with the past."[16] In terms of Mexico and Cuba, the "friendship" relies on this "continuity with the past." For them, the relationship only exists within a history of mutual interests, evidenced in their cooperation with one another against the United States, which has united both nations, according to their solidarity rhetoric. By repeating this discourse-created history, the two countries have hoped to "inculcate certain values," related to the promotion of leftist revolutionary ideals.[17]

The significance of the rhetoric of solidarity can be elucidated also by Maurice Halbwach's assessment of "collective memory." When we observe how news articles from 2002 and 2004 refer to the historically friendly ties of Mexico and Cuba and examine the language of those who still promote the relationship (the PRI, the PRD, and the PRT [Worker's Party], for example), we realize the wisdom of Halbwach's words: "in reality the past does not occur" unconsciously, but instead, "everything seems to indicate that the past is not preserved but is reconstructed on the basis of the present."[18] In this sense, it fits that the two dominant "revolutionary" Mexican political parties reconstruct the past when forming the basis for their policies toward Cuba. The PRI largely supports the strengthening of relations with Cuba based on the notion that historically strong bonds exist between the two nations, whereas the current presidency's party, the National Action Party (PAN) has been anti-Castro since the 1960s. Therefore, it makes perfect sense that PAN would favor its current policy, which conditions its relations with Cuba on the demonstrated improvement of the island's internal freedoms.[19]

Benedict Anderson's notion of the "imagined community" can also be applied to the convenient yet spurious nature of the Mexican-Cuban

▼▼▼

"special friendship." However, the relationship between Cuba and Mexico is an example of a *transnational* "imagined community," promulgated through anti-imperialist, revolutionary rhetoric of mutual affiliation throughout a history of "resistance" to "oppression." That is, the promoters of the Mexican-Cuban friendship have used discourse oriented toward unifying the two nations and equating the histories of both nations and peoples to create what could be considered a transnationalistic community, "imagined" in Anderson's sense of the term but grafted onto the transnationality of Mexican-Cuban friendly relations. While possibly outside the realm of Anderson's original vision, this has not stopped leftist Mexicans and Cubans, whose expressions often convey genuine feelings of solidarity and mutuality, from generating a long-lasting understanding of Mexican-Cuban relations powerful enough to find its way to present-day international headlines, despite evidence that undermines this imagined history. The international headlines from 2002 and 2004 still portray the friendship as "special" based on a standard that belies the complexity and utility of this relationship. Instead, their relations are judged as either stable or not and not in terms of the role the relationship has played in promoting both domestic political legitimacy and Third World agency on the international scene.

Ironically, a strong measure of this "special friendship" lies in its use to thwart one another. Not only did Mexico and the United States cooperate against Castro and Castro support Mexican guerrillas, but right-wing extremist groups in Mexico and the United States joined in opposition to the Mexican-Cuban connection. Cuban American, Mexican, and American anti-Communist groups published extensive literature criticizing what they deemed as Communist sympathies on the part of Mexican and American presidents Adolfo López Mateos (1958–64), Gustavo Díaz Ordaz (1964–70), Luis Echeverría (1970–76), José López Portillo (1976–82), and Jimmy Carter (1977–81).[20]

The extremist groups fundamentally divided, or fragmented, the "two peoples" (dos pueblos) that the leftists themselves claimed were "united" in a history of mutual interests, based on resistance to abuses of power. Furthermore, just as Marxism failed to explain the future of human societies, so too this constructed history of mutual interest between both nations is inadequate. If there were only a few exceptions, this work would matter little, but the evidence contradicting this "special" notion of relations created by leftists and politicians with interests, and "verified" by the mass media, deserves more scholarly attention.

This project aims to address this problem by piercing the surface of this constructed history between Mexico and Cuba, which is real as well as imagined. Important to this analysis is the Mexican foreign policy of respect for self-determination and nonintervention that played a role in the government's decision not to sever relations with Cuba, for both the U.S. and Mexican governments took advantage of the newfound unique position Mexico found itself in as a result of its maintaining ties. Soon after the July 1964 OAS vote that expelled Cuba from the international community, Secretary of State Dean Rusk informed President Lyndon B. Johnson (1963–69) that he and other foreign ministers had decided on "the practical desirability" of keeping one Latin American nation's embassy in Cuba in order to have a channel of communication with the island.[21] Journalist Carl Migdail asserts the same, quoting Secretary Rusk in an interview: "we decided it would be in the best interests of all countries if one country maintained relations with Cuba and acted as a listening post for all of us. That country was Mexico."[22]

The recently discovered evidence showing that Mexico and the United States cooperated in an effort to gather and share information on Cuban affairs through the Mexican embassy in Havana demonstrates how strong their new relationship was. The Mexican ambassador in Cuba between 1953 and 1964 passed information back to Mexico City related only to matters between the embassy and the Cuban government, such as meetings, celebrations, and so forth. In contrast, the correspondence leaving the Mexican embassy between 1966 and 1974 contained sensitive information and often critical rhetoric on the part of the ambassadors pertinent to the Castro government's activities and Cuban society. The information was always received by the Mexican foreign relations secretariat, and at least once, it made its way to the desk of President Lyndon B. Johnson.

▼▼▼

During the period in which these ambassadors gathered information, the relations between Mexico and Cuba were at their lowest, which made sense as Díaz Ordaz was a right-of-center, anti-Communist president. However, it is this very period (1964–70) that is referred to by promoters of the Mexican-Cuban friendship as proof of the strength of their relationship. At the same time, Mexican anti-Communists expressed concerns over connections between Mexicans and Cuban Communists, always with the view that Cuba was an enemy of the Mexican people, as were Mexicans affiliated with the Castro government. Many examples illustrate the complexities of the Mexican-Cuban connection and often complicate the popular understanding promoted by sectors with interests in this concept of "mutualized" history.

Although this project focuses on Castro-era Mexican-Cuban connections, at the suggestion of my Mexican and Cuban interviewees and fellow scholars, I have compiled an initial chapter on the relationship's pre-1959 foundations. Chapter 2 examines the impact Castro's arrival to power had on Mexican-Cuban relations from 1959–64, delving into the reaction to his ascendancy from leftists, anti-Communists, and the Mexican government. Chapter 3 analyzes how the Americans perceived the Mexican-Cuban connection from 1957–61, a period of time during which the United States shaped a hemispheric policy based on thwarting the spread of Cuban revolutionary influence. Mexico's respect for self-determination and non-intervention prevented the United States from obtaining hemispheric unanimity with regard to its anti-Castro policies during the 1962–64 period, the scope of which is the subject of chapter 4.

Chapters 5 and 6 cover the "special" era of Mexican-Cuban relations from 1964–76. Introducing the reader to many sources previously undisclosed along with others only recently unearthed, these chapters pay particular attention to the role of the United States in the Mexican-Cuban connection during this period in which the United States and Mexico improved their official relations by cooperating to counter Cuban influence and thereby challenge the popularized "revolutionary" notion of a special friendship between Mexico and Cuba. These chapters, perhaps more than the others, illustrate the "rational" policies of the Mexican government. In its role as a U.S. ally, it was inherently anti-Communist, despite its "revolutionary" rhetoric; at the same time, it sought to compete with Cuba and the United States for Third World leadership.

Chapter 7 and the epilogue address the state of Mexican-Cuban relations during the road toward U.S.-Mexican free trade, which coincided with the end of the Cold War, and which I cover from 1976 to 2006, as well as the state of Mexican-Cuban relations during the Vicente Fox administration. This last section importantly asks how friendly the history of Mexican-Cuban relations could hope to be given the demands imposed on both the governments of Mexico and the United States, whose political/economic/social trajectories diverge considerably from Castro's. A simple assertion of unified Mexican-Cuban interests belies the complexities inherent in any assessment of international relations and ignores the variegated interests of civil and government sectors with interests in this bilateral connection. These chapters also highlight the levels of agency and independence Third World actors operating in the midst of the superpower-led Cold War were able to achieve. The epilogue comes at the question of the true nature of Mexican-Cuban relations from another angle by comparing the foreign policies of the PRI and the PAN, who took power of the Mexican presidency in 2000 and 2006. While the PRI has no doubt been attempting to placate the left by defending Cuban sovereignty, the PAN has always been anti-Communist and never pretended to legitimate itself based on the so-called "revolutionary" principles of the Mexican Revolution, as has the PRI.

The PAN and Castro thus have very little in common, whereas the PRI has the legacy of the Mexican Revolution, which, even according to Fidel Castro himself, inspired the Cuban Revolution.[23] Hence the PAN's foreign policy position, which parallels former U.S. president Jimmy Carter's and is based on human rights verification. This policy position has formed the basis of the party's relationships with Cuban exiles and led to its voting in favor of the UN Human Rights Commission Resolution to censure Cuba in 2002. Before attempting to understand the present context of Mexican-Cuban relations, we should take a step back and question the very notion that nations can have relationships as such. The competing sectors

▼▼▼

within governments, along with the various interest groups involved in the Mexican-Cuban connection, all deserve examination in order to contextualize the current understanding of so-called "Mexican-Cuban relations."

A "THIRD" WORLD

One must also examine the term "Third World" and how it functions as a conceptual device. First, I use it in geographical-economical terms to refer to the developing world. Second, I use it to refer to a *third* zone of influence outside the control of either of the two superpowers. Third, I use it to refer to an alternative or *third* ideological path from the two set out by the superpowers. All three definitions serve me in demonstrating that Mexico and Cuba represent both a Third World response to the pressures of being caught between the two superpowers during the Cold War and the extent to which Third World actors can indeed determine their role in international affairs. In spite of the fact that developing world concerns are often ignored by outside powers and the scholars of those countries who view the conflict in terms of superpower interests, many Third World nations did indeed respond in their own voices to this power and also played a large role in determining the trajectory of the Cold War.

CHAPTER ONE

CROSS-PATRIOTISM DEFINED

HISTORICAL APPROPRIATION AND
PRE-CASTRO MEXICAN-CUBAN RELATIONS

[W]e will never forget that . . . [Mexico] was
asylum and home . . . for Cuban patriots in the
past century . . .

—Cuban leader Fulgencio Batista in a letter to the Mexican
Ambassador, December 1953

COLONIAL BEGINNINGS

LONG BEFORE THE STATES of Mexico and Cuba became "united in history," as Jorge L. Tamayo put it, geography brought the two countries together. The short distance between the westernmost tip of Cuba and the northeasternmost tip of the Yucatán (122 miles) meant that pre-Columbian indigenous peoples would not have had far to travel from the Caribbean to Tierra Firme via Yucatán and vice versa. In 1508, Spanish vessels sailed from Cuba to the Yucatán peninsula, establishing the first contacts between the Spanish explorers and the Mexican natives. The desire to discover more of Mexico resulted in despair for many Spaniards in 1511 when the first vessels were attacked by Mayan Indians, who left only two survivors: Gonzalo Guerrero and Jerónimo de Aguilar. These two remained with the Maya and were still with them when expeditions arrived in 1517 and 1518, all of which failed in their attempts to conquer the land of the eastern Yucatec Maya. The Maya ambushed the Spaniards and frustrated them to the point of defeat, and so the eastern coast of the Yucatán peninsula remained unconquered.[1]

▼▼▼

By 1519, Hernán Cortez had arrived at the island of Cozumel from Cuba with the intention of finding gold and glory. There he heard of two white men living on the eastern coast of the Yucatán. He sent his emissaries with a message inviting Aguilar and Guerrero to join his mission. Aguilar responded with enthusiasm, but Guerrero chose to remain behind. Aguilar went on to join Cortez's expedition to conquer Mexico, serving as a translator between La Malinche and Cortez. Via Aguilar La Malinche communicated to Cortez the Aztec's version of the legend of Quetzalcoatl. The legend foretold of a white bearded man returning for his crown in Mexico in the year one reed, the year 1519, when Cortez arrived. The conquest of Mexico began in earnest once Cortez heard this story, changing the course of history for both the Mexican natives and the Spanish empire.

The aftermath of this initial exchange between Cuba and Mexico soon became significant owing to Spain's widespread settlement of Mexico, Central America, and the exploration and eventual settlement of the current-day American Southwest. Geography all but guaranteed interrelations between Mexico and Cuba as well as placed the two countries within the future influential domain of the United States. The viceroyalty of the colony of New Spain headquartered itself in the old Aztec capital of Tenochtitlán, now the site of Mexico City, and in the process destroyed the Aztec architecture, marginalized the indigenous population, and reduced their numbers dramatically, largely through disease, overwork, and battle.[2]

Mexico City became the main seat of government for the viceroyalty of New Spain, which also held jurisdiction over Cuba, for the next three hundred years. The two territories were part of the same general political system, even if they were still in separate regional spheres of influence. During the sixteenth century, commercial relations between the peoples of Cuba and Mexico served to form lines of communication. This resulted in a continuous stream of passengers between the two major port cities of Veracruz and Havana and facilitated cultural and political bonds between Mexicans and Cubans. Cuba rose in importance briefly after the conquest of Mexico owing to the increase in demands for goods and services from the mainland, which spurred on the Cuban economy, according to historian Louis A. Pérez: "Sales were brisk, as ranchers and farmers furnished the livestock and food supply for the expeditions."[3]

Yet, Mexico's importance quickly overshadowed Cuba's in the sixteenth and seventeenth centuries not only because the viceroyalty was seated in Mexico City but also because Spaniards in Mexico profited greatly from the lucrative mines and further settlement on the mainland.[4] Mining became principally important in north central Mexico, in places such as Guanajuato and Zacatecas, and though profits have fluctuated throughout the centuries they have supported the growth of these cities and many others. Landholdings varied throughout Mexico, ranging from small to medium to large, the last of which was designated usually as an hacienda, or great estate. Although these holdings were often procured through outright conquest, they were also bestowed via crown patronage or purchased. Landholdings succeeded in creating a landed class that engaged in a wide range of economic activities throughout the colonial period, contributing to the growth of the Mexican economy and at the same time promoting an interchange between the urban and the rural regions of the country. The implications for the expansion of Spanish power on the mainland were such that their Caribbean possessions dwindled in importance by comparison.[5]

Soon great amounts of money leaving Mexico passed through Havana via merchant ships on their way to Europe. The high quantity of goods and bullion being extracted in Latin America and valued Asian luxuries such as porcelain and silk that came from the annual Manila Galleon voyages between Mexico and the Philippines made the sea-land connection between Mexico and Cuba the target of pirates. The pirates were funded by the French, English, and Dutch empires that were also competing for power, wealth, territory, markets, and glory on the high seas. This led to the extensive buildup of military garrisons in both Havana and Veracruz, with the latter becoming the most fortified port city in all of the Americas during the colonial period. The famous Fort of San Juan de Ulúa that until the twentieth century defended (and sometimes failed to defend) the city of Veracruz, Mexico, stands as a monument to the dangers of piracy and foreign invasion that the Mexico-Cuba connection exposed the region to

▼▼▼

during the colonial period. Havana's Morro Castle was no small fort either and also stands today as an example of the significance of this initial connection.[6]

Mexico and Cuba's commercial ties led to educational and cultural links between the two during the seventeenth century. Beginning in the 1630s, Creoles from Cuba sought their higher learning in Mexico City, as Cuba did not have a university at the time, which brought elite Cubans and Mexicans together in Mexico. There the two cultures mingled and influenced the other's music and literature and shared their revolutionary aspirations. One important outcome of this exchange of ideas came in the form of contraband. The Spanish crown declared certain books illegal for possession among the colonists, but Cuban and Mexican travelers obtained this banned European literature through links with Europe and established what later became a route for contraband of other sorts to enter the region in the postcolonial period. Cubans also brought with them the dance of *chuchumbé*, a dance prohibited by the Inquisition in Mexico because of its non-Catholic roots. These examples of illicit exchange between Mexicans and Cubans in resistance to Spanish colonial authority foreshadowed their future cooperation in opposing the Spanish empire during the nineteenth century. The common experiences under the yoke of Spain and the surge of new Enlightenment ideas united many Cuban and Mexican intellectuals and other progressive thinkers during the colonial era. This trend continued after both colonies gained independence.[7]

THE ROOTS OF MUTUALITY:
THE CUBAN LIBERATION MOVEMENT OF THE 1820S

The beginnings of mutual Cuban-Mexican resistance to Spanish rule represented an instance of a much larger revolutionary mood that took hold in Latin America at the same time during the 1810–26 period.[8] Mexico, along with Venezuela and Argentina, all erupted in revolutionary fervor in 1810, as Ferdinand sat in exile. However, there had been independence movements that erupted and failed prior to 1810. For example, in 1809, before Father Miguel Hidalgo y Costilla's famous Grito de Dolores declaring Mexican independence, Cuban-born Dr. Joaquín Infante, along with

Mexican Captain Luis F. Bazave and Román de la Luz, attempted the liberation of Cuba from their base in Mexico. Dr. Infante later became secretary to Antonio López de Santa Anna, who served as commander general of Yucatán. It may be that Infante influenced Santa Anna because Santa Anna went on to initiate a liberation movement in the 1820s.[9] His personal reasons for doing so seem to have been to rid the Caribbean basin of Spain, but his plans to free Cuba never materialized.[10]

While Cuban independence would have to wait until 1898, Mexico achieved independence in 1821 through a compromise between royalists and insurgents that resulted in monarchy.[11] The rest of Latin America, save Puerto Rico, the Dominican Republic, and Cuba, had gained independence from Spain and Portugal by 1826, which marginalized the Spanish crown. The Caribbean presence of their former master concerned newly independent Latin American nations, and in response, several plots were undertaken by revolutionary leaders in Latin America to rid the hemisphere of the Spanish crown. One such plot by Mexican secretary of foreign relations Lucas Alamán rallied support among Mexican officials to liberate Cuba in 1824 after he discovered that Simón Bolívar, too, was developing a plan to liberate Cuba and Puerto Rico. Both Gran Colombia and Mexico must have felt threatened by the proximity of the strategic Spanish colony to their shores, which may have motivated them to work together against Spain.[12]

However, maintaining armies in both Gran Colombia and Mexico proved too difficult, and so the rebellion leaders drew up plans instead for a joint Gran Colombian–Mexican expedition based in Mexico.[13] A link between Guadalupe Victoria, the commander general of Jalapa (and future Mexican president), and Cuban ex-friar Simón de Chávez, both of whom were part of the Gran Legión del Aguila Negra, ensured that the Junta Promotora de la Libertad Cubana, which represented the Cuban exile community living in Mexico, had a voice in the decision-making process of the expedition.[14] The plan was to drive the lingering Spanish army unit at the Fort of San Juan de Ulúa in Veracruz out of Mexico and then proceed onward to liberate Cuba.[15]

The United States had profited considerably from the turmoil in Latin America and the Caribbean during the early nineteenth century. It

▼▼▼

had acquired the Louisiana Purchase from France and Florida from the Spanish, which helped make it the most powerful nation in the hemisphere by 1823. This was the year President James Monroe (1817–25) declared the Monroe Doctrine, which proclaimed America's intention to curb European influence in the Americas as well as increase its own influence therein. Washington applied the doctrine to the Mexican-Cuban relationship in 1825. Cuba was the United States' number two trading partner after England, and so it is not surprising that, as Lucila Flamand shows, U.S. officials were concerned about the joint Mexican/Colombian expedition because they thought it might disrupt U.S.-Cuban trade.[16] To counter their plans, the United States tried to convince Spain to make peace with her former colonies and to convince Mexico and Gran Colombia to abandon their invasion plans.[17] The U.S. ambassador to Russia, Henry Middleton, received orders to oversee the Spanish recognition of its former colonies. The United States hoped that this gesture of goodwill would mitigate Mexico and Gran Colombia's fears of the Spanish colonial presence in Cuba.[18] The U.S. delegation leader in Mexico, Joel Poinsett, pleaded with Mexican foreign relations secretary Sebastián Camacho to pursue peace with Spain to no avail.[19] Poinsett openly expressed disdain for the Mexican people during his tenure, referring to them as "an ignorant and immoral race," which gives a sense of the character of foreign relations between the United States and Latin America at this time.[20] The plot was not, in the end, thwarted.

Apparently undaunted by the diplomatic row with the U.S. government, the Mexican Senate under President Guadalupe Victoria (1824–28) officially approved the military expedition to liberate Cuba in 1826. In response to this escalation in the planning, U.S. Secretary of State Henry Clay, "the Great Compromiser," tried to convince Colombian and Mexican delegates in Washington to desist in their liberation adventure. Colombia agreed to wait until a decision of all American states could be reached in Panama, but the Mexican government remained defiant, in spite of Clay's mediation and negotiation skills. The Mexican government had little choice but to attempt to oppose Spain militarily because it had recently augmented its forces at the Fort of San Juan de Ulúa. Still, it was not until

1828 that Mexican president Guadalupe Victoria finally authorized the departure of Mexican troops to Cuba, and then, for unknown reasons, this deployment never materialized.[21]

Despite the problems inherent in mounting an invasion of Cuba from Mexico, the Spanish presence in the Caribbean remained a nuisance to be dealt with. The following year, in 1829, Mexican president Vicente Guerrero (1829) enacted a law to expel most of the remaining Spaniards from the country. This expulsion, and the expedition that was prepared to launch an invasion of Cuba, coincided with the Spanish attempt at reconquest in the region, which signaled a further escalation in hostilities, making Mexico's need to defend itself from Spanish forces being supplied through Havana an urgent one.[22] The original Spanish invasion plans of Mexico aimed at the Mexican shores closest to Cuba, namely the Yucatán. Named the Real Orden, Spanish authorities had been planning this venture since August 1828, but the invasion was eventually abandoned in favor of the attack on Tampico the following year.[23] Led by Spanish General Isidro Barradas, the Spanish forces attacked Mexico's east coast port at Tampico in July of 1829 and were quickly repelled by Santa Anna's army, rapidly elevating Santa Anna's hero status, a crucial element in his future ascendancy to power and eleven-term tenure as president.[24] After several exchanges of authority in the Mexican presidential palace, strongly foreshadowing the turmoil to come for the next three decades in Mexico, in 1836, Mexico signed a peace treaty with Spain specifying that Mexico would respect Spanish rule over Cuba, thus precluding any further official Mexican attempts at liberating the island.[25] Although these efforts on the part of Mexico to secure Cuban liberation failed, "the struggle" against "imperialism" and the centrality of "revolution" in the Mexican-Cuban relationship form the root of their shared history, as Rodolfo Ruz Menéndez and Lucila Flamand show.

As Spain valued immensely its remaining Caribbean possessions, it is understandable that it regarded the Mexican–Gran Colombian plans as a menace, which perhaps added urgency to its reconquest agenda. Although no Mexican expedition ever came to fruition against Spanish dominion over Cuba, the ties forged between the Cuban exile communities in

▼▼▼

Mexico and the Mexican government during this movement created an incentive to cultivate the Mexican-Cuban relationship along these revolutionary lines.

At the same time, in the 1820s an uneven power struggle that has characterized U.S.–Latin American relations through to the present was set in motion. While neither the United States nor Mexico used force to carry out their goals during the Cuban liberation movement, in the end, even though Mexico did not give in to U.S. pressure, Gran Colombia did, and no doubt that capitulation made Mexican officials rethink the feasibility of their expedition to liberate Cuba.

This power struggle is also reflected in the way the United States handled the question of whether to recognize former Spanish colonies as countries, most of which had gained independence from Spain by the time of the Cuban liberation movement. As a sign of the times, three years before the Cuban liberation movement got underway, in 1821, Secretary of State John Quincy Adams (1817–25), who later served as president (1825–29), summarized the official U.S. attitude toward Latin Americans on this matter:

> [Latin Americans] have not the first elements of good or free government. Arbitrary power, military and ecclesiastical, was stamped upon their education, upon their habits, and upon all their institutions. Civil dissension was infused into all their seminal principles. War and mutual destruction was in every member of their organization, moral, political, and physical.[26]

This blatantly superior attitude was perceived by Mexicans and Cubans and had a deep effect on the direction of U.S.–Latin American relations in general.

The following decades would see the further enhancement of Mexican-Cuban relations with the advent of several armed conflicts as well as the further spread of U.S. influence and power in the region. The relationship continued to be defined in terms of mutual experience with opposing outside forces, namely Spain and the United States, especially after the

▼▼▼

latter had intervened several times in Mexico and Cuba between the mid-nineteenth and early twentieth centuries. What's more, by the time the Spanish had been pushed out of Mexico permanently in 1829 by Santa Anna's forces, Stephen Austin had seven years since led a band of settlers to the Mexican territory of Texas, paving the road for armed conflict between the United States and Mexico.

WHEN THE UNITED STATES SNEEZES, MEXICO AND CUBA CATCH COLDS, 1836–66

Many elements that shaped the U.S.–Latin American relationship from 1836–66 have remained as factors to this day. This era was a period of struggle for Mexico because its northern neighbor expanded territorily and grew in strength partly because of Mexico's instability. The initial problems between the United States and Mexico centered around disputes over the Texas territory originally settled by followers of Stephen Austin in 1822 that was part of the Mexican state of Chihuahua. Conflicts between the English-speaking, slaveholding Protestants of Texas and the Spanish-speaking, antislavery Catholics in Mexico City erupted when the Mexican military under General Antonio López de Santa Anna attacked the Texas independence movement begun in 1836. The infamous massacres of hundreds of Texans by Santa Anna's troops at Goliad and the Alamo only spurred the Texas revolt, leading to Santa Anna's capture and defeat after the ambush at San Jacinto where the Mexican leader granted Texas its independence. Texas became an independent republic for the next nine years until President John Tyler (1841–45) approved its annexation as a U.S. state in 1845, a decision backed by President James K. Polk (1845–49). Polk later convinced Congress to declare war on Mexico over a border dispute in 1846. The ensuing invasion resulted in a resounding U.S. victory by September 1847 and the Treaty of Guadalupe Hidalgo of February 1848, which ceded the Southwest territory to the United States.[27]

The issue of slavery rose in importance considerably as a result of the Mexican War's land spoils, as southerners and northerners in Congress fought over the status of the new territories. Meanwhile, the U.S.-Cuban relationship had been developing in a different direction since the early

▼▼▼

1800s owing to a steady increase in sugar sales from Cuba and the fact that a number of Cuban migrants were flowing into New York and Florida. During Polk's tenure, as Mexico was under U.S. occupation, the president attempted to secure the purchase of Cuba from Spain at a price of $100 million, a bid that failed. This was to be outdone by $30 million by President Franklin Pierce (1853–57) in 1854, but his offer was also refused.[28]

The U.S. expansionist policies of the 1840s and 1850s were supported by many Cubans upset with Spanish rule. One such group, called the Consejo de Gobierno Cubano, made up of exiles in New York, disseminated the annexationist vision openly in the United States and underground in Cuba with their newsletter, *La Verdad*. Cubans on the island also mounted a campaign to promote U.S. annexation through the Club de la Habana, which supported the failed filibustering adventure of Narciso López in his 1848, 1849, and 1851 attempts to make Cuba a U.S. territory. Southern interests supporting this effort stemmed from a desire to add more slave states to the Union, which explains why the vast majority of the filibusters who joined López's cause were American.[29]

Mexico also had its share of American filibustering. The infamous William Walker annexed Sonora for the United States in 1854 and then annexed Nicaragua in 1856, although the first annexation was quickly overturned by locals. The shared experience of Mexicans and Cubans in dealing with northern intervention and integration explains a lot about this triangular relationship. The three parties could not escape one another, for their interests often converge as well as diverge.

With the problems of forced annexation of Mexico and Cuba by filibusters extinguished, the early to mid-1860s signaled a new era of connections primarily due to the U.S. Civil War (1861–65) and the French occupation of Mexico (1862–67). President Abraham Lincoln (1861–65) saw the presence of French troops in Mexico as a violation of the Monroe Doctrine and sent assistance to Benito Juárez's guerrilla army fighting the resistance against Emperor Maximiliano. The emperor in turn developed a contraband trade with Confederates, which assisted both sides, and then invited two thousand ex-Confederates to settle in Mexico after the Civil War. These two thousand settlers were each given between three and six hundred acres of land, mostly in Veracruz, but by 1867, Juarez's army had overwhelmed the French, executed Emperor Maximiliano, and driven the majority of the Confederates out of the country.[30] The relationship between the United States and Cuba was likewise complicated by the Civil War. Lincoln's Emancipation Proclamation of 1863 caused a reversal in sentiment among many Cuban planters with annexationist aspirations who now feared the spread of abolition to Cuba. Planters' fears grew when many rebels in the Ten Years' War (1868–78) took up the abolitionist cause.

The three decades following the Civil War only drove the countries closer together. But the overwhelmingly unbalanced power relationship between the United States and its Latin American neighbors also drove a wedge between the United States on the one hand, and Cuba and Mexico on the other. Mexico and Cuba were thrust together through a cultural affinity of mutual experience in dealing with dominant powers.

Cross-Patriotism through Battle and Immigration during the Ten Years' War, 1868–78

Cuban rebels took up arms against the Spanish colonial regime on October 10, 1868. Led by Carlos Manuel de Céspedes, the Grito de Yara ("the call to rebellion"), as the uprising is known, included several Mexican and Cuban leaders who had also served under Benito Juárez (Mexican president, 1858–72) in the War of the Reform (1858–61) and in the Mexican war against the French (1862–67).[31] The Mexican government and press gave valuable support and solidarity to the Céspedes's insurgency and opened its doors to Cuban immigrants fleeing the chaos of the war, spawning a new era of cultural affinity, particularly between Yucatán and Cuba, that lasted well into the twentieth century.[32]

The decision by the Mexican high military officers to fight the Spanish legitimated and strengthened Céspedes's movement. Prominent Mexican officers such as Ramón Cantú, José Medinas, Rafael Estéves, Felipe Herreros, and José Inclán Riasco, whose recent victory under Benito Juárez when he expelled the French from Mexico had filled them with confidence, fought for Céspedes with valor.[33] Cuban-born Manuel

▼▼▼

Quesada and his brother Rafael had both fought for Juárez as generals in the War of the Reform and against the French, after which Manuel went on to Cuba to serve as commander of all insurgent armies during the Ten Years' War.[34]

A look at the case of José Inclán serves as an extraordinary example of the Cuban-Mexican cross-patriotic link. Born in Puebla, Inclán helped defend that city from the French in 1862. The French captured and deported him to France, from where he escaped, returned to Mexico, and was awarded the rank of colonel. In 1868, Inclán rebelled against the Juárez government. He was sentenced to death but was allowed instead go into exile in Cuba. There, Inclán joined Céspedes and rose to the rank of brigadier general, serving faithfully until he was captured by the Spanish and executed in 1872.[35] President Juárez himself was affected by this interrelationship, for he soon discovered that his friend, Domingo Goicuria, had been captured by the Spanish while fighting for Céspedes and hung in May of 1870.[36]

Extensive political backing for Céspedes in Mexico accompanied Mexican troop involvement. Political endorsement came from Mexican congressional representatives who requested "immediate support" for the insurgents in Cuba at official meetings in December 1868.[37] Financial assistance was, however, not forthcoming from official Mexico. But it did answer a request for a different sort of assistance entered by a Cuban exile group in Matamoros on March 9, 1869, to the governor of Tamaulipas. The group asked if the Mexican government could recognize the belligerency of Céspedes's insurgency in order to afford the rebels the credibility they desired. On April 5, the Mexican congress voted ninety-seven to eleven in favor of belligerent-status recognition of the Céspedes forces.[38] Several of those opposed claimed that they in fact supported Cuban independence yet had voted against the resolution because according to the 1857 Constitution, the Congress did not have the power to determine foreign policy. Rather it was only able to reject or ratify the decisions of the president who was the ultimate authority.[39] President Juárez did recognize the belligerency of Céspedes's Republic in Arms, after which, on June 9, Céspedes praised Juárez in a letter, stating "I am highly satisfied that Mexico has been the first nation of [the Americas] that has demonstrated its generous sympathies like this to the cause of the independence and liberty of Cuba."[40]

The press also played a role in the expression of mutual solidarity between Mexicans and Cubans in the Cuban independence movement. The Mexican press published many works by people sympathetic to Cuba's struggle and gave much attention to the congressional meetings that concerned the debate over the Céspedes movement's belligerency status. During his consular service in Cuba, Cuban-born Mexican consul to Havana Andrés Clemente Vázques wrote articles covering the independence struggle that were published in the news daily *Siglo 19* and in a book entitled *La cuestión de Cuba*.[41] Once Cuban immigrants began to flow into Mexico, especially into Yucatán during the Ten Years' War, they also began to play a prominent role in the Mexican press. The best known of these Cuban visitors was José Martí, the future father of Cuban independence, who wrote for *El Universal* from 1875–76 during what was just one visit to Mexico.[42]

By 1870, between two and three thousand Cubans fleeing the war had emigrated to Mexico.[43] As a result, according to Rodolfo Ruz Menéndez, Cuban culture became so prevalent in Yucatán that even today "Yucatán is similar to Cuba, like no other region."[44] The Cuban immigrants were made up of doctors, educators, revolutionaries fleeing persecution, and farmers.[45] The farmers set up sugar and tobacco plantations in Veracruz, as the climate is similar to that of Cuba, which had a long history of cultivating these crops.[46] Public education in Yucatán was perhaps the most influenced by Cuban immigrants, and the contributors to journalism, literature, and history spread extensively throughout Mexico, with some ending up in politics.[47] Languages also intermingled in Yucatán, as is evident today to visitors who still hear the Cuban word "*guagua*" for "bus" in Mérida occasionally. Cuba also feels this influence, as Havana has a neighborhood named "Barrio Campeche."[48] Even today, trolling through Mérida, one has the feeling of walking through the streets of Matanzas, Cuba, and the Cuban guayabera shirt has become more commonplace in Yucatán than in Cuba. It was the difficulties of the Ten Years' War that spurred Cuban emigration from 1868–78, but emigration continued well after the war had ended.

▼▼▼

The United States, in contrast to Mexico and against its own earlier annexationist intentions, opposed Mexico's recognition of the belligerency of Céspedes's movement. U.S. president Ulysses S. Grant (1869–77) refused to recognize the insurgents' right to rebel, in spite of Céspedes's declaration that the uprising's aims were to pave the way toward annexation to the United States.[49] Grant's refusal symbolized a larger historical pattern of U.S. intentions in Cuba. According to historian John S. C. Abbott, who traveled to the island in 1859, for the United States there were "but two conceivable measures of annexation, namely *purchase* or *seizure*."[50] That the United States viewed Cuba as a resource for American consumption was quite apparent to Cubans leery of U.S. influence on the island, some of whom viewed U.S. intentions there in the context of its actions against Mexico. According to Louis A. Pérez, "Cubans feared, too, that they would share the fate of the Hispano-Mexican population in the territories seized from Mexico in 1848, when longtime residents were displaced and dispossessed of their homes and property by a myriad of bewildering new laws and legal proceedings rigged to favor Anglo-American litigants."[51] Nineteenth-century American traveler Richard Dana confirms that these fears existed, writing that Cuban Creoles were concerned in the 1850s "that the Anglo-Saxon race would swallow up the power and property of the island, as they have done in California and Texas, and that the Creoles would go to the wall."[52] These portrayals of the Mexican experience with the United States that is reflected in Cuban fears of U.S. annexation of Cuba was by no means universal, as noted above, but they do sufficiently demonstrate commonality of perspective among Mexicans and Cubans who were wary of U.S. influence in their countries and who would become more so in the years to come.

JOSÉ MARTÍ: SPREADING CROSS-PATRIOTIC VALUES IN MEXICO

Known as the "apostle" in Cuba, José Martí is idealized for his leadership of the Cuban liberation movement of the late 1800s. Although he was killed in his first battle in the beginning of the 1895–98 war against Spain, Martí had been building a constituency for the movement all over North America for two decades prior. He made trips to Mexico in 1875,

1877, 1884, and 1894, during times when greater numbers of Cubans were emigrating to Mexico. Immigration from 1878–95 brought many other notable Cubans to Yucatán, such as the Betancourts, the Urzaizes, and the Loret de Molas. These families and others formed revolutionary clubs in Mérida and Progreso. Club members produced two newspapers, *La Estrella Solitaria* and *La Bandera Cubana*, to promote the interests of Cuban exiles in Mexico and to form the basis for the future revolutionary struggle that supported Martí's efforts to oust the Spanish crown from the Americas.[53]

José Martí established connections with these clubs during his stays in Mexico in 1875 and 1877, gaining the general support for Cuban independence from these prominent Cuban exiles.[54] The information disseminated in the revolutionary newspapers came from correspondence between the clubs and José Martí, who maintained connections with revolutionary leaders in Cuba such as Tomás Estrada Palma, José Antonio Maceo, and the generalissimo, Máximo Gómez.[55] Martí wrote a regular column for *El Universal* out of Mexico City during the year 1875–76, astutely commenting on internal Mexican affairs. Martí wrote about the turmoil surrounding the elections of 1876, and he expressed suspicion of the emerging power of Porfirio Díaz (Mexican president, 1876–1911). By 1892, two revolutionary clubs, Máximo Gómez No. 2 and Aponte No. 1, in Mexico City and Veracruz, respectively, represented the foundation of the Cuban Revolutionary Party.[56] Eventually, the clubs began to gather support for the evolving Cuban independence movement being led by José Martí.[57]

Martí's trips to Mexico in the 1870s facilitated his mission to Mexico in 1894 because by then he had established a network of Cuban exile friends with connections to the Mexican elite. According to Cuban author, Ramón de Armas, Martí visited Mexico in 1894 for three reasons: to confirm financial support from the Cuban immigrant community, "to counteract the anti-Cuban activity of the resident Spaniards there," and "to arrange for the dual help of the Mexican government: economic [first]; [and] political, immediately after."[58] Martí hoped to obtain financial support from Porfirio Díaz, but he solicited help from other powerful Mexicans as well, according de Armas.[59]

▼▼▼

Martí wrote several very respectful letters to Díaz in 1894 in which he requested meetings, appealing to the Mexican leader's sense of responsibility by explaining that Cuba's freedom from Spain affected all of Central and South America.[60] Martí emphasized that especially "those of the northern part of the continent" were adversely affected by Spanish control of Cuba.[61] There are a couple of different accounts of the meeting that then took place between Díaz and Martí.[62] Mexican novelist Federico Gamboa Díaz asserts that Manuel A. Mercado witnessed Díaz present Martí with funds "from his own private supply" to support Martí's revolt.[63] Carlos Díaz Dufoó claims to have conducted the interview between the two political leaders, and his testimony agrees with that of Gamboa Díaz. Author Ramón de Armas reports Ramón Prida as having confirmed that Martí spoke with Díaz but being unsure whether Díaz gave Martí any money.[64] However, Alfonso Herrera Franyutti cites Prida as claiming that Díaz presented Martí with $20,000, and that Díaz asserted that Mexico could not officially recognize the insurgent forces as belligerent.[65] Although President Díaz may have assisted Martí's cause, his official stance was neutral in this conflict.[66] The motivation for Mexico's diplomatic stance most likely resided in its own political interests, given that there were pro-Spanish elements within Mexico at this time as well as pro-Cuban.[67]

Whether Martí's meeting with Díaz was a success or not, Martí certainly triumphed in his mission to gain support among the Cuban immigrant community in Mexico. After meeting with powerful Cubans in Mexico City, the word of the Cuban independence movement's vision spread to native Mexicans and exiled Cubans alike, and by 1895, five more Cuban revolutionary clubs had cropped up in Mexico, including one for women. Martí also spent considerable time in New York City during his campaign, after arriving there in exile in 1880. This helped connect the exile communities of the United States with the Cuban independence movement in Cuba and Mexico, thus completing the triangle. After residing in the United States for fifteen years, Martí had developed a political philosophy that transformed the notion of "Cuba Libre," first invented among annexationists in the United States and Cuba, into the idea of a liberation both from Spain and the United States. Martí had begun to view the United States as more of a threat to Cuban sovereignty than Spain, in fact.[68] One event in particular disillusioned Martí's view of the role of the U.S. government: the Haymarket Affair of 1886, in which Chicago police were accused of killing and beating workers in Haymarket Square. Martí also soon learned not to rely on help from Cuban exiles living in New York City. At the same time, however, he found a wide base of support in Tampa, Florida's cigar-making community. By 1895, Tampa supplied ample backing for the independence war that began that year.[69]

Mexico had developed extensive trade and political relations with Spain by then, and this may have prevented it from taking concrete sides in the war.[70] However, it did volunteer to mediate to end the war in 1896 after the Spaniard general Valeriano Weyler began his infamous "reconcentration policy" that forced thousands of Cubans into concentration camps where many died.[71] On March 17, the Mexican representative to Spain proposed that Spain grant political and administrative autonomy to Cuba along with amnesty to the rebels. Spain refused, which caused Díaz to shift attention away from mediation efforts. He soon faced a dilemma involving the United States.[72]

According to author Rafael Rojas, the U.S. congressional recognition of the belligerent status of the Cuban insurgents on March 27, 1896, provoked a surprising shift in Mexico's diplomatic position vis-à-vis the Cuban War of Independence.[73] Fearing expansionist motives in the U.S. Congress's decision, Mexico briefly sided with Spain against the insurgents. For example, Díaz encouraged the Spanish colony in Puebla to support the counterinsurgency effort against Cuban independence fighters. In June, Puebla's Spanish colony sent an armed contingent to Cuba, and two Havana dailies claimed Mexico would side with Spain if the United States invaded Cuba. To support his point, Rojas reports that Díaz ordered the suppression of anti-Spanish elements operating in Veracruz during the Mexican Independence Day festivities of September 15 and 16.[74]

Mexicans also debated the possibility of annexing Cuba to Mexico as an alternative to continuing the war. The Mexican press, legislators, and other groups were the main proponents of this proposal both before and during the war, but Díaz declined to consider it. In 1884, Cuban-born

▼▼▼

Mexican congressman Carlos Américo Lera began espousing Mexican annexation of Cuba in the press and in Congress and even published a book called *Cuba mexicana* in 1896. This tract promulgated the benefits of a merger of the two countries, and U.S. Senator John Sherman supported Lera's proposal in the hope it would prevent the U.S. efforts to acquire Cuba. However, factors such as the financial burden of Cuban wartime damages and a general lack of Mexican interest in the idea made annexation impractical.[75] Racial prejudice against the 33 percent Afro-Cuban, and 1 percent Chinese-Cuban populations expressed by Mexico's consul to Havana Andrés Clemente Vázquez may have also played a role in undermining support for annexation.[76]

Of course, after the sinking of the USS *Maine* in Havana Harbor in February 1898, the issue of annexation evaporated as the United States entered the war against Spain.[77] Soon, Joseph Pulitzer's and William Randolph Hearst's newspaper machines were engaging in sensationalist jingoism to rally support for the Spanish-American War. The hope was to expel Spain from the hemisphere and advance U.S. influence in the Caribbean and eventually the Pacific. The U.S. military invaded Cuba, Puerto Rico, and the Philippines, and within four years of the American defeat of the Spanish in 1898 Cuba became a protectorate of the United States under the Platt Amendment of 1902. The United States has maintained the right to a naval base in Guantánamo Bay ever since.[78]

The U.S.-Mexican economic and political relationship grew substantially throughout this period, particularly under the leadership of Porfirio Díaz. The Mexican dictator amplified the liberal economic policies begun under Juárez by coaxing foreign investments into Mexico and extending trade networks with Europe and the United States. This eventually led to unprecedented growth in Mexico, which resulted both in the intensification of economic integration between the United States and Mexico and some mistrust among Mexicans leery of U.S. interests there.

This period symbolized the growing convergence of interests among Cubans and Mexicans over the role of the United States in their own affairs. The Cuban-Mexican connections during the Ten Years' War and beyond, unified many from both countries along revolutionary and cultural lines, promoting solidarity that has resonated through to the present. Likewise, the growing U.S. financial interests in Cuba and Mexico generated deeper political concerns for American officials seeking to preserve this relationship. José Martí's movement helped bring all three countries together through his travels and his message, which worried some and unified others. Eventual official U.S. involvement in the Cuban independence fight shaped Mexico's stance on the war in Cuba and soon ignited a wave of anti-American sentiment among Cubans who viewed the U.S. presence in the same terms espoused by their martyred leader: "the greatest threat to Cuban independence."[79] This was also the increasingly popular view of many in Mexico, who had witnessed not only the loss of half of their territory between 1836 and 1848 but also the growing wealth of U.S. business interests into their country, as Mexican poverty mounted. Eventually, Mexico experienced a repeat of U.S. intervention during the Mexican Revolution (1910–20) that further enhanced Mexican-Cuban affinities. The Mexican Revolution is yet another example of how conflict has served to drive the United States, Cuba, and Mexico together historically.

MEXICAN IMMIGRATION TO CUBA
IN THE MIDST OF LA REVOLUCIÓN, 1910–27

The Mexican Revolution of 1910–20 stands alone in twentieth-century Latin American revolutions for its success, length, and human and economic toll, among other attributes. This important stage in Mexican history paved Mexico's way toward Latin American revolutionary leadership. Soon political exiles from all over Latin America found refuge there, and the legacy of agrarian, economic, political, educational, and other reforms carried out by the Mexican Revolution (embodied in its 1917 Constitution) proved to other Latin Americans that change was possible. The liberal reforms of the late nineteenth century occurring across Latin America had set the first stage for revolution, but many Latin American nations had opted for a more austere form of liberalism (inspired by positivism) that placed export-oriented growth above all other priorities, including

▼▼▼

democratization. Thus, dictatorships, such as that of Porfirio Díaz in Mexico, took root in several Latin American nations. When Mexican revolutionaries such as Francisco Madero, Emiliano Zapata, and Pancho Villa took up arms against Díaz in 1910, they sought to overthrow the neocolonialism of the positivist era, which had perpetuated the colonially entrenched disenfranchisement of the masses for the socioeconomic benefit of the minority.

At the same time, the advent of the Mexican Revolution in 1910 brought a wave of human and economic desperation to Mexico, and the level of destruction of the war from 1911 to 1917 forced a mass exodus during which more than double the number of people left Mexico for Cuba than had left between 1904 and 1910.[80] The Mexicans who emigrated to Cuba from 1910–27 included businessmen, laborers, domestic servants, politicians, artists, and journalists, totaling at least 5,680 documented cases.[81] Mexicans were second only to the Spanish in immigration to Cuba between 1910 and 1927, and a 1931 census found 3,352 Mexicans living in Cuba, which, when compared to the 1907 number of 1,187, indicates that their repatriation may have been minimal even more than a decade after the fighting ended.[82] These numbers suggest that Cuba returned the favor to Mexico for its assistance with Cuba's refugee problem during the Ten Years' War and after.

The economic classes of the Mexican immigrants reflect the nature of the Mexican Revolution. A strong correlation exists between the peak years of the war and the high number of businessmen comprising the Mexican immigrants from 1911–17. This contrasts with the 1917–27 immigrants, who were composed of high numbers of laborers and domestic workers. This wave brought Mexican and Cuban lower socioeconomic classes together, whose interests fused temporarily when thirty Yucatecs, hired as strikebreakers for the United Railroads Company, defied their employers by condemning them in the press.[83]

Repeated change in Mexican leadership during this period meant that there were waves of immigrant groups loyal to ousted presidents arriving in Cuba. For example, in 1916, after the death of Porfirio Díaz, the Mexican colony in Cuba had a funeral in his honor.[84] In 1913, the family of the slain

Francisco I. Madero (Mexican president, 1911–13) spent several days in Havana on its way to the United States, and supporters of the assassinated Mexican president also emigrated to Cuba, bringing their political practices with them.[85] Supporters of Madero formed the Junta Constitucionalista del Movimiento Restaurador in Havana, which received support from the Cuban community, who wanted to see Madero's successor, Victoriano Huerta (1913–14), ousted. Cuban press support came from the *Heraldo de Cuba*. The Cuban government also lent official support.[86] Cuban president José Miguel Gómez disapproved of Huerta's ascension to power and therefore "facilitated the entry of numerous refugees, many of whom were able to carry out their conspiratorial activities without having many obstacles."[87]

The next Cuban president, Mario García Menocal, also refused to recognize the Huerta government. Author Luis Angel Argüelles Espinosa contends that this conservative leader was probably not acting out of solidarity for the legitimate government under Madero but rather more likely had been influenced by the U.S. government's nonrecognition policy.[88] The notion that Menocal was following the United States finds support in the fact that Menocal recognized the Mexican government of Venustiano Carranza (who was officially elected in 1917 and remained president until 1920) in 1915, soon after the United States had done the same.[89] However, beginning in 1914, after Huerta's downfall, President Menocal appears to have enabled the immigration of many Huertistas as well, who included politicians, generals, and clergymen, who worked to discredit the constitutionalist Mexican government of Venustiano Carranza. The Huertista group formed the Centro Mexicano de Auxilios Mutuos in Havana, and the Cuban newspaper *Diario de la Marina* served as a Huertista anti-Carranza propaganda machine.[90]

The Villista and Zapatista immigrant political positions also found representation in the Cuban press. Emiliano Zapata's "official representative," General Jenaro Amezcua, wrote for the Cuban newspapers *La Discusión, El Mundo, Solidaridad,* and others.[91] Notable within the Villa camp's immigrant group were General Roque González Garza, one of his wives and her son (Luz Corral and Agustín), his brother (Hipólito Villa), and his head surgeon (Miguel Silva).[92] The fact that several sides of the complex Mexican conflict found representation and succor in Cuba speaks to the integrated nature of Mexican-Cuban relations and lends some credence to the claims on the part of modern Mexican and Cuban officials that this relationship is special owing to its history of revolutionary mutuality.

This mutuality became ever more solid for future generations of revolutionaries as conflict with the "norteamericanos" grew. The United States intervened three times in Mexico's revolutionary process, in fact. First, U.S. Ambassador to Mexico Henry Lane Wilson, apparently operating without the consent of President Woodrow Wilson (1913–21), supported the overthrow of revolutionary leader and Mexican president Francisco Madero in February 1913. Second, in 1914 Wilson sent the Marines to Veracruz, who forcibly occupied the port city. Third, Wilson sent troops under General John "Blackjack" Pershing into Mexico in 1916 to hunt down Pancho Villa to punish him for his raid on Columbus, New Mexico, that year. These three interventions were largely seen by Mexicans as examples of U.S. intrusion in Latin American affairs and worked to increase the mutual understanding among Cubans and Mexicans that U.S. interests sought to infringe on Latin American autonomy.

MEXICAN AND CUBAN REVOLUTIONS INTERTWINED

This commonality of experience soon grew to monumental proportions with the rise of the Mexico's Institutional Revolutionary Party (PRI) and the advent of the Cuban Revolution. Mexico's series of revolutionary presidents, including Alvaro Obregon (1920–24, 1929), Plutarco Elias Calles (1924–28), and especially, Lázaro Cárdenas (1934–40), established the Mexican Revolution as a force for reform. Cárdenas is remembered popularly today as "Tata Cárdenas," a president of "the people" who put social welfare at the top of his agenda. Most importantly for Mexicans and Cubans alike, he is known for his massive agrarian reform policy that distributed close to fifty million acres of land to the people during his presidency.[93] One Cuban author expresses the role of President Cárdenas as "historic . . . in the Cuban revolutionary process" and in the lives of the Cuban and Mexican people.[94] The author goes on to say, referring to what Cárdenas accomplished, that "the historic deed of the Mexican people is the threshold of a new society that the Cuban people inaugurate[d] in 1959."[95] In any case, the Mexican Revolution's tenets of agrarian, labor, political, and economic reforms formed the closest model to socialism Latin America had ever seen and, according to Castro and other Cuban revolutionaries themselves, greatly influenced the Cuban Revolution that began in 1953. In an interview with *Siempre!* on July 26, 1959, Castro said, "You could say that the Mexican Revolution influenced the Cuban Revolution very much."[96] Essential to our understanding of Mexico's influence on Cuba is the role played by Mexican president Lázaro Cárdenas in the Cuban Revolution and the training of the participants in Castro's July 26 movement in Mexico from 1955–56.

However, the Cuban Revolution had rocky beginnings that jeopardized its success. On July 26, 1953, Castro initiated the revolution with a failed attack against the Moncada army barracks in Santiago de Cuba. Most of Castro's followers were either killed or captured. At his trial, he made his famous "History Will Absolve Me" speech in which he articulated the illegality of the Batista regime, which had come to power via coup d'etat in 1952, as well as the righteousness of his own struggle to liberate Cuba. Communism did not drive the Cuban Revolution at this stage, and this fact no doubt helped lend sympathy to Castro during his imprisonment until 1955. Under national and international pressure, Batista granted him and his followers amnesty and they left for Mexico City soon afterward.[97]

Castro's time in Mexico City would serve him well; he had entered the traditional safe haven for exiles of all nationalities. There he slowly built up his base of support among Cuban exiles and Mexicans. This too was also not without precedent but rather dated back to the 1800s when, as we have seen, Cuban and Mexican revolutionaries worked to liberate Cuba and to defend Mexico. Castro and his brother Raul formed a guerrilla band there that included Ernesto "Che" Guevara, who eventually became the most famous Latin American revolutionary symbol in history. For the next year and a half, Castro organized a training regimen and fund-raising operation in Mexico.[98] However, the movement nearly dissolved in

▼▼▼

mid-June 1956 after Mexican police arrested Castro and many of the other guerrilla recruits on the charge of conspiring to assassinate Batista.[99] Castro publicly denied the charges, but Batista urged Mexican president Adolfo Ruiz Cortines (1952–58) to extradite the men to Cuba.[100]

Several prominent Mexican officials and popular organizations soon led an effort to obtain their release. On June 29, 1956, Mexico daily *Excelsior* printed an open letter to President Ruiz Cortines from the Cuban student group, Ateneo IV Centenario, whose long list of signatories pleaded for their release. The letter invoked Mexico's reputation as an historically hospitable location for exiles and Cuba's reputation for helping Mexicans in their times of national crisis as well.[101] *Excelsior* also published a letter to President Ruiz Cortines on July 7 from another Cuban group with the same request but who aimed their criticism more at Batista: "We are not those who aspire to break the bonds of traditional fraternity between Mexico and Cuba, they are the scheming members of the Cuban Military Intelligence Service."[102] The authors of this letter also recognized the long-standing friendship between Mexico and Cuba and equated Batista's request for Castro's extradition with counterrevolution. After letters of solidarity such as this, one of the most influential Mexican ex-presidents, Lázaro Cárdenas, helped persuade President Ruiz Cortines to release Castro and his group in late July.[103] This foreshadowed the solidarity that Cárdenas would later show for Castro's Cuba, a deed for which Castro has remained grateful to this day.

U.S. CONCERNS

At the same time as the Cuban Revolution was gaining extensive international attention, the U.S. government was busy focusing on the threat of the "international Communist conspiracy." The House Committee on Un-American Activities put itself at the vanguard of this defensive front, and its 1958 report on prominent Communist leaders around the world included among such names as Nikita Khrushchev and Ho Chi Minh the two prominent Latin American socialists, Vicente Lombardo Toledano, secretary general of Mexico's Popular Party (PP), and Luis Carlos Prestes, secretary general of the Brazilian Communist Party.

Lombardo holds a special place in radical Mexican politics, not only for his links to ex-President Cárdenas but also for the extent of his influence in Mexico. A former governor of Puebla, a union leader, federal deputy, and head of the Workers' University until his death in 1968, Lombardo participated in Mexican public life over half of a century. He created the Mexican Workers' Confederation (CTM) in 1936 and later ran for president as a candidate of the PP in 1952, which became the Popular Socialist Party (PPS) in 1960. More than any other Marxist Mexican figure, Lombardo represented a radical alternative to the PRI, if only for a small percentage of the Mexican populace.[104]

The introduction to the Latin America section of the House Committee on Un-American Activities report, written by committee chair Francis E. Walter, stated that "despite ostensible changes in Soviet policy, the ultimate objective of international communism remains constant world conquest. We can disregard the records of the leaders of international communism only at the price of our freedom."[105] In order to support his case for concern over the spread of the Communist threat in Latin America, he asserted that "Lombardo and Prestes rank as two of the Kremlin's key agents in the Western Hemisphere; they command enormous influence in two nations whose resources and geographical location are vital to the defense of the United States and the Western Hemisphere."[106] Thus, U.S. concern over Mexico's role in spreading what would later be spread by Castro's revolution preceded U.S. concern over Castro's influence on Latin American leftists. This worry would increase considerably after Castro's success in 1959, soon after which the island nation became the focal point of U.S. hemispheric security policy.

An interesting side note to this era is the interaction between Mexican ambassador Gilberto Bosques and Cuban dictator Fulgencio Batista. In December 1953, six months after Castro's attack on the Moncada Barracks, the two officials exchanged friendly comments that spoke to the historically rooted relationship that existed between Mexico and Cuba even before the Cuban Revolution. Bosques wrote to Batista that "Cuba and Mexico are people of substantial affinities, united through historical causes."[107] He went on to observe that both nations celebrated the centennials of Mexican

▼▼▼

Figure 1: Lithograph by Angel Bracho, title unknown
(Source: MLN, *Programa y llamamiento* [Mexico City:
República del Salvador, 1961], 19).

and Cuban national martyrs, José Martí and Miguel Hidalgo y Costilla, that year: this signified the "historical causes" that "united" Cuba and Mexico, as it would for years to come in political rhetoric.[108]

In fact, Martí became the symbolic unifier between Mexico and Cuba in a lithograph produced by Angel Bracho, from the Mexican leftist art workshop, the Taller de Gráfica Popular, which depicts men and women from both countries shaking hands in solidarity, holding each other's national flag, with Martí looking over the two sides from above.[109] Bosques ended his letter emphasizing the honor he felt in serving his country in the "glorious fatherland of Martí, which all Mexicans love so much."[110] Batista responded with the words that serve as the epigraph to this chapter: "[W]e will never forget that . . . [Mexico] was asylum and home . . . for Cuban patriots in the past century," and he commented on the "appreciable cooperation from Mexico, in the sad days of [the Cuban patriots'] exile in other lands," a reference to the nineteenth-century exile of many Cubans who had resisted the Spanish and fled to Mexico.[111] Several Cuban papers covered this exchange, and if nothing else, the language used depicting the long-running history of friendly relations between Mexico and Cuba at this time further demonstrates the foundations of Mexican-Cuban relations prior to 1959.

Mexican and Cuban nationalism thus began to coincide with Castro's rise to power. The similarities between the revolutions played no small part in this new era, which increasingly aligned the revolutionaries in both countries along transnationally mutual lines. The basic reforms of the Cuban Revolution (agrarian, economic, labor, and education reforms) were the same ones that drove the Mexican Revolution and formed the basis of its 1917 Constitution. However, the revolutions played themselves out differently as much as similarly. For example, while Mexico maintained a semblance of an electoral system, rooted in basic, albeit corruptible, federalism, Cuba has been a totalitarian Communist system under Fidel Castro for over four decades. And though the state-owned industries in both countries represented parallel interests that linked public ownership over resources to revolutionary nationalism, in the end, Cuban revolutionary ideals were deliberately exported to many other countries, often at the request of

▼▼▼

governments and just as often against their wishes, whereas Mexico restricted its concerns during its revolution to domestic Mexico. Cuba's revolutionary exploits beyond its borders also in a sense delegitimized its revolution and contributed to its increasing isolation in the hemisphere.

In the end, the pre-1959 era has been used by self-proclaimed revolutionaries in Cuba and Mexico in the post-1959 era in particular as a means of historically appropriating the meaning of several events in Mexican-Cuban relations history. To the extent that Mexican-Cuban relations are understood to be unique or special in light of Mexico's stance since Castro's rise to power, we must consider the pre-1959 era as the initial building block on which this history rests. Consequently, any bilateral relations history can be scrutinized in the same vein, for we see how select events over the course of two centuries, when represented as perpetuating a positive relationship between two nations, can take on a life of their own.

CHAPTER TWO

CASTRO'S SPLASH IN MEXICO, 1959–64

[Fidel Castro is] a young intellectual with a
vehement temperament and the blood of a fighter.

—Former Mexican president Lázaro Cárdenas
speaking of Fidel Castro immediately after the
triumph of Castro's Revolution in January 1959

THE PERIOD FROM 1959–64 witnessed a dramatic shift in inter-American relations that stemmed largely from Castro's rise to power and the subsequent U.S. response. The gradual demise of U.S.-Cuban relations, Castro's public announcement that the Cuban Revolution was Marxist-Leninist, and the ostracism of Cuba in the Americas was only balanced by Mexico's stance as the sole Latin American nation to maintain relations with Cuba for six years after the rest of the countries in the Organization of American States (OAS) voted to sever relations with Cuba in 1964. This established Mexico's international revolutionary legitimacy as Third World liberation movements from Africa to Asia to Latin America surged during this same period. All three nations soon became engaged in a delicate balancing act only moderated by the precarious environment created by the Cuban Revolution. In its wake U.S. anti-Communist concerns in Latin America focused largely on Castro's influence as it grew with the emergence of guerrilla, labor, and official leftist movements in Bolivia, Peru, Chile, Central America, Argentina, Uruguay, Brazil, Jamaica, Colombia, Guyana, the Dominican Republic, and Mexico. Castro's influence and the U.S. response simultaneously increased Latin American anti-U.S. sentiment as well as forged anti-Communist links across the Americas.

The emerging triangle of relations therefore signified a new trajectory in intrahemispheric relations. Mexico and Cuba now decisively stood out as major players in the Cold War. Of course, the fact that "Third World" nations had a say in matters related to international security did not mean they had the only say, and these nations were indeed shaped by events beyond their control. However, they demonstrated an eagerness to participate on their own terms as well as in conjunction with the rest of the global community. This must be seen as a major factor affecting U.S.-Mexican relations, which improved markedly in the 1960s. This in turn affected Mexican-Cuban relations. Castro's defiant position toward U.S. hegemony was countered by a U.S. policy that much of the hemisphere eventually adopted. Meanwhile Mexico's relation with Cuba was tempered by its cooperation with the United States in controlling Castro's influence on Mexico. As a result of the policy positions of all three nations, Mexico ultimately found itself in the unique position of maintaining close relations with two countries that were bitter enemies. U.S. officials sometimes used Mexico as a mediator between Cuba and the United States over issues such as the Central American conflicts of the 1980s and the so-called "baseball diplomacy" of the 1970s.[1] In addition, Mexico stood out internationally during this period for its immediate recognition of Cuba's legitimacy after Castro's January 1959 victory.

In fact, the United States followed quickly thereafter, a policy line it would soon repeal. However, this stance made considerable sense at the time because the United States had cut off aid to Batista during the Cuban Revolution just as Castro's rebels surged in strength.[2] This act was not entirely without merit. Despite the perception that the United States consistently supported regimes involved in counterinsurgency campaigns, in fact, during the Cold War it pulled support from a pro-U.S. regime during a revolution two times, from Cuba in 1958 and Nicaragua in 1979. In both cases, the regimes had become increasingly brutal in the eyes of their own people as well as the U.S. government. In Cuba, Batista's human rights abuses had escalated in response to Castro's revolutionary activities and his rising popularity in the cities and countryside, and it was these abuses that compelled the State Department to withdraw its support for the Cuban dictator. In Nicaragua over two decades later, the Somoza government's escalation of repression against the population occurred in tandem with the growing support for the Sandinista uprising, and this repression elicited the cutoff of support for Somoza from the Carter White House. The ensuing defeats of these governments perhaps were spurred on by the lack of U.S. official support for them, among other things.

Richard Weitz has argued that official U.S. support was one of four crucial elements for a successful Latin American revolution during the Cold War. In examining four cases where insurgency and counterinsurgency took place (Bolivia, Cuba, Nicaragua, and Venezuela), he attempts to isolate the variables in the successful insurgencies (Nicaragua and Cuba) to establish a model that should describe which conditions are most conducive to triumphant insurgencies in Latin America.[3] Weitz also explores aspects of each society under study that had an undetermined impact on the insurgents' failure or success, which included "the performance of the economy at the time of the insurgency; the existence of ethnic cleavages in these nations; the geographic location of the guerrilla's main base operations; and the quality of the insurgents' leadership."[4]

The four variables Weitz identifies illuminate another commonality between Mexico and Cuba as revolutionary nations. The first, "the strategy and the tactics of the guerrillas," has had an effect on revolutions throughout the Cold War and even before in Latin America. For example, the insurgents had moderate reform goals in both Cuba and Nicaragua and their strikes against their opponents were surgically planned in an attempt to avoid civilian casualties. The initial stage of the Mexican Revolution (1910–11), led by Francisco Madero, was also moderate in its aims. The unifying goal across the country was the overthrow of the dictator Porfirio Díaz. During the Cold War, moderation helped the two successful revolutions in Cuba and Nicaragua appear less threatening internally and internationally. Conversely, in Venezuela (one counterexample provided by Weitz) the radical left conducted a campaign of "urban terrorism in the futile hope that they could engender a military coup against the popularly-elected government."[5] Likewise in Bolivia, Che Guevara's ill-fated plan to overthrow the Barrientos regime stemmed from Communist aspirations, the likes of which frightened rather than motivated the average Bolivian.[6]

The second variable for success was rural-urban coordination. The

▼▼▼

movements in Cuba and Nicaragua in the 1950s and 1970s, respectively, achieved this by building up their vanguards in the cities and in the countrysides, while the movements in Venezuela or Bolivia both failed. As Weitz notes, "In all four cases, the government confronted an active urban opposition. But it was only when the rebels were able to link their activities with those of the urban opposition that they succeeded."[7] Urban Sandinista National Liberation Front (FSLN) leaders such as Carlos Fonseca and Omar Cabezas spent years organizing and educating the people on the campuses of Nicaragua while simultaneously coordinating the movement in the countryside.[8] In Cuba, leaders like Frank País were part of a strong urban movement that coordinated with Fidel Castro's revolt in the Sierra Maestra.[9] Likewise, the pre–Cold War era revolution in Mexico included rural and urban revolutionaries.

The third variable was the recent loss of U.S. support for the regime under guerrilla attack. Weitz notes that there is no Cold War–era case in which insurgents overthrew a U.S.-supported Latin American government. Only in Cuba and Nicaragua were the governments overthrown and in both cases they had lost U.S. support, making them vulnerable to insurgent victories. Likewise, the United States did not protect the Díaz regime (a longtime U.S. ally) during the 1910–11 revolution.[10]

In Cuba, the U.S. arms embargo against Batista was, according to Louis A. Pérez in his monumental study on Cuba, *Cuba: Between Reform and Revolution*, "tantamount to a withdrawal of support" from the U.S. government.[11] The arms embargo "helped weaken Batista's hold over his supporters, both civil and military" at a moment of particular importance in the government's counterinsurgency campaign in the spring of 1958.[12] The cutoff of U.S. arms had reversed an era of "unqualified support from Washington" (which was how the United States typically reacted when faced with Latin American governments engaged in countering guerrilla warfare during the Cold War.)[13] An indication of the significance of this divergence in U.S. policy came from Ambassador Earle E. T. Smith who stated that the embargo against Batista's army "had a devastating psychological effect" and that it "was the most effective step taken by the Department of State in bringing about the downfall of Batista."[14] The same year, the Eisenhower administration refused to recognize the Cuban election results that would have placed Batista's candidate, Andres Rivero Aguero, in presidential office. This, coupled with the arms embargo, was part of Washington's plan "to ease Batista out of office," Pérez claims.[15]

The last variable involves the type of government that is target of the coup. The less repressive the government and the more legitimate it is, the less likely insurgents will succeed because they will lack popular support, and vice versa: the more fraudulent, corrupt, and oppressive the government is, the more likely the revolution will succeed. In the cases of Bolivia and Venezuela, Weitz contends that the Barrientos and Betancourt governments enjoyed political legitimacy in the eyes of their populations. Conversely, the regimes of Batista in Cuba and Somoza in Nicaragua were considered largely to be corrupt.[16] To an extent, this was also true of the Díaz regime in Mexico. Overall, Díaz's decision to run for the presidency in 1910 hurt his legitimacy, especially after he had already claimed he would not, and this, coupled with his repressive measures, made successful revolt more likely. Further, Madero, who led the 1910–11 revolt, was jailed during the 1910 election, which elevated his legitimacy.

Weitz's structural approach supplies a context in which we can understand the solidarity between the Mexican and Cuban peoples despite the fact that he does not mention Mexico specifically. According to Weitz, revolutions work especially well when all four variables line up, and the fact that they did in the case of Cuba helps explain how it was able to succeed technically and also suggests that the similarity in the fundamental structures of Mexican and Cuban nationalism is the result of their similar revolutionary processes. Also, the fact that these two revolutions stood, above all other revolutionary movements, for ideals that spoke to disillusioned, poor, disenfranchised, and progressive Latin American masses considerably strengthened Mexican-Cuban transnationalism. That disillusionment resonated throughout the Latin America of the Cold War despite the economic growth much of the region experienced at the time, including Mexico and Cuba. In addition, that the United States was largely regarded as an interventionist, exploitative, powerful, "hovering giant," the principal extractor of wealth from the Americas as so many went hungry and ill, often added legitimacy to revolutionary movements in Latin America.[17]

Though the Cuban insurgency succeeded, U.S. acceptance of the Cuban revolutionary government did not last long. The Eisenhower administration was soon drawing up plans to overthrow Castro. Such offensives as the Bay of Pigs invasion and Operation Mongoose as well as the embargo that is still in effect today aimed to topple the Castro government. Between 1960 and 1962, U.S.-Cuban relations deteriorated in the wake of the Bay of Pigs invasion of April 1961 and the Cuban Missile Crisis of October 1962 and as Cuba and the Soviet Union formed an alliance.

It was during the first five years of Castro's rule that the United States government and public demonstrated an interest in the Mexican-Cuban relationship as a foreign policy issue, which indicates just how relevant Third World actors had become on the Cold War stage. The Senate Judiciary Committee even held official inquiries into the connections between Castro's Cuba and Mexican officials. American State Department personnel in Mexico and the U.S. news dailies also displayed a genuine concern over these connections. Official U.S. interest in the Mexican-Cuban connection was reflected in anti-Communist publications sponsored by Mexicans, Cuban exiles, and Americans during this time, too, demonstrating the influence of the Cold War atmosphere on public as well as official opinion. U.S.-Mexican relations improved further under the Johnson administration (1963–69), which expressed more official interest than did Eisenhower or Kennedy by reaching out to Mexico's leadership and establishing a bilateral understanding whereby the countries would cooperate on Cuban information sharing.

THE PRO-CASTRO MEXICAN LEFT

When Mexican president López Mateos (1958–64) took office in 1958, he most likely did not consider the possibility that Cuba would become much of a foreign policy concern. At the time, neither he nor the PRI in general was likely thinking about the implications of Mexico's stance regarding Cuba in terms of its power to serve as a source of credibility for the PRI in promoting its "revolutionary" status. Nor could he have been aware that the Mexican-Cuban relationship would come to exemplify in wide-reaching ways the voices and agency of Third World primary actors in building the Cold War along Third World lines, in cooperation and resistance to that propagated by the superpowers.

On the national level, however, Castro's assumption of the Cuban leadership placed the new Mexican president square in the midst of a left-right division in Mexican politics. An added source of pressure for this new president was the rising tide of Mexican leftism that by 1959 had become strongly affiliated with the Cuban Revolution. At the same time, sectors of the Mexican business community as well as the Church became leery of the new president as a result of his apparently ambivalent approach to Cuba. These traditionally right-wing groups weighed in on Cuba as they had weighed in on the policies of past leftist presidents who implemented agrarian, labor, and education reform measures of a leftist nature. Anti-Communist Mexican groups with roots in the Sinarquistas, dating back to the 1930s, as well as the National Union of Civic Action (UNAC) and many others began to cull their resources in the early 1960s to thwart the actions of pro-Cuban Mexicans. On the other hand, the strength of the growing leftist movement in government, academia, and labor was such that if President López Mateos ignored it, he risked losing a much-needed constituency. So he tried to strike a balance that would placate the left but not disregard U.S. and Mexican right-wing interests.[18] At the same time, Mexico's relations with Cuba and the United States necessitated a balancing act never before seen in postrevolutionary Mexico. Such is the case when international relations occur triangularly.

This triangular balance was offset by Castro's influence and by top Mexican revolutionary-era figures who soon inaugurated a movement with a joint Mexican-Cuban platform called the National Liberation Movement (MLN). Former president Lázaro Cárdenas (1934–40), his former labor representative, Vicente Lombardo Toledano, the famous muralist, David Alfaro Siqueiros, Cuauhtémoc Cárdenas (the son of Lázaro Cárdenas), and many other prominent names comprised this movement that pushed for Mexican-Cuban solidarity. Although he had left office twenty years before, Lázaro Cárdenas was still politically active and his legacy lived on.

▼▼▼

The Cuban Revolution reanimated his revolutionary visions for Mexico; its social, governmental, and economic reform measures, as well as the Mexican left's enthusiasm for the Cuban experiment, encouraged Cárdenas to help form and lead the MLN, which consisted of labor leaders, congressional representatives, academics, peasants, and others. The group's founding in August 1961 came just four months after the April Bay of Pigs invasion, and it provided reform-minded Mexicans and Cubans with another cause derived from resistance to U.S. policies in the region.

Mexican and Cuban anti-Communists also found common cause in opposing Cuban influence. Movements founded on religious and business-oriented principles threatened by the rise in leftist political philosophies erupted in Mexico in Guadalajara, Puebla, and Monterrey and spread across Latin America eventually. One notable example of right-wing solidarity was the band of South American dictators that created Operation Condor. This cooperative effort among the regimes of Argentina, Chile, Paraguay, Uruguay, Brazil, and Bolivia involved hunting down leftist dissidents in South America, North America, and Europe.[19]

No such operation was undertaken in Mexico, but general U.S. support of anti-Communist regimes in Latin American led to the spread of anti-Communism as a way of life. The United States provided military support in the form of weapons sales and aid as well as "humanitarian" and development aid under Kennedy's Alliance for Progress and Food for Peace, for example. The aim of programs such as these was to thwart the spread of Castro-like revolutionary ideas in the Americas, but often the conservative regimes supported by the United States went much further and used the resources the United States provided to oppress and repress their people.

Often, these anti-Communist regimes carried out extreme measures to quash dissent in a manner that even exceeded the initial brutality of the Castro regime. For example, while perhaps seventy-five hundred executions took place under the Castro regime in the initial years of the revolution, between nine and thirty thousand victims were "disappeared" under the Argentine generals during the Dirty War years (1976–82). And death tolls were much higher in places such as El Salvador, Guatemala, and Nicaragua during the civil wars of Central America in the 1970s and 1980s.[20] There, as many as two hundred, seventy-five, and fifty thousand, respectively, died, and recent reports from Peru indicate a death toll of sixty-nine thousand during the counterinsurgency campaign against the Shining Path from 1980–92. Thus, the Cold War took its human toll in Latin America, much more so than it ever did in the United States. It is a toll that, at the very least, indicates the extent to which Latin Americans were involved in the Cold War.

Although anti-Communists were as a matter of course conservative and so opposed to the left as such, still, they ought to have acknowledged the distinction between Moscow-run "Communists" and Latin American nationalists with a leftist bent. Lázaro Cárdenas, for example, had established his leftist nationalist credentials while serving as president in the 1930s. He was no Communist, nor was he run by Moscow. It is true that he was awarded the Stalin Peace Prize (the Eastern equivalent of the Nobel Peace Prize at the time) at the World Congress of Peace at Helsinki in 1956 and that he received other socialist bloc awards, and his assistance in garnering Castro's release from a Mexican prison in July 1956 endeared him even further to the Cuban and Mexican revolutionaries, but a Communist he was not. Cárdenas was a nationalist, and his kind could not always be characterized as "Communist" purely on the grounds of "guilt by association." Nor, by the same token, could Pinochet be characterized as a Republican party member simply because Nixon avidly supported his coup d'etat in 1973 that overthrew the democratically elected government of Salvador Allende (1970–73).

Instead, Cárdenas and Castro represented mutually reinforcing revolutionary icons in Mexico and Cuba that signified the beginning of the process I refer to as "creating a Third World." That is, because the superpowers had globalized the struggles of the Third World, which before then had been considered regionally specific, it became imperative that Third World leaders participate on the stage of international relations. They built their platform on common ideals such as resistance, defiance to "imperialism," and alleviating the suffering of the poor Latin American majority. Further, Castro and Cárdenas admired each other considerably, as is the case among

leftist leaders even today in Latin America, and this enhanced the friendship for years to come. For example, when in January 1959 Cárdenas called
Castro "a young intellectual with a vehement temperament and the blood
of a fighter," he was identifying him as full of new ideas that would be
conducive to inclusion, rather than exclusion, and no doubt expressing his
hope that Castro would indeed be open to cooperation rather than tyranny.
On July 26, 1959, at Castro's announcement of his decision to reassume
the position of Cuban premier, Cárdenas stood behind him, waving to the
crowd as an honored guest of the Cuban revolutionary regime. The former
Mexican president viewed Castro as the provider of a "luminous future"
for the Cuban people and regarded the new regime's initiatives "as a mirror
of his hopes for Mexico."[21]

As agrarian and economic reforms were two of Castro's priorities as
well as two of the main reasons why Cárdenas is remembered in Mexico, it
is easy to see why Cárdenas would have an affinity for Castro. The idea that
their reforms were of a piece was something both Cubans and Mexicans
understood. In a conversation with Mexican writer Elena Poniatowska on
return from a trip to Cuba, Cárdenas mentioned how he felt that the agrarian reform introduced into Cuba would put Mexico in a better position
to push its own agrarian reform further. If Cuba succeeded it would give
Cárdenas the credibility he needed to request a five-fold increase in loans
(from 1 billion to 5 billion pesos annually) for seeds, machinery, education,
and health services.[22]

Cárdenas put a high degree of trust in Castro and hoped he could
revive revolutionary aspirations among Mexicans, Cubans, and other
Latin Americans. In a January 1960 letter to Miguel A. Duque de Estrada,
the head of Cuba's Department of Latin American Affairs, Cárdenas wrote
with idealistic romanticism of a revolution he hoped would reinvigorate
the Mexican Revolution: "the Cuban Revolution has a basic objective: to
maintain its independence and its sovereignty; distribute 'bread, justice,
and culture' to its people through administrative honesty, transformation
of the land tenure system, industrial development and a fair distribution of the product of the people's work."[23] Aside from the letters and
visits to Cuba, Cárdenas showed unwavering loyalty by his activism in

▼▼▼

defending the Cuban people. He even boarded a plane bound for Cuba during the Bay of Pigs invasion to lend support to Castro's defense of the island only to be thwarted at the Mexico City airport on orders from Mexican president Adolfo López Mateos to stop him.[24] Of course, Cárdenas was only at the helm of a much larger movement on the Mexican left that also developed a collectively overromanticized perception of the Cuban Revolution.

In return, Castro spoke highly of Cárdenas in an interview with the Mexican daily *Siempre!* on July 26, 1959. Castro stated that he had invited Cárdenas to the July 26 celebrations owing to his legacy in Mexico's agrarian reform program as well as because of what he meant for Mexican-Cuban relations: "[H]is visit constitutes for us a motivation for profound satisfaction and true honor, and the people of Cuba will appreciate him much for making this visit in these moments in order to, as he says, see with his own eyes, up close and personal, the Cuban people."[25] Castro then stated that the revolutionary movement owed its success to Cárdenas and its inspiration to Mexico: "I credit Cárdenas with [our] freedom," and "I credit Mexico with [our] inspiration."[26]

Castro was referring to the Mexican Revolution's ideals of agrarian reform and economic independence. These were fundamental elements of the war cries of revolutionary heroes Zapata and Villa during the Mexican Revolution of 1910–20 and represent to this day the pillars of Mexican nationalism, especially in the left-leaning self-proclaimed revolutionary political parties.[27] The agrarian reform clause of article 27 in the Mexican Constitution was implemented to redistribute land previously held by a select few to the needy masses of Mexico. This idea had originated with Zapata's Plan de Ayala, which sought a widespread dispersal of the concentration of land into the hands of the landless peasants.[28] Although Zapata would never see the plan's fruition, the Constitution of 1917 guaranteed a form of its implementation. In 1921, Vincente Lombardo Toledano, who would later go on to become a close friend and confidant to President Lázaro Cárdenas, wrote a pamphlet entitled *The Distribution of Land to the Poor is not Opposed to the Teachings of Our Lord Jesus Christ and the Holy Mother Church* that sought to make an expansive agrarian reform

▼▼▼

policy more palatable to Mexicans.[29] This commitment to agrarian reform helped to further establish the Mexican Revolution as a precursor to future Latin American revolutions, despite its non-Marxist foundations, although Lombardo, a well-known Marxist, later promoted the agrarian reform program, which reflected the rising influx of Soviet-style revolutionary thinking in Latin America as well as the growth of Latin American revolutionary nationalism. Cárdenas's nationalization of the oil industry in 1938 also enhanced Mexico's status as revolutionary along these same lines, and Cuba later patterned itself on Mexico, though it took its reforms to a much higher level.[30]

The Cuban agrarian reform process, which was both similar to and different from the Mexican process, has been detailed in several sources. Its differences do not detract from Mexico's role in inspiring the Cuban agrarian reform program but instead explain more about the trajectory of the revolution as its leaders, who were operating under different constraints from the Mexican revolutionaries of the pre–Cold War era, struggled in its wake to consolidate their vision and shape their government. For example, as opposed to Mexico, Cuba's revolution was seen by the United States as a threat because of what it implied for the global struggle between the superpowers of the East and the West. The Mexican revolutionaries did witness a U.S. policy shaped in part by fears of German encroachment in the Americas, but the globalizing reach of the Cold War struggle led to a more concerned U.S. foreign policy establishment regarding Third World revolutionary movements in general. This policy viewed Latin America not just as part of the "backyard" of the "Colossus to the North" but in effect placed Latin America within the larger sphere of the U.S. policy of containment that extended from Eastern Europe and Asia initially, then on to Africa, the Middle East, and Latin America. Therefore, even though the roots of Cuban revolutionary aspirations in the 1950s paralleled Mexico's in the 1910s, the advent of the Cold War located the Cuban affair within the context of the "better safe than sorry" type of foreign policy reflected by the United States, and as a result, Cuban revolutionary programs were seen as part of the larger threat the Soviet Union's influence posed to U.S. national security.

The collectives established by the Cuban government in place of foreign and domestic agrarian corporations as well as the nationalization of U.S. and other foreign businesses mirrored the Mexican Revolution's *ejido* system in part but also reflected the Soviet philosophy of state ownership, that is, communism. The base of the Mexican Revolution, on the other hand, was domestic proponents of wealth and resource redistribution.[31] According to the Cuban Agrarian Reform Law of 1959, "all real estate holdings were restricted in size to 1,000 acres, with the exception of land engaged in the production of sugar, rice, and livestock, where maximum limits were set at 3,333 acres."[32] The land reform program soon divided all excess land into state cooperatives and individual plots according to individual and state collective needs, and this system was overseen by the Agrarian Reform Institute (INRA).[33]

The focus on agrarian reform in the Mexican and Cuban revolutions, even if the process played out differently in each country, turned Mexico and Cuba into the two most notable revolutionary regimes in Latin American history, and from 1959–64 the strong relationship between Castro and Cárdenas epitomized this Mexican-Cuban connection. Other groups were inspired to follow the example set by Castro and Cárdenas. For example, in May 1960, a Mexican delegation named the Encuentro de la Solidaridad con Cuba praised Cuba as "the current example of America," outlining its agrarian reform program and addressing the question of counterrevolutionaries, sovereignty, and other revolutionary issues in its report.[34] Among others, the delegation included future members of the MLN such as Carlos Fuentes, Vicente Lombardo Toledano, Ignacio Acosta, and Enrique Cabrera, and two of the three top Mexican muralists, David Alfaro Siqueiros and José Clemente Orozco.[35]

The growing affiliation between Mexican and Cuban revolutionaries was also apparent in Lombardo's denunciations to the OAS and the United Nations on October 30, 1960, amid rumors of Cuban exiles training in Guatemala with the CIA for a future invasion of Cuba.[36] At the same time, Cárdenas became heavily involved in the pro-Cuba cause by signing the "Declaration of Solidarity with Cuba," after which López Mateos invited Cuban president Osvaldo Dorticós to Mexico for five days. Meanwhile,

President Eisenhower had cut off Cuba's sugar quota that year, U.S.-Cuban relations were severed, and American oil refineries had refused to refine Soviet crude oil. This last act provoked Cárdenas to proclaim the "Guaymas Declaration," in which he drew parallels between U.S. behavior toward Cuba in 1960 with U.S. behavior toward Mexico when it nationalized foreign oil companies back in 1938.[37]

Cárdenas's pro-Cuban activism escalated in March 1961, when he convoked the Latin American Conference for National Sovereignty, Economic Emancipation, and Peace, in Mexico City. With the Bay of Pigs still over a month away, the conference called attention to Cuba as well as the marginalized people of Latin America and denounced the actions of the United States in the region. Cárdenas gave a speech at the conference in which he stated that the Cuban Revolution was the way forward to ending U.S. domination in the region. According to Cárdenas, "The main force that impedes the development of Latin America is U.S. imperialism."[38] However, some people believed that Cárdenas was defending the Cuban Revolution to enhance his position within the PRI while others thought that he was defending it in an attempt to split the PRI into left and right factions.[39]

Cárdenas's words could furthermore be viewed as his interpretation of the original tenets of the Mexican Revolution. For example, instead of advocating a Communist route to liberation, he addressed "the patriots and progressives of Mexico" and "all of the people of Latin America" who, "despite the internal and external pressures, are sure of themselves, convinced of their rights and prepared to defend them."[40] Neither Simón de Bolívar nor Hugo Chávez said it better than Cárdenas when he further framed the necessity for defending these rights collectively by identifying all of Latin America as having suffered from outside control: "All of the peoples of America have had to struggle since their Independence against conservative and retarding interests," have had to struggle through wars of independence, reform, and revolution, but never before have the people "confronted forces and dominant oligarchies" such as "the political clerics and U.S. imperialism, as occurs today."[41] He then called Latin Americans to action: "Mexico, like all the nations of Latin America, has to organize itself, and unite for the collective defense of [Latin America's] interests."[42]

Cárdenas was the embodiment of a politically constructed concept of a revolutionary leader with the highest credibility. The MLN and the Cuban Revolution only reinforced this image of revolutionary legitimacy, as they each represented proactive, vanguard-based movements whose ideals spread across political ideological lines and extended even across national boundaries, the implications of which concerned the United States. In fact, Mexican and Cuban anti-Communists' belief that Cárdenas aimed to carry out Moscow's objectives in the same manner as Castro found resonance in contemporary newspaper commentary and U.S. congressional inquiry.

And indeed Cárdenas's activism was by no means limited to defending Cuba's sovereignty. In August 1961, Cárdenas went a step further and helped create the MLN in an attempt to unite movements of the left such as intellectuals, disillusioned members of the PRI, labor, Communists, and Trotskyists. It was here that he hoped to provide a forum for activists who were upset with Mexico's political system and who had come to favor Mexican and Cuban revolutionary ideals. Speaking of the group, Cárdenas said the activists formed "the most gallant tree of Mexico" and embodied the revival of the Mexican Revolution.[43]

The MLN felt that the Mexican government showed weakness by not taking a definite stand on Cuba. Cárdenas took the lead in defending the leftist interpretation of the Mexican Revolution for those of the MLN who believed that the PRI had betrayed the ideals of the cause for which blood was shed from 1910–20.[44] The Mexican Communist Party (PCM), the Mexican Farm-Labor Party (POCM), the Popular Socialist Party (PPS), the Circle of Mexican Studies (CEM), and several dozen other organizations, led by Lázaro Cárdenas, helped form the sixty-member committee that carried out the MLN's proposals.[45] Among the MLN's leaders were Cárdenas and his son Cuauhtémoc, who ended up running for president three times between 1988 and 2000.[46]

The MLN's August 1961 meeting outlined and approved several resolutions, among them rules on external sovereignty, which focused on Cuba. First among them was the principle of "juridical equality of states," followed by self-determination and nonintervention, the two foundational principles of the PRI's foreign policy as well.[47] A separate section concentrated solely on "the struggle against imperialism," much of which attacked U.S. policy in Latin America. This program is outlined in three principles, which call for "[an] organized and systematic struggle for the liberation of the country from U.S. imperialism," "rescuing, in accordance with Article 27 of the Constitution, the national riches that are found in the hands of foreign monopolies," and "struggling for the repealing of the treaties . . . that attempt to revive the 'Monroe Doctrine.'"[48]

The basic tenets of the March Latin American Conference for National Sovereignty, Economic Emancipation, and Peace were adopted under the rubric of the institutionalization of a reified Mexican revolutionary doctrine that assimilated the Cuban Revolution and invoked rhetoric that identified Mexico with the struggles of all Latin Americans. This message resonated quite powerfully with many Latin Americans as is evidenced by the intensification of Fidel Castro's and Che Guevara's personality cults as well as the student movements of 1968 and the rise of pro-Castro guerrilla movements from Mexico to Argentina from the 1960s to the 1980s.

The MLN was not itself a guerrilla or Communist movement, and yet it made perfect sense for its members to draft resolutions in "solidarity with Cuba." At the top of this section of the report is a reproduction of the Bracho lithograph.[49] The section elaborates on the foundations of the MLN's relationship to Cuba, pointing to the countries' mutual identification through struggle as well as to Mexico's leadership role in Latin America and its concept of revolution. For example, the MLN explained that because Mexico was "a country of old culture in the continent and a nation gravely damaged by U.S. imperialism, an historic and continental responsibility corresponds to Mexicans when U.S. imperialism threatens the development and the peace of Latin America."[50] This responsibility rhetorically and effectively located the MLN's perspective as one of established (that is, "old," in the sense that the Mexican Revolution occurred over four decades before the Cuban Revolution) credibility within the overall revolutionary leadership now represented by the Cuban Revolution. In addition, it legitimated Mexican-Cuban solidarity because Cuba had adopted the basic tenets of the Mexican Revolution:

Because the Cuban Revolution's realizations accord with the aspirations and struggles of the Mexican people in favor of agrarian reform, of the diversification of foreign commerce, of literacy and of education, in defense of the national culture, against imperialism, the anti-national forces and of the reactionary forces, it interests all Mexicans to identify with and defend the Cuban Revolution.[51]

The MLN then went on to adopt seven resolutions vowing to support the Cuban Revolution. The National Committees of Solidarity with Cuba and Committees of Defense of the Cuban Revolution would represent this sentiment as well as promote knowledge about "the trajectory, the accomplishments and the objectives of the Cuban Revolution" with "the utmost social and geographic amplitude" and "denounce" any actions taken against Cuba.[52] Lastly, it called for the continuation and increase of "commercial relations with Cuba, which, within the past two years have fallen notably."[53] The signatories to this meeting included thirty-two organizations and notable National Executive Committee (CEN) members such as Carlos Fuentes and Cuauhtémoc Cárdenas.[54]

Lázaro Cárdenas even spoke favorably of Cuba outside of official circles. For example, he wrote letters of solidarity to the Cuban people. In December 1961, he conveyed his support for Castro in a letter in which he identified Mexico and Cuba as friends struggling against a mutual enemy: "we maintain sincere optimism that the revolutionary government and people of your country will consolidate their social conquests, and that they will bring a better way of life to themselves, in spite of the imperialist consortia and over which they will definitively triumph."[55] The announcements at the Mexico City conference and the MLN meeting thus were not just political rhetoric; rather Cárdenas appears to have genuinely seen Castro's revolutionary spirit as a source of rejuvenation for Mexico's dying revolution.

THE BAY OF PIGS

The Bay of Pigs invasion was one of those moments in U.S.–Latin American relations history that resonated across the broadest of possible spectrums. The failure of the U.S. attempt to overthrow the Castro regime through

CIA-trained Cuban exiles signified not only a defeat for the United States against a weak rival but also a defeat in the Cold War as well as a setback in its relationship with Latin Americans, who saw the invasion as an unjust effort to use force against Cuban nationalism. What's more, it reflected the failure of the U.S. government to comprehend Latin American history, which has many examples of localized resistance to injustice, a cause many in Latin America sympathized with. Mexicans' sympathy for the Cuban Revolution stemmed from their identification with this cause.

The PPS explained its position in this regard quite clearly, in a pamphlet produced on the eve of the April invasion of Cuba. Its title said it all: "To the Mexican People: To Defend Cuba Is to Defend Mexico and Latin America." The PPS defined the struggle in terms of U.S. "imperialism" and its attempts to crush the aspirations of the already weakened Latin American majority, whose poverty and lack of access to resources should serve, according to the Socialists, as a unifying factor, rather than as a source of division.[56] In fact, the group, led by Lombardo, took its analysis even further, incorporating the postcolonial struggles of Africa and Asia, and throughout its pages it refers to Mexico's allegiance with Cuba as part of this larger Third World struggle. According to the PPS, the Mexican people want "the Algerian people [to] gain their complete autonomy," and they want "the people of the small kingdom of Laos [to] resolve their difficulties without the intervention of anyone," especially the United States.[57]

The pamphlet also made special mention of the reasons for Mexico's mutual affiliation with Cuba's plight:

> The yankee imperialism and other forces of exploitation of the weak peoples wish to coax us into saying that Mexico is the model of America, when those same people know that our country is nothing but a paradise for a privileged national minority and for the North American monopolies and that the march forward of our society is full of daily contradictions and of still unsolvable problems. That praise has no other purpose than to try to separate us from what happens in Cuba, so that we will ignore the popular movements that exist on the continent against the

most primitive and bloody tyrants and so that we will condemn all the popular manifestations of inconformity and the rebellions of the people that rise up against misery, the lack of democratic freedoms, and the turnover of the vital interests of their country to foreign imperialism.[58]

These sentiments paralleled those being expressed by the larger movement led by Cárdenas at the same time. Cárdenas's involvement in the MLN spurred the pro-Cuba momentum, and its influence spread quickly across Mexico. Leftists from all over the country came together, their agenda being to convince the Mexican government to return to its revolutionary roots. On some matters, the MLN and the president were of like mind; López Mateos, for example, stood up for Cuba during the Bay of Pigs invasion. In fact, the president spoke to the public of his opposition to the U.S.-sponsored invasion and sent his ambassador to the United Nations, Luis Padilla Nervo, to put forth a resolution to denounce nations that attempt to force out a government simply because they dislike it.[59] The president also showed his official support for Cuba's sovereignty, if not for the regime, in OAS meetings between 1962 and 1964. Such endorsement was important for Cuba especially after Castro proclaimed himself Marxist-Leninist in December 1961.[60]

Cárdenas and the rest of Mexico's pro-Cuban crowd became more animated in their cause after the April 1961 Bay of Pigs fiasco. The Mexican president's reaction to the invasion demonstrated Mexico's independence from U.S. policy as well as its adherence to its own foreign policy principles, which it had stood by more or less consistently throughout the twentieth century, beginning with the Carranza and Estrada Doctrines of 1917 and 1928. Mexican Foreign Minister Manuel Tello asked the United Nations to reject the use of member nations' territories for the purposes of invading Cuba. In support of Cuba during the crisis, López Mateos recounted to a group of pro-Castro intellectuals the several different occasions his administration had shown solidarity for Cuba and reiterated that he opposed the U.S. invasion at the Bay of Pigs.[61]

Response to the Bay of Pigs invasion from the Mexican left came

▼▼▼

from several notable figures. Literary icon Carlos Fuentes wrote an article in *Siempre!* praising socialism in Cuba after the failed invasion. Cárdenas, after he was prevented from boarding the plane to Cuba, later spoke to a crowd of mostly students and declared that it was better for Mexicans to give moral, rather than physical, support to the Cuban people; such moral support, he hoped, would make the United States think twice before escalating.[62]

The Cuban people appreciated Mexico's solidarity greatly, and this was reflected in Castro's speeches as well as in newspaper commentaries. For example, on September 16, 1961, the Havana newspaper *Independencia* commemorated Mexican Independence Day with an article entitled "Independencia de México." After giving a short background on the significance of Mexican Independence Day, the author stated, "Cubans in particular have powerful motives for fraternally incorporating ourselves into [Mexican Independence Day]."[63] He supported this contention by citing examples of Mexico's solidarity with Cuba, such as the hospitality given to Cuban exiles in the nineteenth-century resistance against Spain.[64]

Not everyone in Mexico supported the Cuban Revolution. The anti-Communists, who became the support base for the PAN (National Action Party) and who dictate Mexican foreign policy today, were vocal in their opposition. After the April 1961 Bay of Pigs invasion, a protest in Puebla resulted in a clash between anti-Castro Catholic and pro-Castro university students. This gave further impetus to religious organizations to fight Communism and the new Mexican left. Soon, with the slogan "Cristianismo Si, Comunismo No" leading the way, industrial and commercial groups in Puebla formed the Coordinating Committee of Private Initiative with the purposes of defending themselves from "red vandalism" and to pressure the government into "repressing the [pro-Castro] student movement."[65]

Perhaps in an effort to placate right-wing interests and U.S. concerns over the PRI's loyalties, the Mexican government responded by cracking down on leftist dissidence after the Bay of Pigs fiasco. According to Enrique Krauze:

After the failed invasion at the Bay of Pigs, the Mexican government began to harass political demonstrations of solidarity with Cuba, impose severe police controls on travel to and from the island, confiscate pro-Cuban propaganda, and display a tolerant attitude toward business and Church groups that were waging an intense campaign to discredit the Cuban Revolution.[66]

Other Mexicans became anti-Communist after visiting Castro's Cuba. For example, on May 25, the nation woke to a story written in the leftist daily *Siempre!* stating that "Mexico was to be the initial objective of a campaign to spread the Cuban revolution."[67] The well-known leftist author Carlos Coccioli had recently returned from a trip to Castro's island that showed him a dark side of the Communist regime. Fearing that Castro's revolution would embroil Mexico in his brand of despotism, Coccioli stated that "I have ceased being a friend of Cuba."[68] Other Mexican dailies picked up his story, and the PAN recirculated it in conservative papers.[69] That the *New York Times* also wrote about this on May 26, in an article entitled "A Warning on Cuba Stirs Mexico City," demonstrates that the United States was interested in the Mexican-Cuban connection as a matter of international relations and potential concern over national security.[70]

It was former president Cárdenas, however, who remained above all the main Mexican agitator in the eyes of conservative Mexico especially after he convoked the conference in Mexico City. PAN, the main opposition party to the PRI, and groups such as the Regional Anti-Communist Crusade (CRAC) and, in the words of the *New York Times*, "the pro-Fascist Sinarquist Union party" targeted Cárdenas and Castro particularly.[71] In fact, on May 28, the PAN and the Sinarquist Union submitted a request to the López Mateos government to inquire into "growing rumors pertaining to activities of Gen. Lázaro Cárdenas in the State of Yucatan."[72] The PAN/Sinarquist Union complaints began close to the midterm elections scheduled for July 2 and speculated that Cárdenas had both consented to "violent demonstrations" in the state of Michoacán and that the general had secret meetings with Cubans in Yucatán, where he was known to have spoken with farmers displeased with the agrarian reform programs associated with the sisal industry.[73] The Michoacán demonstrations, according to a PAN statement, "are of such gravity and so coincidental in so many respects that the Government is obliged to institute an investigation."[74]

Another anti-Communist organization, the MHN, representing the business and Church sectors, countered Cárdenas's and the MLN's initiatives with political activism as well.[75] They struggled to convince the Mexican public of the evils of Communism and challenged President López Mateos' ambivalent position on Cuba. The MHN included the Confederation of National Chambers of Commerce (Concanaco), the Confederation of Industrial Chambers (Concamin), and the Managerial Confederation of the Mexican Republic (Coparmex), while groups such as CRAC, renamed National Union of Civic Action (UNAC), of Monterrey, and the Mexican Anti-Communist Federation (FEMACO), out of Guadalajara, began producing regular anti-Communist publications.[76] All of these groups demonstrated an allegiance to the PAN in their literature.

To bolster their cause, Mexico's ex-presidents Abelardo L. Rodríguez and Miguel Alemán Valdés joined the MHN, thus countering some of Cárdenas's momentum generated on the left. Rodríguez even went so far as to call for the formation of vigilante groups to suppress the pro-Castro demonstrations going on in Mexico at that time.[77] Both the MHN and CRAC scrutinized López Mateos and the MLN, focusing on Castro's and Cárdenas's influence. CRAC also took special initiatives in condemning leftism in the universities, deemed as the battlegrounds for political indoctrination.

In the early 1960s, articles in CRAC's publication, *Mensaje Quincenal,* made great efforts to persuade its readers of the evils of Castro's Communism. Articles such as "They Have Killed Christmas: The Tragedy of a Cuban Town" (January 5, 1962), and "More than 1000 Executions in Two Years!" (April 3, 1963) as well as many others illustrated CRAC's tenacity in countering Castro's influence within Mexico. FEMACO's primary publication was *Réplica,* which by 1971 in particular began scrutinizing Mexican-Cuban official connections under presidents Luis Echeverría (1970–76) and José López Portillo (1976–82). Needless to say, the fundamental concerns of the Cold War permeated the political atmosphere of Mexico once its connections to Cuba were spotlighted by Cubans, Mexicans, and, eventually, Americans concerned with the significance of these connections. In the end, because President López Mateos demonstrated a willingness to work with both Havana and Washington, Mexico City became a useful conduit of trust in the post-1959 Cold War arena.

Still, the level of sophistication in the anti-Communist papers likely reinforced Mexican national identity, thus making it easier for the government to suppress internal Communist influences. Specifically, the anti-Communists attempted to define Mexican nationalism as founded on both revolutionary (1910–20) and Christian ideals. Oftentimes the pages of *Mensaje Quincenal* would mention how if Pancho Villa and Emiliano Zapata were alive they would reject Communism and would be opposed to the direction the revolutionary left had gone in. Also, they often based their arguments on religious freedoms and "traditional" family values. In one of its first editions in November 1961, an article highlighted the Cuban president's new secular laws, which "prohibit teaching minors all types of disciplines based on religion." Similar limitations had been placed on Mexican religious practices under President Plutarco Elias Calles in the 1920s, which led to both the Cristero resistance as well as facilitated the rise of opposition parties such as the Sinarquistas, whom the anti-Communist group FEMACO expressed support for in their 1967 manifesto.[78]

As was common with anti-Communist literature, the family was of concern as well, and different aspects of family life were invoked in order to appeal to potential contemporary Mexican anti-Communists. An article entitled "A Father of 10 Children Explains How He Escaped from the Grip of Fidel Castro" attempted to play to readers' sentiments by showing how Cuban Communism was so horrible that parents were forced to risk their lives to remove their children from the island and highlighted the negative impact a Communist regime had on children.[79] The universities were also shown to be dangerous to the young minds of Mexico. CRAC's December 20, 1961, edition headlined with the article "The Students and the People Repudiate the New Rector: The Microbe of Communism Does Not Belong in Our Classrooms."

Pieces in later years focused on the gendered problems of Communism, demonstrating an even higher level of argumentative sophistication on the part of the anti-Communists by the way they appealed to leftist ideals. Articles such as "Women in the Red Brigades" (November 1964) and "Men, Women, and Children: There are Plenty of Rifles for All except . . . the Articles of First Necessity Are Lacking" (March 1965) illustrated this quite well. The latter article was accompanied by a picture of a platoon of uniformed Cubans with women in front as well as by a picture of several children in uniform holding rifles. Perhaps the most blatant article of a gendered nature was the one entitled "A Sexual Problem in Cuba" (May 22, 1965); it alleged that male homosexuality was on the rise in Cuba because of the state's common practice of lodging large numbers of young men together during labor obligation details. Clearly, CRAC realized that the most strategic way to approach the Mexican left was through the various positions they espoused, such as sexual freedom, gender equality, educational freedom, family safety, and the ideals of the revolution.

CRAC also found time to highlight the alleged Communist activities of the pro-Cuban MLN. Its May 31, 1962, edition headlined with the article "Communist Congress in Monterrey" that focused on a conference put on by the MLN on May 27. The article began by observing that "Communism in Mexico" was "disguised now with the name of the Movement of National Liberation" and then noted that the conference had been led by Lázaro Cárdenas and Dr. Guillermo Montaño.[80] The article went on to describe the MLN's positions against "the charrista politics of the government," "charro" being the political elements associated with the right wing, and pointed out how in addition to condemning "Yankee Imperialism," the MLN spoke out against "the independent and autonomous syndicates, against Sinarquismo, against the PAN, against the Church, against the ex-Presidents Aleman and Abelardo Rodríguez," in essence, many important elements associated with the anti-Communist right-wing and opposition parties.[81] CRAC's associating itself with the Sinarquistas, the PAN, and the MHN (of which the two former presidents were leaders) planted the seeds of what has become a long-standing

▼▼▼

Figure 2: Former president Lázaro Cárdenas portrayed
as a Communist agitator (Source: CRAC, "Intensificación
de la 'Guerra Fría' entre Pueblo y Gobierno de México,"
Mensaje Quincenal, May 31, 1962, 7).

division between the PAN's foreign policy and that of the PRI, which have
diverging policies with regard to Cuba.

Fidel Castro became the main foreign focal point of ridicule for the
CRAC, even more than the Soviet leaders Nikita Khrushchev and Leonid
Brezhnev, as titles and subtitles such as "Castro Unmasked: Speaking
of his Two Faced Politics" (December 20, 1961), "How Castro's Agents
Assassinated my Son" (January 20, 1962), "Dean Rusk Won the Battle,"
"Unanimous Condemnation of the Crimes of Castro and Repudiation of
Communism: The Man on the Bolivian Street Speaks" (March 5, 1962)
and many others for years to come demonstrate. Cartoons depicting the
bearded leader portrayed him as a deceptive buffoon, both capable of fooling and of being fooled.

▼▼▼

Lázaro Cárdenas, on the other hand, was portrayed by CRAC not as a buffoon but as a deceptive Communist agitator. CRAC used his image to highlight its perception that he was using the Mexican people for the purposes of installing Communism in an otherwise trusting country that considered Cárdenas to be a father figure looking out for its interests. Articles condemned him for his alleged Communism in leading the MLN, and a cartoon from *Mensaje Quincenal's* May 31, 1962, edition portrayed him sitting in a chair labeled "Mexican Regime," dangling the Soviet hammer and sickle symbol above a small child with one hand and feeding the words, "education," "economy," and "agro" to a pig labeled "international Communism" with the other.[82]

An article the following week entitled "The Cuban Gestapo in Mexico?" elaborated on this portrayal of Cárdenas's deception and subversion. This piece reported that Cuban terrorists were using Mexico as a base "for fomenting armed revolt in other Latin American nations" and were using "Mexican citizens for the services of said foreign government" and that "bank accounts [had been] established for paying the Communist agitators that operate in our country."[83] Predictably, Lázaro Cárdenas is reserved a space of condemnation for his role in leading the MLN. The article is accompanied by a picture of the ex-president with the caption "Cárdenas, whose political activities should be investigated."[84] Thus, CRAC represented Cárdenas in the same way it represented Castro: as a Communist in need of crushing.

The Mexican president was also placed in a tight political spot; he faced pressure from the left and right wings of his own country as well as from the United States, whose anti-Communism dictated hemispheric security policy throughout the Cold War. The U.S. interest in Mexican-Cuban connections was voiced in the pages of the anti-Communist publications of *National Review* and *Free Cuba News* as well as in the Senate Judiciary Committee. We now turn to the way the so-called "Colossus of the North" viewed Mexican-Cuban relations.

CHAPTER THREE

COMMIES IN OUR BACKYARD

U.S. CONCERNS OVER MEXICO-CUBA CONNECTIONS, 1957–61

The works of the Cuban Revolution point the

road to ending foreign domination. Its instructive

revolutionary process constitutes an effective

contribution to our cause of liberation.

The fundamental force that blocks the development

of Latin America is U.S. imperialism.

> —Quotes included in a U.S. Senate inquiry into
> Mexican-Cuban relations taken from the final
> declaration produced by participants in the
> Latin American Conference for National
> Sovereignty, Economic Emancipation and
> Peace, held in Mexico City in 1961

THIS CHAPTER EXAMINES the official and public view in the United States of the emerging Mexico-Cuba connection during the initial years of Castro's rise to power in Cuba. At the time, American politicians and anti-Communists were concerned over the spread of Castro's influence in the Americas. In fact, the Kennedy administration created the Alliance for Progress, a program under which billions of dollars in aid was sent to Latin America to deflect Castro's power. As Robert A. Pastor writes, "the real impetus for John F. Kennedy's [Alliance for Progress] initiative was the

▼▼▼

Cuban Revolution and the fear that it would spread."[1] Although the Cubans eventually gravitated toward the Soviets and away from the Americans, according to top Cuban foreign affairs specialist Jorge I. Domínguez, "the evidence clearly shows that Castro was not pushed into Soviet arms by the United States or by domestic conflicts."[2] Rather, Castro's proactive revolutionary attitude was more in line with the Soviet way of thinking than with the American. Cubans very much feared U.S. intervention, especially after the Bay of Pigs invasion and numerous U.S. covert operations in the early 1960s. Castro and his message appealed to the poor and disenfranchised masses of the Third World as well as to labor movements, politicians, and intellectuals of the left wing. As a result Cuba became a formidable transnational and transideological Third World institution that quickly changed the trajectory of U.S. policy in the region.

At first, the Cuban Revolution elicited little, if any, official hostility from Washington. In fact, Castro traveled there in 1959 and later made a visit to Harlem in 1960, which he still remembers fondly, where he was greeted warmly by the African American community. Although efforts to overthrow and assassinate Castro were in the works shortly afterward, concerns over Mexican-Cuban relations were largely limited to the State Department, which had been monitoring Castro's connections to Mexico since 1957 through the U.S. embassy in Mexico City.

Still, although Eisenhower's internal White House files do not reveal concern over this connection per se, there are indications of an indirect interest. For example, the first paragraph in the State Department's February 1959 briefing paper on Antonio Carrillo Flores, the Mexican ambassador to the United States as of 1958, observes that "Although strongly nationalistic in his thinking, he has cooperated fully with the United States and is considered most friendly."[3] This indicates Washington's awareness of the potential obstacle "nationalistic" Mexican officials might pose to U.S. interests. But Carillo Flores is nonetheless understood to be a trustworthy Mexican nationalist; that is, the ambassador may have valued the tenets of the Mexican Revolution and could perhaps be expected to prioritize Mexico's interests vis-à-vis the United States, but he would still prove a worthy ally to the United States. Carrillo Flores later went on to head the Mexican Foreign Relations Secretariat and was represented quite favorably in the Johnson administration's internal records as well. In fact, he is the only Mexican official to have a documented oral history preserved in President Johnson's Presidential Library, a collection that covers the years 1946–69.[4]

The Eisenhower State Department's briefing paper on President López Mateos also reflected concerns over Mexican nationalism. As with Carrillo Flores, Eisenhower's advisors recognized the importance of a Mexican president who would control radical leftist elements within his country for the sake of U.S.-Mexican relations as well as international security:

> Despite endorsement by Marxist and pro-Communist elements, López Mateos is believed to be genuinely friendly to the United States and there appears to be little doubt that his own personal inclination and style of life are far from proletarian. The support furnished by leftist elements may indicate that they expect more freedom of action, and it is possible that López Mateos' attitude toward domestic Communism may be colored by Mexico's traditional liberalism and tolerance in this regard.[5]

Thus, some U.S. officials recognized as soon as Castro assumed power in 1959 that the Mexican government had the potential to suppress radical leftism. This relative confidence in official Mexico was tempered by anti-Communist worries over Castro's influence in Mexico, as evidenced by CIA security briefs prior to Kennedy's and Johnson's visits to Mexico.[6] However, because both countries had mutual anti-Communist policies, security relations between Mexico and the United States in the end improved, and the basic alignment between the two counties would persist throughout the Castro era. Through leftist and rightist Mexican presidencies, the United States rarely if ever lost faith in the Institutional Revolutionary Party's (PRI) ability to maintain dominance over the political system in a manner that more or less jibed with the United States on matters of anti-Communist state action.

Still, the United States' relative trust in the PRI's anti-Communist

▼▼▼

credentials hinged on the PRI's ability to provide evidence of its strength. For example, in a February 1959 position paper produced by the State Department before Eisenhower was scheduled visit to Mexico, an official stated that the Mexican government's "tolerance" of Communists as well as the "freedom of action" it granted those Communists operating in its country should be viewed as problematic for U.S. interests because "it has been repeatedly proved that there is no such thing as a solely 'domestic' Communist," and the official further warned U.S. delegates that Mexican officials tended to downplay the Communist problem.[7] Finally, the official recommended that Mexico "take effective steps to protect itself from internal Communist influence and aggression" by "denying Communist adherents positions of influence in Government and, to the extent possible, in such key institutions as labor unions, farm associations, schools and universities."[8] In a sense, the U.S. State Department was advocating even more limitations on Mexican political expression than Mexico itself had imposed up to that point for the sake of curtailing possible Communist aspirations there.

Despite the State Department's assessment, Eisenhower's foreign policy advisers were keenly aware of the importance of respecting the PRI government's decisions. The PRI was a stable political machine that had brought about economic growth in a developing country, enabling it to embrace a wide range of political ideologies and still maintain internal stability. Unlike many other governments in Latin America at the time that faced violent internal strife between the left and the right, the PRI in the 1950s and early 1960s was largely able to limit problems by accommodating all interests under the umbrella of the one-party state.

As U.S. trust with and confidence in Mexico's ability to maintain stability grew, relations between Cuba and the United states became increasingly antagonistic. Several events, including Cuba's integration with the Soviet bloc, provoked the United States and Cuba to react in ways that drove wedges further and further between them. Castro's nationalization of American businesses beginning in 1960 strained relations considerably, prompting the United States to impose a trade embargo on the island in October that as of 2007 was still in effect. In January 1961, the two nations severed diplomatic relations, and October 1962 witnessed the Cuban Missile Crisis, which has had a lasting negative impact on the way Americans view Fidel Castro's place in the hemisphere.[9]

Public Spotlighting of the
Mexican-Cuban Connection, 1961

Within two months of the complete deterioration of U.S.-Cuban relations, the Senate Judiciary Committee began to take official notice of the role of Cuban Communism in Mexico, holding several hearings, one of which was entitled *Cuban Aftermath—Red Seeds Blow South: Implications for the United States of the Latin American Conference for National Sovereignty and Economic Emancipation and Peace.* The conference drew the attention of the American public as well as the government, which began to investigate the Mexico-Cuba connection as a result.[10] The conference's participants came from important Latin American nations like Mexico, Cuba, Argentina, Brazil, and Chile, and, reportedly, from the United States as well, and a list of the endorsees of each of these countries was included in the report submitted to the U.S. Senate Judiciary Committee within eight days of the conclusion of the conference.[11]

While the stated official purpose of the conference was to promote general Latin American empowerment, its pro-Cuba and anti-U.S. policy rhetoric, which the epigraphs to this chapter represent angered many Americans.[12] No clearer verbal challenge to U.S. legitimacy in its own backyard was needed. U.S. anti-Communist watchdogs quickly responded. On March 16, 1961, Dr. Joseph F. Thorning, professor of Latin American history at Marymount College, went before the Senate Judiciary Committee to explain the meaning of the Mexico City conference. Dr. Thorning was a dedicated anti-Communist who had written about the Mexico-Cuba connection in the popular conservative magazine, the *National Review*, edited by William F. Buckley, in 1960. This piece informed his 1961 Senate testimony in which he testified that the conference aimed to spread Communism throughout the Americas. In his words, the conference, "was, in reality, a propaganda show to promote political enslavement of all the American Republics under a Soviet regime . . . by means of Fidel

▼▼▼

Castro type revolutions."[13] He went on to paint former Mexican president Lázaro Cárdenas (1934–40) as a Communist as well: "The truth is that Lázaro Cárdenas . . . has been most effective in carrying out Soviet general directives and policies."[14] To illustrate his point, he submitted the following evidence of Cárdenas's activities:

> In August 1950, Lázaro Cárdenas was elected a member of the presidium of the World Peace Council by the World Peace Congress, Warsaw, Soviet Poland. In May 1951, he wrote a letter of adherence to Mexico's First National Peace Congress, Mexico City. In August 1955, Cárdenas was listed as one of the several vice presidents of the World Peace Council in Helsinki, Finland. . . . In February 1956, Cárdenas accepted the Stalin Peace Prize in Mexico City. In October 1956, he was listed as a vice president of the World Peace Council in Stockholm, Sweden. On Oct 12, 1958, Cárdenas left Mexico on a world tour that took him to many Iron Curtain countries, including the U.S.S.R., Soviet Czechoslovakia, Soviet Hungary and Red China.[15]

Dr. Thorning concluded his testimony by suggesting that the outcome of the conference could ultimately be that "the Castro-Soviet forces" would take over all of Latin America, isolating the United States in a sea of Communist Latin American states.[16]

Dr. Thorning's testimony served to heighten official Washington's awareness of the power of international connections among Third World countries whose shared plights led them to solidarity. This mutuality of Third World interests became a force for change in Latin America during the Cold War, the likes of which had never been seen before. The level of Latin American autonomy in creating a third path of their own in international affairs is demonstrated, for example, in the list of the signatories that the Senate included in its report. Many Mexican government officials as well as other well-known figures signed on, along with many professors, judges, lawyers, union leaders, engineers, journalists, and university rectors.[17] Prominent among these was Ignacio García Tellez, former Interior Secretary, former rector of Mexico's prominent university, the UNAM, former secretary of public relations, former secretary of education, and founder of the Institute of Social Security. In addition, at least twenty-three federal congressional representatives signed the final resolution. Lázaro Cárdenas's son, and future presidential candidate (1988, 1994, 2000) Cuauhtémoc Cárdenas, also signed on, as did Vicente Lombardo Toledano.[18] The conference thus led American anti-Communists to take a closer look at Mexico. Castro was seen as the main catalyst there; his rhetorical skills were such that even former Mexican presidents fell under his spell and were willing to help extend his influence in the hemisphere. The scrutiny the United States put Mexico under might seem excessive, and yet when one considers that Mexico was probably the target of the fewest incidents of U.S. intervention during the Cold War, it becomes clear just how worried the United States was about Castro's influence in the hemisphere. Many more U.S. covert and overt activities were undertaken in places like Cuba, the Dominican Republic, Ecuador, Chile, Brazil, and Central America than in Mexico.

U.S. concerns over Mexico's political direction found a considerable audience among anti-Communists. In his December 1960 *National Review* piece Dr. Thorning described Lázaro Cárdenas as "increasingly active . . . in the worldwide Marxist conspiracy" and claimed that "the vast influence exercised by Cárdenas is one explanation for the support of Castro by many powerful Mexican officials."[19] He cited Cárdenas's positive descriptions of Chinese popular communes and Cuba's Institute of Agrarian Reform as proof of his power to manipulate the direction of Mexican politics through deception based on his own ideologically leftist convictions.[20]

That same month, the *National Review* gave a more in-depth assessment of the Mexican-Cuban connection in a piece that, addressing the danger of Mexican Communism as well as Cárdenas's influence there, came to the same conclusion as Thorning. In "No Communism in Mexico," subtitled "Says the Government: There's No Organized Communist Party in Mexico, No Communist Threat. For All the World as if Wishing Could Make It So," Philip Burnham, author of the monthly column "The Third World War," argued that the PRI government's denials that an

▼▼▼

official Communist Party existed in Mexico disguised its own reluctance to acknowledge and combat the threat that Communism posed at that time: "For various reasons of pragmatic power politics, some groups in the party studiously want to recognize no enemy on the Left. So Communism does not exist."[21] The sarcasm was intended to emphasize, in his assessment, how dangerous a wavering-on-Communism PRI regime could be to U.S. national security. He then made Cárdenas's role in this threat quite clear: "Lázaro Cárdenas, labeled by so many critics and by so many of his own words and acts as—for practical purposes—a Communist, has never broken with the PRI which he once led."[22]

Not surprisingly, Burnham's opinion of the National Action Party (PAN), on the other hand, was positive. Noting that the PAN was the only opposition party, he observed that "in Mexico the showing of political parties in elections does not reflect in any detail, nor at all clearly, the political trends, and the more intimate and meaningful political associations of the people."[23] He went on to portray the PRI the same way the PAN did: "The 'Government Party,' the PRI, is too big. It is the legatee of the tough, violent, crooked and domineering ways of Calles and other caudillos of Revolution."[24] The reference to President Plutarco Elías Calles is pointed, for his administration was well known for its suppression of the Catholic Church. The Church's cause was later taken up by the extreme right-wing Sinarquista movement in the 1930s and 1940s, which had allied itself with the PAN in mutual opposition to Mexican leftism at least by the 1960s. In fact, the Sinarquistas and the PAN, founded during the Cárdenas presidency (in 1937 and in 1939, respectively) found common ground in their opposition to leftist or revolutionary policies of Lázaro Cárdenas. Anti-Communist, both the PAN and the Sinarquistas received support from the Catholic Church and served as the principal opposition to the PRI by the time of their founding.[25]

American interest in and concern over Mexican connections to Cuba piqued by the Latin America conference received a sounding board in the U.S mainstream press as well. Before the March 1961 conference, titles such as "Mexicans Promote Pro-Castro Parley" (*New York Times*, February 12), "Red Carpet Spread for 'Peace' Meet" (*Miami News*, February

19), and "Kisses for Castro Theme of Mexico Meeting" (*Miami News*, February 22), sprinkled the pages of American newspapers, revealing that the American public had begun to regard the Mexican-Cuban connection with suspicion.[26] *New York Times* articles during the conference confirmed the existence of this growing wariness: "Leftists Stress Latin Solidarity: Meeting in Mexico Steps up Attacks on U.S.—Role of Cárdenas in Doubt" (March 7) and "Leftists Consider Latin Secretariat" (March 7).

After the conference, response from inside the United States intensified and spread throughout the print media. A *New York Times* March 9 article, "U.S. is Condemned in a Leftist Parley of Latin Americans," which followed the end of the ceremonies, announced that the "Communist-oriented World Peace Council" sponsored the event and focused on Cárdenas's denunciation of U.S. policy, particularly its "military pacts" in Latin America. The article leaves no doubt that the Conference for National Sovereignty, Economic Emancipation, and Peace was antagonistic to U.S. policy. The *New York Times* was not alone. Every U.S. newspaper I looked at that covered the conference took special care to describe it as anti-American, which demonstrates the level of national anxiety that was emerging over the Cuban-Mexican connection, despite the air of confidence emanating from the office of the president and the intelligence community.

Other articles speak volumes about how the relationship between Mexico and Cuba fit into the Cold War. A March 11 article by *Diario de las Americas* author Jaime Plenn entitled "Plan of Agitation against the United States" outrightly accused the conference participants of planning a Communist takeover: "as a conclusion of the Communist conference in Mexico City, the Cuban Revolution was acclaimed as an example for Latin America." On July 13, a *Washington Daily News* article, "Fidel's Red Pals to 'Demonstrate'—Plan Latin Riots," stated that at the Mexico City conference "Communists and supporters of Cuban Premier Fidel Castro are believed" to have mapped out "plans for hemisphere wide demonstrations." It went on to say that the plans aimed to promote a "Communist 'show of force'" that "during the week of July 19 to 26 . . . will seek to intimidate Latin American governments into avoiding any political,

▼▼▼

economic, or military action against Castro's regime." The article thus implied that Mexico served as a haven for coordinating Communist agitation; this allegation was voiced in other newspapers as well as in overtly anti-Communist magazines during the 1960s.

TRENDS IN U.S. OPINION: THE LARGER CONTEXT

Many articles in the *New York Times, Miami News, Washington Evening Star,* and *Washington Daily News* and from the Hearst Headline Service before, during, and after the conference (between February and July) demonstrated a high level of concern from a national security perspective over the connections between the two countries. As preeminent Mexican political scientist Sergio Aguayo documents in his 1998 book *Myths and [Mis]perceptions: Changing U.S. Elite Visions of Mexico,* the articles and editorials published in the news media about the conference were part of a larger pattern of negative public expression with respect to Mexican-Cuban relations. According to Aguayo's examination of the 6,903 *New York Times* articles written about Mexico and Mexican affairs between 1946 and 1986, "it was the Cuban Revolution that awakened U.S. interest" more than any other issue, and particularly during the early 1960s.[27] For example, in 1961, 10 percent of the articles referred negatively to the Mexican Communist Party-Mexican Unified Socialist Party (PPS-PSUM), and 21 percent referred negatively to Lázaro Cárdenas.[28] These statistics clearly reflect the fear of international Communism of the times, which was heightened by the fact that Cuba had recently fallen under its influence, and suggest that the prospect of Communist infiltration in Mexico seemed real enough because of its Cuba connections. In the end, however, this public and sometimes official concern only played a minor role in policy making owing to Mexico's pragmatic approach to security relations with the United States, as the intelligence briefings and State Department memos revealing the extensive anti-Cuban cooperation between Mexico and the United States beginning in the 1960s attest to. The offices of the heads of state in Mexico and the United States were able to both acknowledge public and Congressional concerns as well as work together in order to combat the spread of Castro's influence.

▼▼▼

New Concerns: The State Department and
Mexican-Cuban Connections, 1957–61

Unreported in the mainstream news or elsewhere during this same period (March to June specifically) was a series of hearings in the Senate Judiciary Committee referred to as the *Communist Threat to the United States through the Caribbean*. These hearings revealed a concern over the growth of Communism in the hemisphere as a result of the presence of Castro and his associates in Mexico and also revealed a level of trilateral cooperation on intelligence gathering in Mexico on the part of Cuban, Mexican, and U.S. officials interested in Castro's Communist associates in Mexico.[29]

Two weeks after Dr. Thorning's testimony, the committee's attention turned to the possibility that William Wieland, the U.S. State Department director of Caribbean and Mexican Affairs from 1957–61, might have assisted Castro's revolution. This allegation was rooted in suspicions about Wieland's possible pro-Castro leanings, stemming from the halt in U.S. military aid to Batista in 1957 in the midst of the Cuban Revolution. The committee was no doubt motivated to investigate Wieland in early 1961 because that was when Castro's Communist leanings became public.[30] Testimony to the committee also harshly alleged that Wieland had deliberately blocked the flow of intelligence from Cuban, Mexican, and U.S. sources alluding to Castro's Communist connections as early as 1957.[31]

Andres Pérez-Chaumont, former Cuban lieutenant colonel who served as military attaché to Mexico and Central America from 1957–58 under Fulgencio Batista (1934–58, on and off), testified first as part of the Wieland case on March 29, 1961.[32] His testimony revealed how intelligence cooperation began between Cuba and the United States through the U.S. embassy in Mexico City during the Cuban Revolution from 1957–59, and it complements a 1958 report from the House Committee on Un-American Activities on Vicente Lombardo Toledano.[33] However, the report on Lombardo mentions nothing of any connections to Castro or Cuba, for connections between Castro and Lombardo or, for that matter, between Cuban and Mexican Communists, may not have solidified enough at that point to be detected by Cuban, Mexican, or U.S. intelligence.[34]

Still, the testimony of Pérez-Chaumont notified Congress that intelligence sharing had begun early enough during the Cuban Revolution to raise the specter of anti-Communist policies as a factor of official Mexico-Cuba-U.S. solidarity. He explained how he passed intelligence to the embassy, then run by Robert C. Hill (1957–61), whose superior was Wieland. Pérez-Chaumont noted how he transmitted extensive, detailed, and verified data on alleged Communist Cubans operating in Mexico. The "proof" consisted in the fact that Cuba had connections with the Czech commercial attaché and the Russian embassy in Mexico as well as in the fact that Che Guevara's wife was a Communist living in Mexico.[35] In addition, Pérez-Chaumont claimed to have come into possession of further proof of Castro's Communist affiliations and leanings in 1953 while serving as the officer in charge of the Moncada Barracks in Santiago de Cuba during Fidel Castro's initial launch of the Cuban Revolution on July 26, 1953. The Cuban officer testified that he had captured Castro's recordings at Moncada and that these recordings professed a Communist agenda of agrarian reform, nationalization, and redistribution of wealth.[36] Pérez-Chaumont also specified that he had passed a large amount of information on to the Batista regime in Cuba and gave copies of that information to the U.S. embassy in Mexico from 1957–58. He also testified that "usually I did not see action concerning all the information I had given" and that he was told that Wieland, who had authority over Ambassador Hill at the embassy, "was the one that sort of had been an obstacle for those reports to have been properly evaluated."[37]

A similar accusation was leveled at Director Wieland three months later by several others who had served with him. On June 1, Raymond Leddy, counselor for political affairs at the U.S. embassy in Mexico for at least the 1957–61 period, testified to the committee about Wieland's conduct during and after the revolution. Leddy testified, as did Ambassador Hill eleven days later, that the embassy had been monitoring the growth of Communism in Mexico since 1957, which had discernibly drawn more adherents along with direct support for Castro's revolution from within Mexico.[38] He then told the committee that after Batista fell from power in January 1959 Cubans poured into the U.S. embassy in Mexico and passed on information about Castro that further convinced embassy officials that the revolution had Communist leanings. The embassy then produced reports that it sent to the U.S. State Department, which, according to Leddy, were not acknowledged until June 30, 1959, a full six months after the embassy began receiving information.[39] The allegation of the delayed State Department reaction validated Pérez-Chaumont's earlier assertion that the State Department had failed to act on his Castro intelligence after he had passed it to the U.S. embassy and that Wieland may have been the obstacle to that information flow.

This anxiety over possible U.S. official sympathies with insurgent movements in the Third World reflected the fear the Cold War elicited as well as of the extent to which Third World nations were now able to influence international relations. Leddy highlights this keenly in his testimony by demonstrating a clear-cut "us vs. them" mentality that excluded nuance and put every player into one of two camps. The U.S. government viewed most Third World leaders and their political movements as either Communist or anti-Communist, and this black-and-white thinking made it hard for it to grasp the Third World problems that led to postcolonial movements in the first place. Castro's revolt, just like Ho Chi Minh's and Patrice Lumumba's, found resonance with Third World populations not because they wanted to align themselves with Russia against the West but out of a need to alleviate the fundamental problems of underdevelopment associated largely with a colonial past.

Leddy's testimony makes clear that his anxiety was not driven by concerns about development problems in the developing world but instead by his belief that the Third World had become a battleground for a cold war that threatened thermonuclear destruction and the spread of Stalinist and Maoist Communism. Leddy voiced this superpower-centered view to the committee when explaining a briefing he gave to President Eisenhower's brother Dr. Milton Eisenhower in August of 1959 on the fifth meeting of foreign ministers that took place in Santiago, Chile. Also present at the briefing were Wieland, Hill, and several others, and all of them heard Leddy state that he and the other foreign ministers had come to the conclusion that "Castro was, himself, pro-Communist and that his government was falling under the control of Communists and that, as such, it constituted a danger to other countries and a matter of serious concern to our government."[40] However, Leddy claimed that Wieland disagreed with Leddy's assessment and asserted that there was no conclusive evidence on this matter. That Wieland did indeed dissent was corroborated eleven days later in Hill's testimony.[41]

This line of reasoning on Leddy's part raises the question of Wieland's culpability. If Castro did not declare his Socialist leanings until 1961, the same year that U.S. and Cuba severed their relations, then Wieland's perspective in 1959 may have influenced U.S. ambivalence on Castro that year. Leddy assumed that Wieland ignored the State Department's assessment that Castro had early Communist affiliations dating back to 1957. According to this reasoning, Wieland may have deliberately covered up evidence that could have informed U.S. policy on Castro before we cut off aid to Batista, which was arguably a deciding factor in Castro's triumph in 1959.[42]

Similar testimonies regarding Wieland's actions were given the same day as Leddy's and further illuminated the depth to which anti-Castroism had gone within a short two-year period. Former Cuban generals Jorge García Tunon and Ricardo Artigas Ravelo, who had served under Batista, leveled the same accusations at Wieland. General García supported Leddy's contention that intelligence on Castro's Communist affiliations had been extensive throughout Wieland's tenure as director of Caribbean affairs.[43] Specifically, he stated that the Cuban ambassador to Mexico himself, Dr. Oscar de la Torre, had passed reports to the U.S. embassy in Mexico claiming that Castro received support from Communists operating in Mexico, the main piece of evidence here being that alleged Communists had attacked the Cuban embassy in Mexico with Molotov cocktails.[44] García also stated that "a Cuban" had informed him that the Mexican police had seized "Communist documents" and "Communist literature" in Castro's apartment during his arrest in June 1956.[45]

García then asserted that when he went on a trip to Washington in January 1958 with General Ravelo to visit Wieland he had passed a document to him indicating that Castro was going Communist. García told the committee that Wieland agreed to examine the document, but that he "never heard from him about it."[46] The Senate committee then asked García about Wieland's role in halting U.S. arms shipments to the Batista regime in 1957, the first year of Castro's grassroots rebellion in the Sierra Maestra mountains of eastern Cuba: "Did [Wieland] tell you that he had stopped shipment of arms to Batista?"[47] The general answered that Director Wieland had denied this allegation, but that he had also questioned Garcia's accusations against Castro on two occasions during visits in 1959, thus discrediting himself.[48]

General Ravelo's testimony also attested to Wieland's silence. Ravelo claimed to have written a letter to Wieland in Mexico from Atlanta in January 1958 stating that two top members of the Communist Party, Carlos Rafael Rodríguez and Ladislao González Carvajal, were involved with Castro's revolution and that Wieland never replied to him. Ravelo then said that on seeing Wieland again later in 1958 he asked what the United States planned to do about Castro's Communist partners and that "[Wieland] replied that the United States could do nothing about the Cuban situation."[49] According to Ravelo, the last time he and Wieland met was in Washington in March 1959. Ravelo and another Cuban army colonel gave him "a military plan to overthrow Castro," but, according to Ravelo, Wieland again asserted that Castro was not a Communist "and defended him as he had done on every occasion in the past when I had brought up Castro's name."[50] Thus, the general's assessment of Wieland's pro-Castro sympathies paralleled that of the previous testimonies as well as that of the U.S. ambassador to Mexico, Robert C. Hill, who testified next.

The committee made clear on opening its questioning of Hill that its task was to evaluate "the part played by certain officials of the United States in Castro's rise to power."[51] Hill told the committee that he felt the situation with Castro had been very serious for some time, indicating that it was his view that Castro's Communism began with his participation in the Bogotazo, which is the name given to the Bogota, Colombia, riots of 1948. His later arrest in Mexico City in 1956 also led Hill to believe "that this fellow might be oriented toward communism."[52] When asked about his impression of Wieland, he responded that he felt he could not be trusted, and as evidence he corroborated Leddy's account of Wieland's response to the August 1959 briefing in which Wieland denied allegations of Castro's Communist leanings and affiliations.[53]

In Hill's opinion, the embassy in Mexico in particular had played an essential role in uncovering the activities of Communists precisely because of "the proximity of Mexico to Cuba" and because the situation had reached the point that

> The agents coming from Moscow and some from China would go back and forth between the Soviet Embassy in Mexico City and Cuba. Propaganda was flowing into Mexico at this time from Cuba and from behind the Iron Curtain. The peasants were very sympathetic to the Castro cause and that is understandable, because he has done something for the peasants of Cuba. The Embassy knew that there would be demonstrations in Mexico which could very seriously affect our relations between the United States and Mexico. If Castroism was not restrained in Mexico, it could continue on to the Central American countries and through the Caribbean into Latin America. If the United States does not act affirmatively, you could have a solid Communist bastion on the doorstep of the United States. We wanted to do our part in Mexico to prevent such a thing happening without intervening in the affairs of the Mexican people.[54]

Hill also corroborated the previous testimonies that there had been a continuous stream of reports from 1957 through 1961 on Castro's Communist connections flowing through the U.S. embassy in Mexico and that Wieland never acted on the information despite his access to it.[55] Hill then went on to accuse the U.S. ambassador to Cuba, Phillip Bonsal, of being too soft on Castro, stating that Bonsal also denied that Castro was a Communist and noting that "patience and forbearance in dealing with a Communist would lead to disaster for the United States."[56]

Hill's "Confidential Report and Suggestions on Latin America" demonstrates a significant level of U.S. concern over the possible repercussions of Mexican-Cuban connections:

To be cowed by the nationalistic and communistic enemies of the American system, is to give up the defense before it is undertaken. American businessmen and industrialists in Latin America are, by and large, disappointed with the lack of spontaneity of official interest in their plight shown by our diplomatic missions. I have seen the rising tide of anti-Americanism, in its economic form, sweep from country to country. It has already engulfed Cuba completely. In Mexico, it has raised a mist of doubt over future investments.[57]

Cuba is deemed to have a natural influence over Mexico and to be the cause of the "rising tide of anti-Americanism" in Latin America.[58] At the same time, even though Hill expressed concern over Cuban Communism in Mexico he seemed more concerned about the perception of instability rather than actual instability in Mexico, which suggests he trusted that the PRI would be able to thwart potential internal Communist threats. What he emphasized was that Mexico was a conduit that the United States could either take advantage of or let go to waste, and that is why he expressed so much concern over Wieland's denials of Cuba's connections to Communism.

The 1961 Senate hearings and reports on Cárdenas and Wieland demonstrate that it was the international security concerns generated by the global Cold War that accounted for the U.S. interest in Cuban-Mexican relations. In essence, as far as the Senate Judiciary Committee and its witnesses were concerned, the connections between Mexico and Cuba made clear the potential gravity of the threat posed by Cuban Communism to the security of the United States, and thus, by definition, that of the hemisphere. If even a popular former Mexican president could become pro-Castro as well as a high U.S. State Department official, then what were the odds that this pro-Castro sentiment would not spread to the rest of Latin America, in places where the United States had less influence than it did in Mexico?

At the same time, American officials' worries over Mexico-Cuba connections highlight the leading role of Third World actors in the Cold War.

▼▼▼

Castro and Cárdenas were deemed both as threats to and inspirations for established norms in international relations, and this is key to recognizing the power the Third World had in shaping the outcomes of superpower policy and perspectives. Castro and Cárdenas also made clear that Third World actors would not allow themselves to be controlled by the superpowers and that autonomy was the main issue of importance for Cuba and Mexico. The Americans, of course, were concerned about the possible instability of Third World actors, for they recognized that the boundaries among developing nations and indeed between that of developing nations and the developed world were fluid.

CHAPTER FOUR

OF OSTRACISM AND FRIENDSHIP, 1962–64

[López Mateos] has followed an "independent"
foreign policy but knows that good relations with us
. . . are essential to his country. At times his foreign
policy has been too independent—for example on
Cuba . . . But when fundamental issues are at stake
we have usually found him understanding and
willing to be helpful.

—U.S. Secretary of State Dean Rusk in a letter to
President Lyndon B. Johnson in February 1964

THE CUBA-MEXICO CONNECTION was a thorn in the side of U.S. officials in 1961, but the relations between Mexico and Cuba gradually became less of a concern to the United States with Cuba's definitive move into the Soviet orbit. By 1962, the U.S. government began to rely on the legitimizing force of the Organization of American States (OAS) to address the threat of Communism rather than explicitly unilateral action against Castro's government. Inter-American protocol is codified in three basic treaties that were signed in 1947 and 1948: the Inter-American Treaty of Reciprocal Assistance of 1947 (also known as the Rio Treaty), the Charter of the Organization of American States of 1948, and the American Treaty on Pacific Settlement of 1948, also known as the Pact of Bogotá.[1] Participation in the Inter-American system requires that member states respect the right to nonintervention and self-determination, that they "resolve disputes in a peaceful manner, and . . .

▼▼▼

to take collective measures, in the event of aggression, to assist [a member] under attack."[2]

The leaders of the hemisphere soon invoked the Rio Treaty and joined together to discuss the future of relations with Cuba. Owing to the urgency of the situation, the Eighth Meeting of Consultation of Ministers of Foreign Affairs was called and held in Punta del Este, Uruguay, from January 22 to 31, 1962. Mexican anti-Communist groups such as the Regional Anti-Communist Crusade (CRAC) attempted to influence the resolution that would exclude Cuba from the OAS before the meeting. A January 20, 1962, article in CRAC's mouthpiece *Mensaje Quincenal* about a former Cuban priest entitled "The Threat of Communism in Latin America: Dr. Ramón Infiesta, ex-Catedrático of the University of Havana, Speaks to a Conference of 'CRAC' Members" focused almost solely on the loss of economic rights under Cuban Communism and was most likely intended to influence Mexicans on the lead-up to the OAS vote regarding Cuba's future, which was two days away.

In the same issue, CRAC wrote a letter to the Mexican president directly in a last-ditch effort to persuade the president to vote along with the U.S.-sponsored plan to expel Cuba from the OAS. The CRAC argued that if Mexico were to apply its traditional foreign policy to Communist Cuba, it would betray "the values of the Mexican people" who had always espoused nonintervention and the right to self-determination.[3] CRAC argued that Cuban disregard for international and domestic sovereignties by its "interven[tion] in Latin America" meant that Mexico's technical adherence to nonintervention and respect for self-determination in the case of Cuba specifically would equal an abandonment of those values.[4]

The OAS debate over Cuba rested on the question of whether and if so to what extent the inter-American nations were willing to tolerate Cuba's Soviet connections. As Secretary of State Dean Rusk put it, the ministers met in order to evaluate the implications of Cuba's complicity in "the Communist conspiracy dedicated to the overthrow of the representative governments of the hemisphere."[5] The Mexican delegation, although not supporting Cuba necessarily, responded to the resolution by stating that "the exclusion of a member state is not juridically possible unless the Charter of the Organization of American States is first amended."[6]

Ultimately, all OAS nations except Cuba agreed that "a Marxist-Leninist government was incompatible with the principles of the inter-American system."[7] In fact, even Mexican foreign minister Manuel Tello made a speech in which he noted that "There appears to be an incompatibility between belonging to the Organization of American States and professing a Marxist-Leninist government, as there would be with a profession of absolute monarchy."[8] Still, six countries abstained (Argentina, Bolivia, Brazil, Chile, Ecuador, and Mexico) from voting on the resolution to expel Cuba while fourteen voted in favor of adopting it.[9] At the same meeting, Mexico voted for the creation of a special security committee to investigate Communist subversion in the hemisphere and endorsed the Alliance for Progress, for free elections, and for condemning the Communist offensive in Latin America. Given the number of the countries that abstained, which made up 75 percent of the population of Latin America, Mexico's position at Punta del Este was not as unique as it would be later on.[10]

The CRAC expressed disappointment with Mexico over the position it took at Punta del Este. A February 5, 1962, article entitled "The Communist Castro Regimen Expelled from the OAS Session," was accompanied by a picture of U.S. Secretary of State Dean Rusk and subtitled "Dean Rusk Won the Battle" but did not praise the Mexican government. Although it mentioned that Mexico did ostensibly represent itself as opposed to Communism, another article "Czech Machineguns," explained that the Mexican government had chosen its centrist OAS policy "against the unanimous opinion of the Mexican people" and that its OAS decision in fact showed it to be "in favor of the Communist Castro . . . who through all means is intervening in Latin America in order to infect it with Communism."[11] CRAC further illustrated its disappointment with the Mexico vote in its March 20, 1962, issue, which included a cartoon of a man with a peasant hat with a star on top, arms and feet tied together, above a caption reading "This is my Self-Determination?"[12]

An October 1, 1962, article in *Mensaje Quincenal* entitled "To Attack the Countryside is to Divide the Country" reprised this theme. It was

▼▼▼

¿Esta es mi Autodeterminación?

Figure 3: Very typical anti-Communist cartoon depicting the slavery
and general oppression of Communism (Source: CRAC, "El socialismo,
municipal y estatal, factor para explotar, el trabajo por medio del jornal,"
Mensaje Quincenal, March 20, 1962, 2).

accompanied by a cartoon, the message of which was that Mexico's foreign
policy toward Cuba was endangering Cubans. The cartoon shows two men
in a rowboat heading down a waterfall, with the United States, represented
by Uncle Sam standing on a cliff across the canyon, waving a white rag
and saying "bon voyage." The river is labeled "neutralism," the rower has
labels on his arm and oar, respectively, that read "nonintervention" and
"self-determination," and passenger "Juan Pueblo" is saying "Careful!
This trip could be the last," as the rowboat goes over the falls into the
crushing rocks below, which are labeled "Communism."[13] In its criticism
of the Mexican government, CRAC was attempting to appeal to the sentiments of Mexicans by representing the Cuban people as in danger, just
as it used gender and family values and the idea that Mexico would be
rejecting its traditional foreign policy norms if it supported Castro to gal-
vanize support for the anti-Communist cause. Castro was also predictably

▼▼▼

ME QUIERE.... NO ME QUIERE.... ME QUIERE....

Figure 4: Cartoon depicting Castro weeping after OAS vote (Source: CRAC, "La 'CRAC' se Dirige al Presidente en Carta Abierta," *Mensaje Quincenal,* January 20, 1962, 2).

Figure 5: Cartoon depicting the false allure of Communism (Source: CRAC, "Atacar a la Provincia es Dividir a México," *Mensaje Quincenal,* October 1, 1962, 3).

ridiculed after Punta del Este. The open letter to President López Mateos was accompanied by a cartoon of Castro kneeling in a field and weeping, pulling petals from a sunflower with both OEA (the Spanish acronym for the OAS) and OAS printed on it, meant to justify a loss of sympathy for the Castro dictatorship.[14]

Mexico's position at Punta del Este, albeit not unique, started Mexico on the path of becoming a mediator between Cuba and other countries. In fact, López Mateos first mentioned his administration's role as mediator between the United States and Cuba during his September 1961 *Informe de gobierno* in which he attempted to articulate Mexico's new direction of wider international integration. He stated that his administration had offered assistance to both countries in the hope of facilitating a productive dialogue and that even though that had as of yet failed to transpire, Mexico would "not shirk its pledge to serve without any limitation the

▼▼▼

cause of friendship and harmony of the American republics."[15] After Punta del Este, López Mateos claimed at his 1962 *Informe* that Mexico would represent Cuban interests in Costa Rica, Honduras, Peru, Panama, and Colombia and represent Honduras, Peru, Panama, Colombia, Venezuela, and Paraguay in Cuba.[16] Mexico's position between these two enemies became especially useful to the North American superpower beginning with the administration of Lyndon Johnson (1963–69).

Cuba responded to the resolutions passed at Punta del Este diplomatically by replacing the ambassador to Mexico, José Antonio Portuondo, who was a Communist, with a non-Communist named Carlos M. Lechuga. Cuba also made a gesture of good faith by significantly reducing the flow of Communist propaganda into Mexico. Finally, Cuba issued the Second Declaration of Havana, which "challenged the assumption of the Alliance for Progress," hoping to raise doubt as to the "benevolent" nature of the U.S. program, and instead contended that Communist revolutions could solve the problems of the hemisphere.[17]

Cuban and Mexican expressions of friendship took other forms as well after Mexico's defense of Cuban sovereignty at the Punta del Este conference. For example, on March 23, 1963, Ambassador Bosques wrote a letter to Alfonso de Rosenweig Díaz Jr., the Mexican foreign relations secretary, telling him that the Benito Juárez School had held a ceremony celebrating the former Mexican president's birthday and that both Cubans and Mexicans were present for the celebration. Ambassador Bosques also wrote that the faculty and students of the school had sung both the Cuban and Mexican national anthems and that the celebrations ended with a guard ceremony that included representatives from the Mexican embassy and the Benito Juárez School.[18] To this day, the statue of Benito Juárez in Havana's downtown Parque de la Fraternidad stands out as one of the most important figures in a park full of heroes of the Americas.

Two days earlier, the Havana daily *El Mundo* had given a short biography of Juárez in an article covering his birthday. The author of the article, citing Juárez's observation that "respect for foreign rights is peace," commented that this phrase "constitutes an example and a formula of good government."[19] This obviously refers to the reasoning Mexico had used in

1962 at the OAS to defend its position not to support Cuba's expulsion from the international community. That both the Havana papers and Ambassador Bosques reported on these acts of solidarity demonstrates the continued importance of the Mexican-Cuban relationship in the midst of the Cold War turmoil unleashed by Castro's presence in a U.S.-dominated policy atmosphere.

Mexico's foreign policy ideology was the most vehement of all the OAS countries in its demand for nonintervention in Cuba. Yet, out of respect for U.S. foreign policy, "in the years 1959 and 1960, Mexico avoided referring to the multiple activities of the U.S. against the Cuban Revolution as acts of intervention," according to Mexican-Cuban relations scholar Olga Pellicer de Brody.[20] The PRI government sometimes used the policy of nonintervention as an excuse for looking the other way when it was too costly to speak out, and neither the leftist National Liberation Movement (MLN) nor the rightist MHN felt their interests could be served sufficiently by turning a blind eye.

To understand leftist and conservative concerns over the Mexican president's foreign policy trajectory it is also important to recognize that López Mateos was known for promoting social welfare. López Mateos, through a reinvigorated agrarian reform program, redistributed thirty million acres of land to the Mexican people (the second highest amount of any Mexican president after Cárdenas).[21] However, "Mexicanization" under López Mateos contrasted markedly with "Castroization." López Mateos expropriated a significant amount of land but the magnitude of the expropriation was not as great as it was in Cuba and the methods López Mateos used were distinct from Castro's. Castro had made the diplomatic blunder of only offering twenty-year bonds as compensation to American companies expropriated in Cuba, which was one reason the United States decided to cut off relations and institute an embargo against the island. On the other hand, López Mateos financially compensated companies that his administration nationalized and thus did not elicit the backlash that Cuba did from the United States.[22]

More specifically, although left-of-center Mexican presidents such as López Mateos expressed solidarity with the Cuban people, they never

▼▼▼

specifically praised Communism as a philosophy. That type of expression was more often than not made by pro-Cuban interest groups and citizens. In fact, in early January 1961, before the Bay of Pigs invasion and long before the Cuban Missile Crisis, López Mateos said the following of Castro's government: "In the beginning, we had a great deal of sympathy with the Cuban Revolution. . . . As for the political regime, we have of it the worst impression."[23] As in the United States, the public and government sectors that appeared to be aligned on foreign policy issues were in fact divided on others. For example, both the MLN and López Mateos opposed the Bay of Pigs invasion as well as supported the PRI's foreign policy of nonintervention and respect for self-determination. However, the two sectors diverged when it came to defending the Cuban Revolution itself. Although the PRI professed its revolutionary foundations, the PRI governments from López Mateos to Ernesto Zedillo Ponce de León (1994–2000) never "allied" themselves with the Castro regime in the same sense that they allied themselves with the United States during this period. That the PRI government did not allow radicals of either side to dominate the government made sense because it in fact already accommodated many different political elements, and of course it wished to preserve its own power.

THE CUBAN MISSILE CRISIS

Until October 1962, Castro had only gradually tested the patience of the United States and its hemispheric anti-Communist allies. But permitting Soviet missiles in Cuba was more serious than claiming to be Marxist-Leninist or expropriating foreign landholdings. This time, when the United States responded with a naval blockade, Mexican leftist groups like the MLN, the Popular Socialist Party (PPS), and the Mexican Communist Party (PCM) denounced the action, but also stated that they did not support the presence of missiles on the island. It was the overt shift to Communism coupled with the arrival of nuclear missiles to Cuba that made the relationship with Cuba a little too close for comfort for the Mexican left. Soon, the pro-Castro bent of the MLN lost much of its allure. Unlike the Bay of Pigs, where there were bona fide grounds for objecting to the U.S. invasion, there was no incentive for Mexico to defend Castro's and Khrushchev's ability to threaten so much destruction to so many people, and there were no pro-Castro demonstrations in Mexico as had been the case during the Bay of Pigs fiasco.

While the hemisphere was certainly opposed to the presence of nuclear weapons in Cuba, there was opposition to the U.S. blockade. For example, in an interview with the Cuban news agency *Prensa Latina*, Cárdenas spoke out against the way the United States reacted to the crisis, calling for "urgent measures by the UN to contain U.S. 'imperialist' designs." Cárdenas also wrote a letter to the *New York Times* placing the blame for the crisis on the United States and its offensive policies against Cuba.[24] Yet, he was not willing to fly to Cuba in support of Castro as he had been during the Bay of Pigs invasion.[25]

The crisis of October 1962 also tested the faith of the Mexican left. Marxists in Mexico were divided over how the missile withdrawal was dealt with. After Khrushchev pulled the missiles out of Cuba, many were disillusioned, but others considered the Soviet premier's decision a responsible move aimed at establishing peace.[26] The MLN itself declined in membership and significance. A significant loss came when Vicente Lombardo Toledano of the PPS abandoned the MLN in 1962 on the grounds that the MLN lacked a base of workers and consisted mainly of intellectuals.[27]

President López Mateos took the middle ground during the crisis. At a meeting in Manila, he responded to the presence of nuclear weapons in Cuba by saying that as long as they were there for defensive purposes, no harm should be done to peace. However, if the intention was to use them offensively, then he would take the opposing side with the United States.[28] But then the OAS called a meeting to discuss the Soviet strategic weapons in Cuba, and all members, Mexico included, called for the unconditional withdrawal of all of the missiles. Brazil, Bolivia, and Mexico requested that a separate vote be taken on the part of the resolution that provided for armed intervention against Cuba as a possibility for resolving the dilemma. On the other hand, "Argentina offered two destroyers; Honduras and Peru offered troops; and, Costa Rica, Nicaragua, Panama, the Dominican Republic, and Guatemala offered temporary use of their

▼▼▼

bases."[29] Mexico maintained its role as moderator of a potentially explosive situation and added that the resolution "should not be used to justify an invasion."[30] President López Mateos wrote a letter to Cuban president Osvaldo Dorticós saying that the presence of nuclear weapons could not be tolerated by Mexico.[31]

Historian Olga Pellicer de Brody argues that Mexico's foreign policy is dictated by the fact that Mexico shares such a long border with the United States: "The dependence of the Mexican economy on the North American market and capital . . . and the assimilation of western values by large groups of Mexican society" makes "any other policy . . . unthinkable."[32] As López Mateos put it, "We are within the ranks of democracy," and so when the United States was affronted by the USSR and Cuba, Mexico sided with its northern neighbor.[33] At the same time, Mexico's friendship with Cuba was damaged by the missile crisis. Interaction between the two countries from 1962–70 was strained at times, yet they did maintain formal diplomatic missions in the other's country throughout this period.[34]

The last straw for the American states came in 1964. After the United States and Venezuela discovered that Communist literature and Cuban arms were being sent to Venezuelan rebels, they decided "to invoke the Rio Treaty of Reciprocal Assistance to combat Communist subversion."[35] In July, the OAS called the Ninth Meeting of Consultation of Ministers of Foreign Relations, at which all of the Americas except Mexico severed relations with and imposed sanctions on Cuba.[36] Adhering to the age-old policy of nonintervention, Mexico opposed the OAS resolution and thereby became the only nation in the hemisphere to maintain relations with Cuba for the rest of the decade. The meeting came shortly after Gustavo Díaz Ordaz had been elected president of Mexico, and López Mateos was still in office.[37]

Cuban and Mexican delegates voiced their reactions to the OAS resolution in October 1964 at the Second Conference of Non-Aligned Nations held in Cairo. Invoking Mexico's long-standing representation of the essence of Mexican-Cuban relations, Mexican delegate Manuel Moreno Sánchez said, "In view of this and of the special circumstances in which Cuba and Mexico have always maintained friendly relations, President

López Mateos resolved to continue diplomatic relations with Cuba."[38] Cuban foreign minister Raúl Roa, who, just like the Castro brothers, had spent time in Mexico in exile before the Cuban Revolution, responded to Mexico's show of solidarity by stating, "Mexico's position, as was to be expected, was a vivid contrast to that of the Latin American observers."[39] Cuban president Osvaldo Torrado Dorticós also had a few kind words for Mexico: "How marked a contrast is the worthy and independent attitude of the Government of Mexico, a country with which we maintain relations, proving the possibility of friendly coexistence within the same part of the world, in spite of different social and political systems."[40]

The 1980 speech by Castro in recognition of Mexican president José López Portillo demonstrates the enduring nature of the political validity of this solidarity language, especially in reference to Mexico's defense of Cuban sovereignty and its refusal to sever relations during the 1964–70 period. That Castro had invoked this language in several speeches throughout the Cold War, and that Mexican officials and academics in turn expressed themselves using similar solidarity rhetoric, reveals the political value of the Mexican-Cuban connection as well as the extent to which the United States (however inadvertently) shaped the character of that relationship. However, at the very same time that, as Castro put it, "Mexico alone maintained the worthy and courageous position of not breaking its relations with Cuba," Mexico was also poised to become a mediator between the two powers, in more ways than one.[41]

MEXICO IN THE MIDDLE

The groundwork for U.S.-Mexican cooperation was being laid in February 1964, when López Mateos was still in office. In a letter to President Johnson before his meeting with the Mexican president, Secretary of State Dean Rusk asserted that

> [López Mateos] has followed an "independent" foreign policy but knows that good relations with us . . . are essential to his country. At times his foreign policy has been too independent—for example on Cuba and in commercial and cultural relations with

Communist China. But when fundamental issues are at stake we have usually found him understanding and willing to be helpful—controlling travel of Castro agents, non recognition on China, offering help on Panama.[42]

Rusk recognized that the PRI needed to maintain its image as independent vis-à-vis the United States so that the it could keep its standing with the Mexican left but also was confident that Mexico could be counted on when it really mattered.[43] Later that year, on November 12, as Johnson prepared to meet with Mexican president-elect Gustavo Díaz Ordaz, Rusk took matters further, advising Johnson that the Mexican-Cuban connection might prove helpful to hemispheric security:

> The background on [Mexico's position on Cuba] is that during our foreign ministers meeting in late July, a number of us, Brazil, and others, talked about the practical desirability of having one Latin American . . . embassy there if possible, but we couldn't find a formula in which we could do that with four having embassies, and so the hemisphere is sort of relaxed about the Mexicans staying on there for a time. I would emphasize to [Díaz Ordaz] the importance of his taking all the steps necessary . . . not to permit the Cubans to use Mexico as a channel for money or agents or for travel of students to Cuba for training and things of that sort. . . . But I wouldn't press him unduly to break relations."[44]

Thus, Rusk admits here that an informal understanding was arrived at among several of the American states (he does not mention whether Mexico was directly involved in that conversation) and that Mexico's position was considered a useful tool for hemispheric security.

When Johnson spoke to Díaz Ordaz on November 23 in Texas, Díaz Ordaz told the American president that the Mexican government would continue to side with the United States on matters of importance even if on other issues of less significance they would have to officially agree to disagree. In the words of a State Department memorandum, Díaz Ordaz's position was that "the United States could be absolutely sure that when the chips were really down, Mexico would be unequivocally by its side. He added that Mexico, for example, might not perhaps know about the details of what was going on in Viet-Nam or Cyprus, but that he and the Mexican Government understood perfectly well what the stakes were and that Mexico's interests in a show-down would be parallel to ours."[45]

Referring to Mexico's position in the OAS with regard to Cuba, the memo also paraphrased Díaz Ordaz as stating that Mexico's "juridical distinctions . . . might not seem logical or profound" but that, according to Díaz Ordaz, "they were a product of Mexico's history and of Mexican tradition and sentiment."[46] The memo even echoed Rusk's February assessment that the PRI needed to appear independent: according to Díaz Ordaz, "there was a considerable advantage when the issues at stake were not great if Mexico could continue to demonstrate its political independence and divergence on relatively minor issues," which "might at times create temporary discomfiture" but that "also demonstrated that the American states did in fact enjoy independence."[47] The key word here is "demonstrate."

Thus, the PRI desired its image of independence vis-à-vis the United States to be "demonstrated" across Latin America, even if only on "minor issues." According to the memo, President Johnson was in full agreement with Díaz Ordaz on these matters. In addition, the unnamed National Security Council official who relayed this memo to the council's executive secretary, Bromley Smith, noted in the cover sheet that, "Part II should be made Limited Distribution. If it should get out to the public it could really hurt Díaz Ordaz."[48]

A staunch anti-Communist, Gustavo Díaz Ordaz had little interest in affiliating himself with Castro. His assignment of General Pamanes Escobedo as ambassador to Cuba in early 1965 opened the shaky chapter of subterfuge and accusation of subterfuge via the Mexican embassy in Havana. Whether Castro's claims about CIA agents infiltrating the embassy were true, it is at the very least clear that some Mexican ambassadors between 1965 and the 1970s passed information of an irregular and often private nature about the Cuban government to the Mexican Foreign Secretary. Documents from 1967 related to the work of Ambassador

Pamanes Escobedo reveal that Mexico and the United States tried to use the Mexican embassy in Havana to gather intelligence. A comparison between eleven years of reports from Mexican ambassador Gilberto Bosques (1953–64) and those of Pamanes in 1967 shows a marked transformation in the purpose of that embassy once Díaz Ordaz took office.[49]

While the U.S. government was growing more comfortable with Mexico's position on Cuba, the anti-Communist voices from the United States were more skeptical. On July 17, 1964, *Free Cuba News*, which was produced by the Citizens Committee for a Free Cuba, Inc., out of Washington, D.C., described Mexico's position as "recalcitrant" with regard to its foreign policy toward Cuba, four days before the OAS conference.[50] Mexico's foreign policy, according to the author, "is viewed by many Latin American diplomats in Washington as a real danger to Hemispheric security."[51] This danger was due to "Mexico's attitude, and U.S. acceptance of the Mexican position," which serves "as a crippling veto to any effective action which the OAS might want to take."[52]

Cuban exile groups also chimed in, expressing perhaps the most openly militant position against pro-Cuban Mexicans of all other interested anti-Communists in advocating the destruction of Communists by any means necessary, including murder. This illustrates how illuminating it can be to analyze both official policy and interest group expression, which amounts to a policy analysis as well but of the public instead of the government, and raises the question of what influence the public has on the government and vice versa in this regard. In this case, although some in government certainly expressed concern over Mexican-Cuban connections, eventually policy accommodated these connections out of pragmatism. Yet, the policy of anti-Communists was even more strident than that of the government. To see why, let us examine the coinciding policies of the U.S. and Mexican administrations of Lyndon B. Johnson and Gustavo Díaz Ordaz.

CHAPTER FIVE

DEFINING DIPLOMATIC

ALLEGIANCES, 1964–70

Mexican leaders have no sympathy for the

Castro regime.

Mexican cooperation has been good.

—John H. Crimmins, U.S. State Department director
of Mexican and Caribbean affairs in February 1964,
regarding U.S.-Mexican cooperation on Cuba

MEXICO BEGAN GROWING important to the United States between the
1970s and the 1990s, according to most scholars of U.S.-Mexican relations. Robert Jones Shafer and Donald Mabry's *Neighbors* (1981) and, more
recently, Jorge I. Domínguez and Rafael Fernández de Castro's *The United
States and Mexico* (2001) point to economics, the drug war, and immigration as primary factors in their emerging closeness. However, a look at the
triangular relationship among the United States, Mexico, and Cuba shows
us how U.S.-Mexican relations were affected by the rise of Castro's influence and, additionally, how they shaped Mexican-Cuban relations.

U.S.-Mexico scholars tend to gloss over the importance of Mexican-
Cuban relations in the evolution of U.S.-Mexican relations. According
to Shafer and Mabry, for example, before the 1970s, the United States
"had little interest" in the country until the OPEC oil cartel unbalanced world prices and Mexico entered its second great oil boom."[1] And
though Domínguez and Fernández de Castro use a more complex, three-
phase model in their account of the evolution of the relationship
between the United States and Mexico, they still fail to concentrate

▼▼▼

sufficiently on the role that the Cold War played, beginning in the 1960s, in its development.

This relationship emerged primarily out of a mutual U.S.-Mexican hostility to Cuban influence. Yet, according to Domínguez and Fernández de Castro, although initially "contemplating alliances with major powers from other continents" in the 1910s, Mexico went on to adopt "an abnegation strategy for most of the century," whereby it sought to maintain its relative independence vis-à-vis their northern neighbor and "cooperated little or not at all with the United States over international security issues" until the 1990s.[2] At that point, "Mexico followed . . . a 'bandwagoning' strategy," in which it "cooperated extensively with the United States over international security issues, especially drug trafficking."[3] However, an examination of Mexican-Cuban relations from 1964–76, more than a decade before Shafer and Mabry contend the two countries began to take an interest in each other and three decades before they did according to Domínguez and Fernández de Castro, reveals that Mexico increasingly aligned itself with the United States on matters of security.

At the same time that the relationship between Mexico and the United States was growing, the Mexican-Cuban relationship was being characterized as one of solidarity in the so-called "struggle" *against* U.S. efforts to isolate Castro. Yet as early as January 1964 Mexico and the United States demonstrated an intelligence sharing capacity within Mexico against Cuba, as a U.S. report that month revealing how Mexican authorities broke up an illegal passport ring makes clear. Mexican foreign ministry officials were selling fake passports with the assistance of the Cuban and Soviet embassies, who were assisting "Latin American Communists" including "Cuban-trained subversive agents . . . to travel to and from Cuba posing as Mexicans."[4] Thus, both U.S.-Mexican relations and Mexican-Cuban relations have been incompletely understood by scholars. The level of intelligence sharing between the United States and Mexico suggests that cooperation between Mexico and United States throughout the 1964–70 period and beyond was in fact important to both sides during an era that Mexicans and Cubans often refer to as one in which Mexico stood alone as a *friend* to the Cuban people.

Mexican president Adolfo López Mateos's (1958–64) visit to California in February 1964 increased Mexico-U.S. cooperation, as President Johnson's Mexico briefing book for the visit shows. State Department director of Mexican and Caribbean affairs John H. Crimmins wrote that "Mexican leaders have no sympathy for the Castro regime, and they realize that their vital relations with the United States can be jeopardized by seeming to be neutral on the Cuban issue."[5] Those American officials familiar with Mexican foreign affairs felt that Mexico was allying itself with the United States, not Cuba. Furthermore, Crimmins noted, "with a national election in the offing, Mexican leaders are extremely reluctant to have the Cuban issue emerge as a divisive political force," which he perhaps mentioned to emphasize that the U.S. government should not dwell on it either.[6] This shows how the U.S. understood the role Cuba played in Mexican politics.

Crimmins also noted how Mexico had been cooperating with the United States on Soviet and Cuban connections in Mexico. The report stated that "Mexican cooperation has been good," because its officials "have restricted the issuance of Mexican transition visas and have generally honored the requests by other Latin American Governments not to permit movement of their nationals whose passports were not validated for travel to Cuba. Cuban aircraft of Soviet manufacture have been prevented from landing in Mexico."[7] That same month, Robert W. Adam, counselor of the U.S. embassy in Mexico City, reported on suspicions concerning a pro-Castro Mexican official. Adam's report stated that Mexican authorities stopped Antonia Sánchez Gavito, second secretary of the Mexican embassy in Cuba and sister of the Mexican ambassador to the Organization of American States (OAS), at the Mexico City airport "carrying an official Mexican mail pouch which she refused to open for customs inspectors."[8] This behavior, Adam reported, was suspicious to Mexican and American authorities because of her alleged "very pro-Castro" sentiments.[9] The fact that Adam's report mentions her brother's role in the OAS is important because he, Vicente Sánchez Gavito, represented Mexico at the ninth meeting of foreign ministers in July 25 that year (1964), and as such was the Mexican representative who made history in refusing to sever relations with Cuba, when Cuba was expelled from the OAS.[10]

▼▼▼

That October, U.S. embassy officials reported a similar incident to the State Department in which Mexican authorities seized "Castrista propaganda" at the airport. In the words of the embassy officials, the Mexican authorities made "close observation of travelers returning from Cuba."[11] In this case, the travelers possessing the materials were "the Director of the School of Economics of the University of Sinaloa and five of his students."[12] The report provided details, including their names, length of stay in Cuba, their affiliation with the National Liberation Movement (MLN), and called them "guests of the Castro government."[13]

A letter from Bob Sayre to National Security Advisor McGeorge Bundy in July 1964 showed Mexico taking its cooperation with the United States in the struggle to defeat Communism to a new level. Exactly eighteen days before the ninth meeting of foreign ministers in July 1964, Sayre relayed a request from the Mexican minister of defense to the U.S. Army attaché asking "whether we could arrange to have ten Mexican officers (Majors and Colonels) receive counterinsurgency training in Vietnam for six months by acting as observers."[14] Sayre noted that "this would be good from the point of view of US-Mexican relations. We have tried for years with almost no success to interest the Mexicans in defense cooperation, internal security improvement, etc."[15] It's not known whether the Mexican officers ever went to Vietnam, but the request nonetheless helps contextualize the favorable atmosphere of U.S.-Mexico relations on the eve of Mexico's historic OAS vote not to sever relations with Cuba as well as Mexico's agency in promoting its own role in international relations during the Cold War as opposed to simply cowering to a U.S. demand. Mexican autonomy with respect to both the United States and Cuba exemplifies how the Cold War provided developing world nations the opportunity to find their own voices and thus affect international relations in a way they had never been able to before.

Likewise, the American Consulate's officer in Mérida, Yucatán, described a combined U.S.-Mexican "security improvement" the following February. The report, entitled "Cuban Involvement in Recent Civil Disturbance in Yucatan," told of an intelligence link between the Mexican police and a U.S. consular officer that helped to uncover the pro-Cuban roots of several civil disturbances in Yucatán that year.[16] The report stated that "identification by police elements was facilitated by long-standing and efficient cooperation between a Consulate officer and a local police official."[17] This effort to thwart Cuban influence was particularly significant given the proximity of the Yucatán peninsula to Cuba and demonstrates how the international threat that Castro's influence posed forced Mexico and the United States to further align themselves along national security lines. The report even gave the names of the three pro-Cuban Mexicans captured by the police as well as their backgrounds. For example, it provided information on when they had traveled to Cuba and noted the three men's deep connections with the Cuban-Mexican Cultural Center in Mérida and that their financing came from the Mérida Cuban Consul and the Cuban embassy in Mexico City.[18] The author of this report, Paul S. Dwyer, also complimented the Mexican police, stating that "it is gratifying to note the quick police action against these young agitators."[19] The gesture typifies the Johnson administration's approach to the Díaz Ordaz administration.

Cooperation against Cuban activities in Mérida continued at least into 1965, as Mexican officials began to treat Cuban vessels suspiciously, drawing praise from American officials. On April 12, the American Consulate in Mérida sent a report to Washington entitled "Indications of New Attitude of Mexican Military Authorities with Respect to Cuban Fishing Vessels."[20] This report detailed how Mexican military officials had starting imposing uncommon restrictions on Cuban vessel passengers after "forced arrivals" at Mérida owing to alleged onboard emergencies.[21] The American Consulate's report suggested that the U.S. government "may wish to exploit this newly developing Mexican attitude," deemed by the consulate to amount to "hostile Mexican treatment" of Cuban vessels: "The Consulate, in noting this new Mexican manner of treating Cuban fishing vessels, attaches substantial importance to this matter. The Consulate thinks the word will spread among Cuban fishing crews," who are "already badly demoralized" and "will become more so" as this type of "hostile Mexican treatment" continues.[22]

The consulate also astutely described the delicate nature of Mexican-Cuban relations in its report. It expressed hope that "the Cuban goverment,

▼▼▼

anxious as it may be to avoid any unpleasantness with Mexico, may order Cuban fishing vessels to curtail their landings at Mexican ports." The vessels entered the port for repairs and shelter from storms, and the U.S. authorities alleged that they were also trading illicitly with Mérida merchants.[23] The consulate hoped "this newly developing Mexican attitude" would help the United States achieve its goal of "[harming] the Cuban fishing fleet" by hindering its maintenance, thereby preventing the contraband trade that assisted the Communist island's economy.[24] The reference to the "Mexican attitude" shows both the level of U.S. respect for Mexican autonomy and Mexico's own initiative in conducting its anti-Communist security policy.

This type of official U.S.-Mexican cooperation went straight up the chain of command to the Mexican foreign relations minister, Antonio Carrillo Flores. Carrillo Flores had served both as ambassador to the United States and as a moderator between the United States and the Soviet Union–Cuba in mid-1965. A State Department UN delegation Memorandum of Conversation entitled "LA Nuclear Free Zone and Cuba" noted how Mexico mediated between the United States and Cuba on the nuclear issue. Carrillo Flores had asked the U.S. government if it would consider a Cuban agreement on a nuclear-free Latin America "just a gesture by Cuba or whether it would have real significance in terms of future U.S.-Cuban relationships."[25] The State Department delegation welcomed the gesture but insisted that the agreement "would not be enough at the time to assure our acceptance of the Castro Regime."[26] Carrillo Flores inquired as to U.S. requirements, to which the secretary replied that "Cuba must demonstrate, even though it need not take a public announcement to this effect, that it was withholding its subversive activities in the area" and that the island "must also break its military ties with the Soviet Union."[27]

That this negotiation failed in the end is not at issue here; rather the fact that the U.S. government asked Mexico to convey messages to Cuba concerning vital national security issues demonstrates Mexico's geopolitical importance in the Cold War struggle against Cuba, which only increased as the 1960s progressed. That Mexico had international clout with both the Soviet Union and the United States also speaks clearly to its influence in Cold War relations.

By 1966, the U.S. government had the utmost confidence in the Díaz Ordaz administration's capacity to thwart the pro-Castro Mexican left. The CIA's April 7, 1966, "Security Conditions in Mexico" conveys much the same information as the 1962 report but mentions a couple of notable developments, such as that the Mexican government "has sharply limited pro-Castroite and other anti-US activities" and that the "once-touted Movement of National Liberation (MLN), an anti-US and pro-Cuban mass organization . . . has lost much of its early support and has been weakened by disagreement among its leaders."[28] Furthermore, communication between Díaz Ordaz and President Johnson surpassed that between earlier Mexican and American leaders considerably. In October 1967, both heads of state met in several border cities, which elicited the usual intelligence assessments of pro-Cuban Mexican elements potentially able to sabotage Johnson's visit to the Mexican side of the border. The CIA report noted how "two Cubans who recently entered Mexico clandestinely are in Ciudad Juarez" and that "they reportedly have contact with Mexican Trotskyists and the Communist-dominated National Democratic Students Council (CMED) groups—interested in disrupting the presidential visit. Mexican authorities have been alerted to the Cubans' presence and are attempting to locate them."[29] Taken as a whole, the communication between the Díaz Ordaz and President Johnson administrations showed a high level of enthusiasm and willingness to cooperate together against Cuba.

INTRIGUE ON THE ISLAND: MEXICO IN CUBA, 1966–70

The Mexican embassy in Havana facilitated Mexican access to Cuban internal information from 1966–74. Although Mexican-Cuban inter-governmental relations recovered somewhat in the early 1970s from the deterioration they suffered under Díaz Ordaz, Mexican ambassadorial correspondence from Cuba to Mexico indicates that Mexico was still suspicious of and even hostile to Castro's Cuba. That a fellow "revolutionary" government secretly observed its neighbor challenges the idea that "revolutionary" aspirations formed the core of Mexican-Cuban relations, further illustrating the increasingly parallel interests of Mexico and the

▼▼▼

United States with respect to national security matters as well as the forces that undermined actual Mexican-Cuban solidarity.

A highly decorated Mexican general, Fernando Pamanes Escobedo, fit the new assignment as Mexican ambassador to Cuba quite well. Arriving in March 1965 and leaving in September 1967, Pamanes passed information later characterized as "intelligence" to the Mexican Foreign Relations Secretariat (SRE) from 1966–67. His regular correspondence to the SRE covered the Cuban and sometimes Soviet militaries, Fidel and Raúl Castro's activities, waning Cuban public enthusiasm for the regime, shortages, the presence of Mexican guerrillas training in Cuba, and other information related to Castro's regime that represented an international security concern to both Mexico and the United States.[30] Some of this information made its way directly to the desk of President Johnson as well as to President Díaz Ordaz as well to U.S. consular officer Francis Sherry in Mexico.[31]

Pamanes's file would bear significantly on Mexican-Cuban relations. From May 1965 to February 1966, the files contain no foreign secretariat-oriented correspondence regarding sensitive Cuban information, but on February 24, according to a Mexican SRE memorandum written for President Díaz Ordaz, Pamanes had reported on two instances in which the Cuban military had used weapons in a questionable manner: when they killed a Yugoslav embassy officer and when "anti-aircraft batteries . . . fired at an 'object' that approached the east bank of the bay of Havana, later verified as a commercial plane [that had] veered slightly from its regular route."[32] This type of critical perspective appears nowhere in the eleven years of correspondence between the former Mexican ambassador, Gilberto Bosques, and the SRE. But that does not seem to be because the Mexican government discouraged it or considered it an unworthy thing to do, since Pamanes's critiques of the Cuban government's actions were almost uniformly greeted by the secretariat with interest, as his replies to Pamanes make clear. In this particular case, the secretariat even produced a memo of this information for the Mexican president.[33]

On January 26, 1967, Pamanes sent a letter commenting critically on the new agricultural program requiring Cuban citizens to help in the fields. For some reason, he paid close attention to the rhetoric used by the

Cuban government during the promotion of this program at the exposition of "Industry at the Service of Agriculture," in which he refers to the program as "propaganda."[34] In fact, the subdirector general of the Mexican Diplomatic Service considered Pamanes's report on this matter so important that not only did he respond by praising him for his attention to detail in the report but also he produced a memorandum on it for the Mexican president.[35] Pamanes's February 28 letter to the SRE reported on Castro's speech at the Cubana de Acero factory's "struggle against bureaucracy" campaign. Pamanes believed this event had "social, political, and economic . . . repercussions," but that the campaign could not succeed.[36] Again, the SRE responded that the letter was worthy of their "interest."[37]

On April 12, Pamanes reported on the so-called *llamamiento a la juventud* (call on the youth) by the Cuban government. He noted how peculiar it was that "the Vice Minister of the Armed Forces, Commander Juan Almeida Bosque" rather than Raúl Castro had called on "the Cuban youth to enlist" in the service.[38] The peculiarity, according to Pamanes, lay in the fact that Raúl had hidden himself for some time from the public eye. Pamanes later conveyed this information to U.S. consulate officer Francis Sherry in June in Mexico City, stating that he had not seen Fidel or Raúl "since the winter of 1966."[39] The fact that it found its way from Havana to Mexico City to the U.S. consulate officer demonstrates that Pamanes found it relevant to U.S. and Mexican national security.

Che Guevara even entered the picture in Pamanes's assessments owing to Guevara's 1967 Bolivian insurgent movement. Pamanes asserted that Cubans considered this movement "the beginning of an intense guerrilla movement in the very heart of the South American continent."[40] Pamanes also stated that because the tactics of the guerrillas in Bolivia resembled those of the insurgents during Cuban Revolution "it makes one think . . . that the Bolivian guerrilla leaders could have been trained militarily and instructed ideologically in Cuba."[41] He also commented that some people assumed Che Guevara was in the Santa Cruz province of Bolivia or in Mato Grosso, Brazil, adding that "it is not easy to accept such speculation, but neither can one discard" the possibility that Che was still alive.[42] Perhaps Pamanes's military background compelled him to pass

▼▼▼

such specific information and offer such speculation; by 1967, it would lead to his dismissal.

He further commented on Bolivian guerrillas in his April 21 letter reporting on meetings among leftist organizations in Havana. The Organization of Solidarity of the People of Asia, Africa, and Latin America (OSPAAAL) meeting in Havana as well as the Latin American Organization of Solidarity (OLAS) had, according to Pamanes, "entered an era of intense activity, preparing a vigorous propaganda scheme."[43] His May 9 letter reported on the Week of Solidarity with Latin America in which he observed "that the revolutionary movement in our hemisphere is progressing and that the guerrilla activities in Colombia, Venezuela, Guatemala, Peru and Brazil might direct the final overthrow of their respective governments."[44] His May 10 letter quoted Guatemalan delegate Renato Jiménez as calling on Latin Americans to fulfill their "obligation to take up arms and launch [the revolution] in the mountains," which stemmed from the Cuban notion that it was the duty of all revolutionaries "to make revolution."[45]

Why was Pamanes passing this information? For whom was he reporting? One possible answer is found in a June 10 U.S. State Department memo covering a June 2 meeting between Ambassador Pamanes and Francis Sherry. This memo made its way from Mexico City to Washington, D.C., where both National Security Advisor Walt Rostow and President Johnson viewed its contents. The cover attachment of the memo addressed to President Johnson from Rostow notes that "this first hand account of the situation inside Cuba has some interesting insights."[46] This note indicates the U.S. government's interest Mexico's insider information on Cuba, and the name of the Mexico City CIA station chief, Winston Scott, appears on the cover page.[47] The memo contained military information and addressed issues such as levels of dissent in the Cuban public and repatriation efforts for U.S. citizens. For example, Pamanes told Sherry that dissent within Cuba was high and that it might manifest itself in "much stronger terms than they have up to now."[48]

Pamanes's military intelligence in particular indicated his suspicion of Cuba during this conversation. He told Sherry that the Cuban army had mobilized "along [its] southern coast, particularly in Oriente province."[49] He also revealed details about their movements and activities: "Reservists were not called but Cubans activated numbers of vigilante and guard groups which in turn freed the regular Army troops from guard and other duties."[50] Pamanes even mentioned that over "30 thousand troops were freed for defensive duties along the southern coast by placing guards and militia on alert status" and then demonstrated his inside connections by telling Sherry how "a Cuban official speaking privately" told him "that the Cubans foresaw the extreme possibility" of a Venezuelan attack "along the Cuban coast."[51] According to Sherry, "Pamanes observed the unloading of an unidentified Soviet ship from a distance which included large, long boxes which he felt probably contained small to medium-size ground to air missiles. Four to six were being loaded on trailers of about 30-ton capacity."[52] He went on to report on the possible devolution of Soviet-Cuban relations after Castro became adamant about using violence to establish socialism in Central and South America, information he received during a conversation with the Soviet embassy officials in Havana.[53]

Several aspects of Pamanes's tenure as ambassador would lead one to believe he was possibly operating on the assumption that passing intelligence was expected of him. For example, his July 4, 1967, report described an event that appeared completely unconnected to his normal duties, the visit of Soviet first prime minister Alexei Kosygin to Havana:

On the 26th of the previous month, the Soviet Premier Alexei Kosiguin arrived in this city by surprise for the public and without previous notice, after his visit to the United Nations in New York and his interview with President Johnson in New Jersey. He was received at the airport by [Cuban] President Osvaldo Dorticos, Premier Fidel Castro, the Minister of Armed Forces, Raul Castro, two or three functionaries more from the government and the Communist Party and Vilma Rapin de Castro, President of the Federation of Cuban Women.[54]

▼▼▼

Pamanes then went on to discuss internal Cuban issues such as repression and Castro's support for foreign guerrilla movements that, according to a 1971 report submitted by the Mexican foreign relations secretariat after the Mexican government removed Panames from Cuba in 1967, he ought not to have been concerning himself with.

That report paints Pamanes's intelligence gathering as inappropriate and, as such, as if it were unsolicited. For example, the unidentified SRE author states that Cubans complained Pamanes charged asylum seekers for passage to Mexico.[55] The costs included passing sensitive information, according to section of the report that discussed "[a]ctivities not included in the instructions that Ambassador Pamanes received with respect to his mission in Cuba," which describes Pamanes as being "undoubtedly guided by the best intentions," when he assigned himself "intelligence work."[56] The author notes that the SRE ordered him not to do this "except in cases in which he had a true reason to consider that he could obtain information of direct interest for Mexico."[57] I found no evidence of such an order in searching through Pamanes's file, however. The report goes on to relate information contained in several documents produced by Pamanes concerning intelligence matters, which he apparently received from a Mr. "X," whom, the author says, was the "chief of the section of Cuban intelligence in Mexico."[58] Pamanes was Mexican national defense secretary from 1958–64 and may have established connections with this person during that period. Mr. "X" requested that Pamanes help him gain asylum in Mexico and Mr. "X"'s most interesting information was his "evidence" of Mexican guerrillas training in Cuba.[59] This document also claims Pamanes stated that "Mr. 'X' gave me an envelope for the American Embassy in which he submitted to me a credential that says it is necessary for his organization to have absolute confidence in me and to give me all of the information, which is of the highest importance and gravity."[60] Although this is still unspecific with regard to names, Pamanes apparently gained the trust of Cuban dissident groups that passed him information about internal Cuban affairs. How he was approached by the group is still unclear, but at the very least it can be gleaned that his former position as Defense Secretary and Mr. "X"'s position as intelligence chief in Mexico suggest a possible mutual affiliation through military connections.[61]

Further information from this confidential report highlights possible strong connections between Pamanes and the Cuban dissident community, which gives us reason to believe that Pamanes was actively looking for intelligence in exchange for which he would grant asylum to those seeking it, with Mr. "X" working for him as he passed information on to the SRE. The report told of several letters found in Pamanes's strongbox that he had left behind when he was sent to Indonesia.[62] The letters, addressed to Pamanes, were dated from April to August 1966, and according to the report, "If what [the letters] say is true, people asked Ambassador Pamanes to give asylum to people connected to anti-Castro groups, [such as] the 'Democratic National Front,' with the apparent aim of facilitating the exposure of issues within Cuba that would help the group's cause."[63] The report quotes one letter as saying that Pamanes had already met with "a high leader" of their group.[64]

The letters from Cuban asylum seekers to Pamanes also revealed details of "guerrilla training activities or arms trafficking to Guatemala" and indicated that Pamanes assisted the asylum seekers in gathering intelligence. For example, the Cuban dissident stated the following: "the photos taken with the microfilm that you [Pamanes] provided us, taken of the records of every one of the 17 Mexican citizens that we referred to (people who were trained in Cuban guerrilla camps), sending them to you in order to have the microfilm developed in the laboratories in the intelligence service of your country."[65] The confidential report notes that one roll of undeveloped microfilm was sent directly to the secretaría de gobernación in Mexico City.[66] Further evidence over this matter came to light in 1970, three years after Pamanes had left Cuba and Victor Alfonso Maldonado (1970–74) was installed as ambassador. Ambassador Maldonado and his staff reported finding the strongbox referred to in the 1971 confidential report that contained several letters written to Pamanes apparently from asylum seekers who wrote about "matters related to the Cuban Revolution."[67]

It is important to note here that this type of information passing is similar to what the Cuban government later accused Mexican press attaché Humberto Carrillo Colón of doing as a CIA agent in September 1969.

▼▼▼

After these accusations surfaced and Mexico removed Colón from Havana, the Cuban government produced a book with "evidence" to demonstrate its case against Colón. The book, *El Insólito caso del espía de la CIA bajo el manto de funcionario de la embajada de México en Cuba*, asserted that Colón gathered information on "internal political affairs," "Cuban military capacity," "Cuban-Russian Relations," and "Internal Cuban support for guerrilla movements in other Latin American countries."[68]

The book's introduction makes clear Castro's personal intention of exonerating Mexico in the scandal and placing the blame for the embassy's infiltration on the United States. "[T]he government of Cuba," it stated, does "not implicate . . . the foreign secretary [Carrillo Flores] or [Ambassador] *Covián*" in Colón's activities. The introduction also pointed out that one reason the Cuban government produced the book was to alert Mexico to the fact that there were Mexican government officials engaged in U.S. intelligence activities.[69] The book further expressed the Cuban government's confidence in the Díaz Ordaz administration: "the Government of Mexico, *without any doubt*, will complete by its own methods, an investigation concerning this case."[70]

In light of the Cuban report on Colón, it seems pertinent to consider what may have motivated Pamanes to pass intelligence information. Kate Doyle, National Security Archive researcher, contends that Pamanes is the embodiment of a double-sided foreign policy on the part of Mexico. That is, she contends that Mexico held two contradictory policies: it appeared to be Cuba's friend but at the same time was gathering anti-Castro information behind Cuba's back. This would imply that the information was in fact considered "of direct interest for Mexico," the criteria the report criticizing Pamanes set for the appropriate passing of intelligence information, or, as Walt Rostow put it, a "first hand account of the situation inside Cuba."[71] If so, then it would make sense that each time the SRE received reports from Pamanes it was in fact condoning the use of its embassy for passing sensitive information on Cuban affairs.

Furthermore, isn't it possible that Mexico wasn't fooling Cuban officials? Might Castro have recognized that official Mexico was increasingly aligning itself with the U.S. government over issues of international security? Does it make sense that Castro may have been saving face with his favorable pronouncements toward Mexico even during the era of soured relations from 1964–70? In a way, the type of information ambassadors Miguel Covián Pérez (1967–70) and Victor Alfonso Maldonado sent to Mexico City was no different from what Pamanes had sent. These two ambassadors were quite critical of the Castro regime's domestic and foreign policy and its potential threat to international security. However, while Maldonado's files from 1970–74 contain significant amounts of information, the volume of reports in Covián's files do not approach that of Pamanes, whose files for two years of service are fully four times the size of Covian's, whose service spanned three years.

A March 21, 1968, confidential letter to foreign relations secretary Antonio Carrillo Flores made clear Covián's critical stance regarding the Castro regime. In the letter Covián reported overhearing discussions in public places among Cubans complaining about rationing and noted that "these critical expressions . . . signaled that this country, instead of progressing, is regressing."[72] Covián then added that he believed the discontent did not stem from the rationing alone but also had to do with "the growing distrust in the effectiveness of this system of government to satisfy the major necessities of the people."[73] Commenting on one of Castro's speeches, Covián stated that even though the milk rationing may have been "necessary," Castro's "prolix speech on 'political definitions' ignored the critiques about the viability of his regime to achieve its proposed development goals."[74] He made his strongest statement in response to Castro's announcements for new "government measures" to further the revolution, observing that "the true objective of [Castro's] pronouncement [was]: to organize a new and more violent assault of repression against all the groups that . . . have manifested nonconformity or discrepancy with their system of government."[75]

Castro, according to Covián, only desired loyalty and thus created reasons to enforce that. Covián noted that every Cuban was a potential target of Castro's repression, including people benefiting disproportionately from the revolution and people "seek[ing] to travel to other countries" as well as even "orthodox Marxists who criticize Castro Ruz's government."[76] Castro was using "tactical aspects of great interest," such as "the creation of new motives of revolutionary exaltation," for example, by going after "new enemies of the Revolution" because "the old ones (bourgeoisie), don't exist anymore." Because the bourgeoisie had disappeared and the calls against imperialism no longer had the power to motivate people, Castro needed a new enemy.[77] The government therefore repressed "the last survivals of commercial and industrial private property" and showed itself to be "even against professional activities that are practiced by free initiative."[78] And yet, despite this aggressively critical perspective, Covián's first quoted words by the Havana daily, *El Mundo*, on the ambassador's arrival in Cuba on September 12, 1967, were quite favorable toward Cuba: "I come from a free country and I arrive in a free country."[79] Covián resigned in April 1970 for unspecified reasons. He had truly carried on Pamanes's legacy.

Evidence obtained by the National Security Archive indicates an official understanding Covián's role as legatee. For example, in a confidential telegram from the U.S. embassy in Mexico City dated September 7, 1967, just five days after Pamanes's removal from Havana, U.S. ambassador Tony Freeman reported that Covián would effectively pick up where Pamanes had left off, acting as an "unofficial representative of the U.S." in Cuba.[80] Covián then demonstrated his dedication to Mexican-U.S. international security cooperation by assuring Freeman "he would report all developments promptly to [the foreign secretary] for transmittal to me."[81] Ambassador Freeman also indicated that he understood Mexico's dual position on Cuba, that it wished to support and facilitate U.S. observations of Cuban internal politics as well as defend Cuba's sovereignty in the international community: "[I] will understand should the [Mexican government] decide to abstain from any [resolution] which condemns Cuba . . . and calls for sanctions."[82]

Henry Dearborn, U.S. chief of station in the Mexico City embassy, further pointed out that it was in U.S. interests for Mexico to maintain relations with Cuba, noting in a telegram to the U.S. State Department on June 26, 1967, that he had been told by embassy officials that the Mexican government "has informal understanding with U.S. at highest levels to maintain relations with Cuba so one OAS country can have foot in door which might sometime be helpful."[83] By 1970, however, Covián had left as ambassador and a new, left-of-center president was inaugurated: Luís Echeverría Alvarez (1970–76).

ANTI-COMMUNISM: CUBAN EXILES AND
MEXICAN-CUBAN CONNECTIONS

Meanwhile, anti-Communist groups not operating under the same presumption of solidarity between Mexico and Cuba renewed their efforts to thwart these ties from the 1960s through the 1980s. The anti-Communists used the Mexican-Cuban relationship, ironically and tellingly, for unfriendly ends, not to enhance solidarity but to destroy it and thereby advance their own interests. The Regional Anti-Communist Crusade (CRAC) verbally criticized Cárdenas, López Mateos, and Díaz Ordaz, while the Cuban exile group, the National Christian Movement (MNC), intimidated and threatened the Mexican government with violence over Mexican-Cuban connections. The MNC established its terrorist status early on, in 1965, when it claimed responsibility for a grenade attack on the Mexican newspaper *El Día*, which it targeted for its alleged Communism. The MNC's mission was to battle Communism in all its forms, which included anyone who defended Castro's government as well as the Díaz Ordaz government, which imprisoned MNC commando chief, Henry Agüero, for the July 7, 1965, grenade attack. Its newsletter, *Acción*, repeatedly wrote of the heroism Agüero had displayed and called for his release from the well-known Mexican prison, Lecumberri.

MNC's diatribes, which mostly focused on Mexico during the 1960s, tellingly reveal the Cold War importance of the Mexico-Cuba connection. In *Acción's* June 1968 edition, an article entitled "They Plan to Assassinate Henry Agüero" stated that "an old Red" named Victor Rico Galán had ordered an attempt on the life of Agüero from within Lecumberri.[84] The paper alleged that Galán's imprisonment resulted from "plotting to overthrow the Mexican government . . . but he enjoys all the privileges and prerogatives in prison," and "he counts on the protection of the Mexican Penal Authorities, with large sums of money facilitated by Castro . . . and influential friends in the high levels of the Aztec government."[85] The article then placed responsibility on the Mexican government

▼▼▼

40. ANIVERSARIO

Figure 6: Cartoon depicting three uniformed MNC militants
firing into a car full of unarmed people in front of *El Día*
(Source: MNC, *Acción* 6.39, July 1969, 1).

for any attempt on Agüero's life: "[W]e hold the Mexican government responsible for what might occur to our compatriots and we warn it that if the assassination takes place, the nationalist terror will fall on the representatives of that treacherous government so that they will remember us as long as one nationalist breathes life on this continent."[86] Thus, in contrast to the revolutionary solidarity proponents, the Cuban exiles defined nationalism in transnational anti-Communist terms.

The openly militant attitude of the MNC was further revealed in the issue covering the fourth anniversary of the *El Día* attack. Dubbing the attack as part of its hemispheric "Operation Punishment," the newspaper showed a cartoon of three uniformed MNC militants firing into a car full of unarmed people in front of *El Día*.[87] Agüero's imprisonment in

▼▼▼

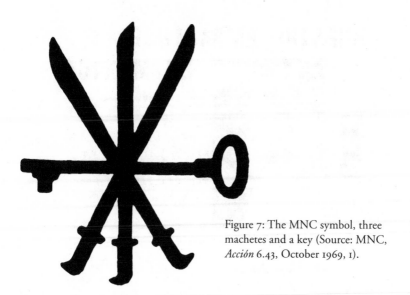

Figure 7: The MNC symbol, three machetes and a key (Source: MNC, *Acción* 6.43, October 1969, 1).

Lecumberri received attention in all *Acción* editions between 1966 and 1969, and the paper continued to issue threats against the Mexican government until at least May 1969. An article that month entitled "Cowardly Aggression" stated that "we will continue denouncing the immoralities of the Mexican government, warning them that to violence we will respond with violence."[88] Even in 1969, MNC was protesting through the streets of Miami in uniform with impunity from the U.S. government, even after the U.S. government had actually acknowledged its threat on the life of President Díaz Ordaz as well as its attacks in Mexico and other Latin American countries to which it had admitted.[89]

The *Miami Herald* had exposed the MNC as early as 1965 in an interview with the group's leadership. The MNC in fact included this August 1, 1965, article by Don Bohning entitled "Cubans Here Push Anti-Red Terror" in *Accion*'s July 1968 edition, as if to emphasize its influence to their readers.[90] Don Bohning reported on the grenade attack on *El Día* of July 7, 1965, the May 21 bombing of the Mexican-Russian Cultural Relations Institute in Mexico City, and a May 1965 machine gun attack on the Mexico City home of a correspondent of a Yugoslav newspaper.[91] Bohning also described the MNC's flag, which had a "key drawn across

▼▼▼

NUESTRO EMBAJADOR
EN MEXICO

pachos mensajes sub-
versivos hacia toda
la América.

La Embajada de Cuba
Libre, integrada por
un solo hombre -NUES-
TRO EMBAJADOR-, com-
parte su habitación
con cinco personas y
sus contactos con el
exterior se limitan a
una carta cada cierto
período de tiempo.

La Embajada castris-
ta, radicada en un
bien cuidado edificio
de la ciudad de Méxi-
co, sirve de trampolín
para la entrada y sa-

HENRY AGUERO.

Figure 8: Henry Agüero, MLN commando
(Source: MNC, *Acción* 5.29, July 1968, 4).

three united machetes," which was meant to represent "Cuba as the 'Key to the Gulf,' situated between Florida and the Yucatán Peninsula."[92] The MNC thus clearly viewed itself as the key to defeating Communism in the hemisphere.

The radicalism of the MNC's anti-communism was unique among anti-Communist groups in Mexico. According to Bohning, the MNC's "terrorism, says the MNC, is directed not at the Castro apparatus but world Communists. Mexican Communists are as bad as Cuban Communists."[93] The leader, Aldo Rosado, commented that executing Latin American Communists was part of the "successive phases of 'Operation Punishment.'"[94] MNC explained its Christian-based philosophy as well: "The Crusades were Christian . . . and the fight against Communism is a crusade."[95] The MNC also attacked the Mexican government's relations with Communist Cuba and the betrayal of Cuban anti-Communists. In another article in the July 1968 issue by Eladio Román, the MNC dubs Agüero as their organization's "Ambassador to Mexico," who is imprisoned for his anti-Communist efforts while privileged treatment, and "impunity" is given to "the Communist Cuban Embassy," where, "from their air conditioned and comfortable offices," hundred of spies are able to dictate "subversive messages to all of America."[96]

The MNC also revealed its anti-Semitism in its article, "Declaration of Moshe Sneh, of Israel."[97] This piece notes how the Mexico-based newspaper *Prensa Israelita* was "founded by Sergio Nudelstaeger, the enthusiastic defender of the Marxist regime of Castro Ruz," who "published an interview with the voice box of Israel, Moshé Sneh, who says: 'I am convinced that in the future Communism will expand through all the countries of the world.'"[98] Sneh was then quoted as praising Communism and stating that Communism "does not contradict the Jewish legacy."[99] The unnamed MNC author observed, "Of course not. Marx was a Jew, as were Engels, Lenin, Beria, Krushchev and Breshnev."[100] The social implications of the anti-Semitic roots of some Mexican anti-Communist groups may challenge their claim to the moral high ground.

The question that arises from the MNC example is, if Cubans and Mexicans are in fact "united in history," as Mexican author Jorge L. Tamayo's anthology title (*Mexico y Cuba: Dos pueblos unidos en la historia*) suggests, then how do they acknowledge the voices of the anti-Communist Cubans and Mexicans?[101]

GUADALAJARA: THE CENTER OF MEXICAN ANTI-COMMUNISM

The Mexican Anti-Communist Federation (FEMACO), established in 1967, expressed distrust in any politician deemed weak on Cuba and Communism in general. It showed considerable zeal in its criticism of the Mexican-Cuban connection and expressed particular concern over leftists within the Mexican and American governments. Like CRAC, FEMACO felt it was necessary to keep vigil over Mexican connections to Cuba. FEMACO's July 1967 report established its Christian-based anti-Communist credentials and emphasized its opposition to Castro's Cuba.

For example, page sixteen states: "In the Cuba tyrannized by the Dictator Fidel Castro, the workers and peasants, instead of obtaining an increase of actual wages, have suffered reductions in their remuneration and an increase in the hours of daily work, living truly in a poverty never known in that sibling nation before the so-called 'socialist revolution.'"[102] The mention of Cuba as a "sibling nation" indicates recognition of an affiliation between Mexico and Cuba, but here it is defined as a struggle against Communism. FEMACO, like CRAC in Monterrey, also targeted Lázaro Cárdenas as a subversive Red agitator and put Díaz Ordaz in a more favorable light. FEMACO wrote about the "Redness and auspicious" acts of "agitation and subversion" carried out by "Lázaro Cárdenas in an attempt to frustrate and nullify the agrarian politics of President Díaz Ordaz."[103]

FEMACO also revealed its Cristero roots in its accusations against former Mexican president Calles:

> Two thousands years ago, . . . the grand doctrine was initiated that gave light to the world, the grand doctrine that promulgated the abolition of slavery. And now the Communists want to plant that flag, . . . hoping to inoculate civilization, which Christianity gave birth to. It is said here . . . that Mexico, that the Mexicans, are learning to be anti-Communist[.] Calles, the tyrant Calles, knows very well, from the place where he is, of the power . . . [of those who] frustrated his communistic plans, because he never could defeat the resistance of the blood of those that were the seed of patriotism and Christianity in Mexico![104]

FEMACO used Communist accusations against Calles to buttress its opposition to leaders of the revolutionary left wing, including Vicente Lombardo Toledano and Lázaro Cárdenas. According to Jon Lee Anderson FEMACO itself was the front organization for Los Tecos of the Universidad Autónoma de Guadalajara.[105] FEMACO expressed its support for Los Tecos in its July 1967 report, referring to the "martyrs of the Teco movement," who were repressed by Calles and who, FECAMO notes, "chose the Rector of the nascent University and the Directors of the Schools."[106] As with CRAC, Los Tecos may have been anti-Semitic, according to investigative journalists Scott and Jon Lee Anderson in their 1986 book, *Inside the League*, which examines the World Anti-Communist League and its affiliates.[107]

The section in the FEMACO report entitled "The Communist Conspiracy in Mexico" focused on chapter 3 of the Mexican Communist Party's (PCM) Central Committee *Informe*, the product of its fourth national congress. FEMACO's attention to the connections between Mexican and Cuban Communism in this report bears resemblance to the focus given to this same period in Mexican history by CRAC. FEMACO author Jorge Prieto Laurens, alleging to be standing up for President Díaz Ordaz, noted that the PMC's assertion that Mexico had the most political prisoners is the claim "of those who defend the bloody tyrant of Cuba, Castro Ruz, who has converted the otherwise joyous [island] . . . into a gigantic prison," and pointed out that "if someone dared to express themselves about the pro-Soviet Government of Cuba in the same way as they have done . . . in speaking about the President of Mexico, they would have already paid for their daring" in front of a firing squad or they would be serving a prison sentence "in any of the disgusting cubes of the ignominious Cuban prison system."[108]

The anti-Castro animosity among the Mexican right wing makes perfect sense, but these right-wingers are unaccounted for in the discourse produced by Mexican and Cuban "revolutionaries" concerning the solidarity and brotherhood between Mexico and Cuba. The remarks of the anti-Castro groups make abundantly clear that there was a large group of Mexicans whose vision of Mexico's relations with Cuba bore no relation to the ideals of the Cuban Revolution; their vision was at complete odds with the standard story of Mexican-Cuban relations, which pro-Castro Mexican author Alberto Bremautz was disseminating just around the same time. In 1966, Bremautz wrote about the ties between Mexico and Cuba in terms of an historically based bond forged through mutual revolutionary interests. His position was tolerated by the PRI because it worked to a certain extent to include the Mexican left in its political orbit. As with Venezuela and Cuba today, the PRI placated those on the Mexican left,

▼▼▼

many of whom respected the PRI's "revolutionary" position, by supporting Cuba and therefore benefited politically from it.[109] Bremauntz was a
former rector of the Universidad Michoacana de San Nicolás de Hidalgo,
and his book, *México y la revolución socialista cubana*, claims that in spite
of U.S. pressure to submit to demands to abandon its "independent foreign policy," Mexico's resolve would not waiver, "especially in reference to
[Washington's] criminal plans against Cuba."[110]

Bremauntz's hostility to U.S. policy toward Cuba is the result of his
belief that the PRI indeed represented the interests of the Mexican left
regarding Cuba. What's more, Bremauntz affirms that the rest of his colleagues at the Casa de Estudios also supported the Cuban Revolution:
"I only have left to express that the participants of this Casa de Estudios
hope that very soon, with the firmness, bravery, and enthusiasm that char-
acterizes them, contained in their motto, 'Fatherland or Death, We will
Triumph,' [the Cuban people] totally complete the goals outlined by their
program of Revolution."[111]

The discourse surrounding the promotion of Mexican-Cuban relations during the Castro era reveals more of the holes in Marxist and revolutionary theories in general, as they have been interpreted throughout the
world. The idea that two nations, encompassing interests of many stripes
as well as governments with their own complexities, could somehow have
the same interests or even consider themselves "the same," solely because
groups of people in each country had found common ground in the past
replicates the Marxist assertion of mass action rooted in common material or class-based experiences and interests. The failure of all Communist
states throughout the past century to achieve classless societies of mutual
interests across populations is further evidence of the failure of Mexican
and Cuban "revolutionaries" to adequately explain how the entirety of
Mexico and Cuba are indeed "united in history." It also reveals the extent
to which the Mexican-Cuban friendship is a construct, promulgated by
those interested in using the relationship as a means of claiming solidarity and legitimizing revolution, and not a representation of a uniformly
understood reality. The Echeverría administration would both clarify and
complicate matters further.

CHAPTER SIX

MEXI-CUBA OR THE ENTRENCHMENT OF U.S.-MEXICAN RELATIONS?

THE AGE OF ECHEVERRÍA, 1970–76

[W]e are not in any kind of a hurry; we can wait
10 years, 20 years. I say that even relations with
the United States can be awaited. As for the economic
blockade, the North Americans become more isolated
each day. The blockade is increasingly losing prestige.
If the North Americans would analyze the blockade,
it would really behoove them to lift it. I do not mean
that it does not hurt us; it does hurt us.

—Interview with Fidel Castro,
published February 15, 1974

INAUGURATED IN DECEMBER 1970, President Luís Echeverría Alvarez (1970–76) shifted Mexico's foreign policy to the left. Where relations with Cuba were put on ice under Díaz Ordaz, Echeverría expanded foreign policy parameters to highlight problems shared by nations in the developing world. More than any previous Mexican president Echeverría used an expanded foreign policy to increase Mexico's leadership in the developing world. He did this by cultivating relations with Africa, Asia, and the Americas in particular and by cultivating more leftist ties. Above all, in the realm of foreign policy, Echeverría became known for his personal

▼▼▼

diplomacy, for unlike his predecessors, Echeverría traveled the world in order to spread Mexico's influence.[1]

Echeverría, who had served under the reactionary presidency of Díaz Ordaz as interior minister and was accused of orchestrating the attack at Tlatelolco on October 2, 1968, was no doubt acting in part out of a desire to placate the Mexican left. Enrique Krauze describes Echeverría's attitude as "trying to reconcile himself with the students and disclaim any responsibility for 1968."[2] As president, "[h]e would become a new Cárdenas," a reference not without irony, for the new president's populism was also offset by his repression against leftist movements operating across the country.[3] Aside from being implicated in the Corpus Cristi massacre of June 1971, in which over fifty student demonstrators were murdered by police, Echeverría also oversaw the disappearance of hundreds of leftist activists during his tenure.[4]

Echeverría, in contrast to his predecessors and like Castro, had a strong ambition to be a leader in the developing world and would champion the cause of tercermundismo, the idea that developing world nations should band together to throw off the dependency that characterized their plight. In 1971, in an early sign of the shift in policy toward Cuba, Echeverría signed the Mexican-Cuban aviation pact establishing a direct exchange in commercial and trade missions between the two countries. The following year, on a visit to the United States, Echeverría called for Cuba's readmission into the inter-American system, an issue the upcoming OAS Permanent Council was to broach. At the council meeting, OAS members Peru, Jamaica, Barbados, and Trinidad and Tobago opened diplomatic relations with Cuba, along with OAS observer nations Canada and Guyana.[5] Of course, Salvador Allende's Chile had established relations with Cuba in 1970.

Although an anti-Communist, Echeverría openly opposed the growing pro-American, anti-Communist military regimes of Latin America. Mexican opposition to U.S. policy toward Cuba increased when evidence surfaced concerning CIA involvement in the coup that overthrew and ended in the death of Salvador Allende in Chile. According to Alan Riding, "Echeverría began openly criticizing the United States, referring routinely to 'imperialism,' language normally used only by leftists in the region."[6] Renewed efforts to improve Cuban-Mexican relations also led, for example, to the construction of a new Cuban embassy building in Mexico, and in 1975, Echeverría visited Cuba where he was received with honors.[7] Mexican-Cuban trade also increased considerably, as Mexico purchased nearly 12 percent of Cuba's exports, valuing $310 million in 1974. That same year, Mexican foreign minister Emilio Rabasa and Fidel Castro oversaw the opening of the Lázaro Cárdenas Technological Institute in Havana.[8]

In all, the Echeverría presidency tried to represent itself as a government that was returning to the values of the Mexican Revolution. This reversed the official cold Mexican-Cuban relations of the Díaz Ordaz administration; at the same time, ironically, the U.S.-Mexico relationship improved too. Echeverría's promulgation of tercermundismo as a way to empower developing countries in the face of the powerful nations on which they depended helped form another bond between Cuba and Mexico. Both assumed leadership roles within the Third World, but one would use its power to change the system from within and the other would use its power to change it from without.

In his fourth annual government address in 1974, Echeverría proclaimed his official position toward Cuba. He stated that "in order to rebuild the inter-American system, Cuba's presence is indispensable and . . . it is necessary to lift the economic blockade that was imposed on it."[9] Mexico subsequently championed the OAS resolution at the fifteenth meeting in 1974 to drop the 1964 sanctions. The campaign failed by one vote, with the United States abstaining.[10] However, the cause to help Cuba no doubt helped Echeverría address the problems that Díaz Ordaz, despite his attempt to take the left into account, had caused with it during his tenure and thereby contributed to Echeverría's attempt to cut a progressive look.

Echeverría used Mexico's relationship with both nations for the benefit of all. During the oil crisis the next year, Echeverría told President Gerald Ford that the United States could be the primary beneficiary of Mexico's oil on the condition that the OAS lift the sanctions against Cuba.[11] At the sixteenth OAS meeting on July 29, 1975, when the United States once

▼▼▼

again abstained on the vote, the resolution passed and the OAS sanctions were lifted (the U.S. embargo of 1962, however, was not lifted).[12] Thus, Echeverría used Mexico's petroleum as economic leverage to facilitate the lifting of sanctions against Cuba. Gradually many Latin American countries reestablished relations with Cuba.[13]

In 1975 Castro received Echeverría in Havana, where they discussed a number of issues that culminated in a joint communiqué. They each condemned apartheid in South Africa, supported Panamanian sovereignty over the Panama Canal, and criticized General Pinochet's dictatorial, repressive regime in Chile. This common ground with Cuba helped Echeverría keep much of the left on his side at home.[14] In the same year, Echeverría and Venezuelan president Carlos Andrés Pérez cosponsored a resolution at the Panama Convention to establish the Latin American Economic System (SELA), an association that would promote economic development in the Americas from which the United States would be excluded. Twenty-five Latin American countries including Cuba supported the resolution.[15]

Still, despite his tercermundismo, President Echeverría knew how to pragmatically balance his left-of-center social leanings with the anti-Communist political leanings of the U.S.-dominated Cold War atmosphere. His foreign relations secretariat touted Echeverría's 1975 visit to Cuba as proof of the island's high priority for Mexico in its 1974–75 *Informe de labores*, stating, "it suffices to remember the posture that Mexico assumed in relation to the decision of the OAS to expel Cuba from the International system, and the unceasing defense that Mexico made for the rights of the Cuban people" to decide which type of system they prefer.[16]

In 1975, Henry Kissinger recognized the PRI's new leftward tilt as an expression of its need to portray itself as independent from the United States. At a staff meeting, he stated that "there is a yearly cause that [President] Echeverría uses to appeal to his left wing."[17] In his published memoirs, Kissinger elaborated on the understanding between the United States and Mexico:

But having paid their dues to the left, Mexican Presidents—including Echeverría—rarely insisted on their rhetoric. When it came to bilateral issues they were generally practical and conciliatory. The many meetings between Mexican Presidents and high-level Americans in the Nixon and Ford administrations were conducted in a friendly atmosphere.[18]

The specifics of how Mexico and the United States worked to thwart Cuban influence indicates that U.S.-Mexican relations improved because Mexico chose the United States *over* its island neighbor on many occasions. For example, at a meeting on June 15, 1972, between Echeverría and President Richard M. Nixon (1969–74), Echeverría stated that he would use his tercermundismo platform as a means of thwarting Castro's influence in the hemisphere: "Because if I don't take this flag in Latin America, Castro will. This is something I am very, very conscious of."[19] Further, he made it clear that he viewed Cuba as a military threat to the hemisphere: "it is clear that Cuba is a Soviet base in every sense of the word, both militarily and ideologically, and we have this right up against our noses." "[W]e are also aware," he noted, "of the fact that Dr. Castro and Cuba are instruments of penetration even into the United States itself, not to mention Mexico and the other countries of Latin America. They are unceasing in their efforts, using one path or another."[20] Echeverría's plan for U.S.-Mexican cooperation followed the logic that "if we in general, and Mexico very much in particular, do not adopt a progressive attitude within a framework of freedom and of friendship with the United States, the [Communist threat] current at this time could proliferate."[21]

According to his plan, "we must take their flags away from them by taking positive steps of cooperation, by using not only government but private enterprise and technical approaches as well," all of which, he argued, would help squelch Castro's growing influence in the Third World.[22] This meeting, like other official and unofficial conversations between the Untied States and Mexico, reveals the dual position that both right- and left-of-center Mexican presidents adopted with respect to Cuba. The difference between the Díaz Ordaz and Echeverría governments is that although both

▼▼▼

worked with the United States to thwart Cuban influence in the hemisphere, the Díaz Ordaz regime rarely expressed solidarity with the Castro government while the Echeverría government often did.

The evidence also suggests that after Ambassador Victor Alfonso Maldonado replaced Ambassador Covián in 1970, information still flowed between Havana, Mexico City, and Washington.[23] Maldonado, an accomplished diplomat with three decades of ambassadorial assignments between 1946 and 1976 behind him, began almost immediately inquiring about sensitive information within Cuba, as his April 22, 1970, report to Mexico City suggests: "upon finishing my official trips it would be convenient if you called me to Mexico City for two or three days, so I can tell you some small things, but which are very necessary that you know about Cuba, but it is not possible to discuss this either by cable or by written letter so it must be in person, in order to avoid suspicions from the Cuban government."[24] He then seemed to offer a good cover pretext for him to visit Mexico: he would ask for "two or three days to go to the world soccer championship."[25]

In October 30, 1971, Maldonado stated that Castro made a speech in which he encouraged potential airplane hijackers. There had been a string of hijackings from 1968–71 between Mexico and Cuba, and Maldonado argued that the people "seem to respond to [Castro's] speech from last September 28. . . . [W]hen referring to an attempted terrorist attack against the people of the eastern region of the country, he said that in Havana plane hijackers still didn't receive medals, but that it would be possible."[26] Whether or not the ambassador interpreted his speech correctly is not at issue here. What is at issue is the fact that the Mexican ambassador, as representative of the nation considered close friends with Cuba, criticized the Cuban leader's speech in a way that suggested Mexico was concerned and on the same page as the United States regarding the international Communist "menace."

In another report, this one dated April 3, 1972, Maldonado analyzed the potential threat posed by the Second Congress of the Union of Communist Youth. He observed that the meeting was "unquestionably an important event for leftist agitation in the Latin American countries and in the entire world."[27] This congress, according to Maldonado, "was organized by the Cuban Communist party" who, "continuing with its program of international political agitation, . . . invited Communist youth delegates from countries with which the government of Cuba does not have diplomatic relations," such as Panama, Argentina, the United States, Puerto Rico, Uruguay, Peru, and Bolivia.[28] He concluded that the result of this congress would be greater organization among "leftists" who carry out "very meditated propaganda of continental diffusion in America and in the world."[29]

His May 2 report also could have proved of interest to the United States. He focused on Cuban military strength and propaganda efforts in other countries in a manner befitting of Pamanes. The report states that Castro announced "that the security of the country is guaranteed" because of its capacity "to mobilize 600,000 men and put them under arms."[30] Maldonado's reporting in September of 1972 was a further testament to Pamanes's legacy. Assessing the extent of Cuban influence in Africa and Latin America, he reported that it had spread propaganda effectively enough between April 24 and August 8 of that year to "have established diplomatic relations with Sierra Leone, Zambia, Somalia and Mauritania" and possibly with Yemen.[31] He went on to express concern about African populations supposedly ripe for indoctrination by Marxist ideologies and issued the following warning:

> The misery and underdevelopment of some African countries that have obtained their freedom are propitious fields for Cuban socialist propaganda, and its diplomatic representatives in those African countries have, among other activities, advanced Communistic propaganda with their eternal call to the masses to struggle against Colonialism and neo-Colonialism and above, all in a very special and systematic manner, against "Yankee Imperialism."[32]

Maldonado was also concerned about the consequences of Latin American nations renewing relations with the island nation. For example, he stated that "official Cuba activity . . . with the renewal of diplomatic relations with Chile and Peru" could spread propaganda "in

Latin America."[33] Maldonado claimed that, according to information he had obtained from the embassy and "other diplomatic circles," "[Cuba] contemplates the possibility" that "imitating Peru, Panama, Ecuador, Colombia, and possibly Argentina, might renew relations with Cuba."[34] To support this point he reported on the dates of visits of Ecuadorian Communist Party members Pedro Saad and Elías Muñoz, and even mentioned that the general secretary of the Canadian Communist Party, William Cashtan, had visited.[35]

Maldonado's account of the arrival of ten Argentine guerrillas rivals Pamanes's reports from 1966–67 for the depth it goes into. They had hijacked a plane from Argentina to Chile and then arrived in Havana to request political asylum, according to Maldonado, who listed their names, rank in political party leadership (there was a general secretary of the Workers Revolutionary Party, for example, as well as "executive member of the People's Revolutionary Army"), guerrilla activities, family information, place of birth, educational background, when they had visited Cuba, and prison backgrounds.[36]

The following month, Maldonado even went so far as to condemn the Castro regime for criticizing the United States. The title of Maldonado's October 30, 1972, report says it all: "Degrading and Vile Cuban Press Campaign against the United States of America." The words "degrading" ("*baja*") and "vile" ("*grosera*") reveal Mexico's true allegiance: "Unfortunately, the campaign that is insistently against the United States is a campaign of insults, jokes, contempt . . . against the U.S. president" and "the most degrading and insulting epithets are utilized, such as . . . 'genocidal clown.'"[37] This rhetoric flies in the face of the general understanding of the touted "special" nature of the Cuban-Mexican relationship, revealing that the relationship was not as friendly as claimed by either government officials in both countries in public or by solidarity enthusiasts who overlooked Mexico's pragmatic alignment with the United States on security issues.

In the same file as the report on Cuba's press campaign against the United States, Maldonado informed Mexico City of the arrival of a Soviet naval ship in Havana, which struck him as "extraordinary."[38] He gave extensive details about the ship, such as its name (*Yuri Gagarin*), the amount of time it was docked in Cuba, who visited the ship (Cuban dignitaries), weight (forty-five thousand tons), and other details.[39] He explained that the ship's purpose was "scientific investigations" and that it could control the movement of space and naval structures from its location in Havana and that it could also "from this cosmic floating center, maintain direct communication with the management center located in USSR territory and even with the very cosmonaut crews of space ships."[40] His analysis of the ship's purpose makes it clear that Maldonado believed his job as ambassador was to pass information of a sensitive nature to the SRE.

Maldonado continued to report on Cuban-connected activities, such as the June arrival of Colombian Communists in Cuba. This "Colombian delegation, presided over by Mr. Hector Herrera, member of the Central Committee of the Colombian Communist party, . . . [attended] to the invitation . . . from the Cuban party" suggests, Maldonado reported on June 7, the extent of "the activit[ies] and propaganda of the Cuban Communist party in relation to other similar parties" as well as its influence.[41] According to Maldonado, "they have changed their minds about the best way to augment and complete the socialist ideological struggle in the underdeveloped countries of Latin America."[42] This type of reporting shows both Mexico's and Cuba's interest in shaping international affairs during the Cold War.

Maldonado follows up on his June 7 report by assessing the possible dangers of Argentine-Cuban connections through an analysis of the language the Cuban delegation used at the inauguration of Argentine president Hector J. Campora that year. The last part of the title of Maldonado's report states succinctly what he thinks the Cuban delegation's purpose was in attending the Argentine presidential inauguration: they hoped to "Tak[e] Advantage of This Trip for Motives of Political Propaganda."[43] He also stated that "the Cuban delegation . . . sent messages not of friendship but of a political character." It offered, he noted, a "'a revolutionary greeting' from the Cuban people to the Argentines," and Cuban president Osvaldo Dorticós, he went on, asserted that "we should swear on the memory of the martyrs and heroes of [Argentina and Cuba], and of

▼▼▼

our hero Ernesto Che Guevara, that Argentina and Cuba continue their struggle against imperialism until [it is] exterminated."[44]

Maldonado argued that President Dorticós's remarks raised important international security issues. For example, he questioned whether the "struggle against imperialism" referred to "the eternal anti-Yankee campaign."[45] He also wondered "how is it that a [delegation] invited" to the inauguration of "the Argentine government" should "take advantage of foreign territory" and "refer to an international position of struggle of the inviting country?"[46] "Did President Dorticós previously speak with President Campora," Maldonado asks, "to be assured of the 'anti-imperialist' position of the new government and also in agreement that Cuba and Argentina TOGETHER, will continue that struggle until imperialism is exterminated?"[47] The Mexican ambassador's tone is striking when we consider the solidarity expressed by the Echeverría and Castro regimes during this same period.

The following month, Maldonado received more information about the connections between Cuba and Argentina. His July 4 report, "Deception in the Official Circles of the Cuban Government with Respect to the Political Situation of the Argentine Government," states that Cuban government propaganda had indicated that the new Argentine government would soon align itself with Cuba, the assumption on Cuba's part being "that each American country that renews diplomatic relations with Cuba could eventually arrive (also supposedly) to make common cause with [Cuba]."[48] According to Maldonado, the "common cause" referred in particular to Cuba's "Communist position and its adhesion to the [socialist] countries of [Eastern Europe] and its uninterrupted campaign against the U.S.A."[49] The Mexican ambassador was clearly reporting on issues he considered posed an international security concern from the perspective of a U.S. ally opposed to the Cuban government.

At the same time, the Mexican-Cuban relationship held considerable significance for the highest officials in both countries, despite the hidden uses of the friendship. For example, on Echeverría's goodwill tour of thirteen countries in 1975, which ended in Cuba, the mutual resistance to U.S. pressure that had historically connected the two countries was the main subject of Castro's public discourse. Mexican journalist Julio Pomar, from the daily newspaper *El Día,* prefaced his question to Castro by observing that "there is historical evidence" suggesting "that Mexico and Cuba have been the two countries in Latin America" most affected "by imperialism" and that "at the same time [they are] the only two countries in Latin America that have developed profound social revolutions, each one in their [own] time and [each one] distinct, accordingly." This was followed with the question, "Do you think that Mexico and Cuba would be prepared and ready to mount an historic alliance that would make them struggle better for independence in all its orders?"[50] The question is an important one when we consider how difficult it was for leftists in the developing world to achieve their goals amid the Cold War paranoia propagated by anti-Communists who operated under "better safe than sorry" assumptions that often placed leftist nationalists within the Communist camp.

Adding to the strain of Mexican-Cuban relations during the 1964–70 era, the correspondence from ambassadors Pamanes, Covián, and Maldonado revealed sensitive Cuban information and offered detailed criticisms of Castro's government, which indicated Mexico's willingness to gather intelligence on Cuba and its alignment with the United States. In addition, the anti-Communist voices more than demonstrate the use of this relationship for politically divisive interests by extremists seeking to profit politically, and, ironically, the way the Mexican-Cuban relationship enabled Third World actors to shape international relations during the Cold War.

CHAPTER SEVEN

THE ROAD TO FREE TRADE, 1976–2000

*Dear friends . . . from Tuxpan, from Veracruz, and
from Mexico [crowd cheers and applauds]. They are
all the same thing, as it is to say that for us Mexico
and Cuba are the same. [applause].*

—Fidel Castro, speech in Tuxpan,
Veracruz, December 5, 1988

THE LATE 1970S USHERED IN another shifting era in Mexican-Cuban relations. In the 1970s, Mexico's economy was centered on the production and
export of its newly discovered petroleum, taking out large loans from the
international banking community at the same time. In the aftermath of the
1982 debt crisis, however, Mexico abandoned its centrally controlled economy, as U.S.-Mexico free trade policies allowed for a greater economic and
political relationship with the United States. The fall of the Soviet Union
in 1991 left Cuba, which had been dependent on Moscow's assistance, faced
with the problem of how to adjust its economic and political system to
make up for that loss of economic support. Meanwhile, the 1994 free trade
partnership among Mexico, the United States, and Canada, known as the
North American Free Trade Agreement (NAFTA), as well as the renewed
U.S. restrictions on business with Cuba reshaped relations between Mexico
and Cuba. Mexico's response was mitigated by the pressures of the Cuban
exiles of Miami as well as the business community in Mexico. In addition, the wars of Central America inevitably drew Mexico and Cuba into
conflict with the United States, providing both Latin American countries a platform on which to influence Cold War international relations.
The Sandinistas in Nicaragua and the Farabundo Martí Liberation Front

▼▼▼

(FMLN) guerrillas of El Salvador were gaining power in the late 1970s, leading the United States, Cuba, and Mexico to view their hemisphere in different terms from before and to the simultaneous convergence and divergence of interests among the three on many issues.

ANTI-COMMUNISM REVISITED

In April 1975, the Mexican Anti-Communist Federation (FEMACO) contacted the Gerald Ford administration (1974–77) to express its concern over the OAS resolution to lift the embargo against Cuba. Earlier, FEMACO had sent a letter addressed to Vice President Rockefeller, Secretary of State Kissinger, "and others" pleading for the United States to oppose the OAS resolution to end the sanctions.[1] After the resolution passed, FEMACO's parent organization, the Latin American Anti-Communist Federation (CAL), wrote at least two letters to the U.S. government, calling for it to stop Latin American nations from resuming relations with Cuba.[2] CAL was a division of the World Anti-Communist League (WACL), an organization allegedly "tied to neo-Nazis and Latin American death squads" as well as to members of the U.S. Congress, various authoritarian military governments in Latin America, and the business and intellectual communities of the United States and Mexico.[3]

From its offices in Guadalajara, the magazine *Réplica* served as a mouthpiece for groups like FEMACO, CAL, and WACL.[4] Some of the regular heroes of *Réplica*, such as Nicaraguan dictator Anastasio Somoza and Paraguayan dictator Alfredo Stroessner, were well-known political and military leaders with human rights abuse records.[5] *Réplica* dedicated itself to disseminating anti-Communist perspectives on Cuba and the Central American conflicts. For example, in 1979, when presidents Jimmy Carter (1977–81) and José López Portillo (1976–82) favored lifting the U.S blockade on Cuba, *Réplica* dedicated at least 20 percent of its pages to speeches, opinion pieces, and reports denouncing these efforts. Several *Réplica* articles accused the PRI of involvement with international Communism and even denounced Carter for withholding military aid from anti-Communist governments, such as Guatemala, because of their human rights abuse records.[6]

Mexican anti-Communism also focused on the PRI's role in Central America in its 1980s issues. A central anti-Communist concern was President López Portillo's attempt to extend the Mexican-Cuban friendship during his tenure, especially after their interests coincided in Central America. For example, he arranged visits between Isidoro Malmierco and Santiago Real, the foreign ministers of Cuba and Mexico, respectively. Subsequently, the two jointly condemned apartheid and supported Panamanian control of the canal, as had Echeverría and Castro before them. López Portillo also signed the General Agreement of Bilateral Collaboration, designed to encourage solidarity between the two countries, and denounced the U.S. economic blockade.[7] In addition, Mexican Foreign Minister Jorge Castañeda spoke at the sixth meeting of the Non-Aligned Movement in Havana of Mexican-Cuban agreement regarding U.S. hegemony in the region and the Sandinistas.[8]

Just three months before the Sandinista triumph in Nicaragua, López Portillo had hosted a Cuban legislative delegation in Mexico City for the eighteenth anniversary of the failed Bay of Pigs invasion at which the Cuban delegation praised former president Cárdenas for his support during the invasion. In the end, both leaders issued a joint communiqué calling for the elimination of the United States naval mission at Guantánamo Bay as well as for an end to the economic blockade.[9] López Portillo also ignored the United States boycott of the 1980 Olympics in Moscow and, after having granted asylum to the Shah of Iran, a U.S. ally, at the request of the Carter administration, refused to readmit him after his hospitalization in the United States.[10]

In 1980, Mexican-Cuban official relations received a further boost when Castro hosted a Friendship Rally for López Portillo. The day before the rally, Castro presented the Mexican president with the José Martí National Order. Castro's speech echoed the long-held understanding of camaraderie between the two nations. The next day, Castro began his speech by describing Cuba and Mexico as united in the same struggle, against U.S. "imperialism," to the applause of the crowd, which chanted "Fidel, for sure, hit the Yankees hard." Castro responded: "Let's leave the Yankees alone today. We are receiving the president of Mexico. We have

146 / CHAPTER SEVEN

▼▼▼

to dedicate this day to Mexico, to friendship (shouts of 'Long live Fidel,' 'Long live Mexico,' 'Cuba, Mexico, united [we] shall win')."[11] The crowd's response might have been a command performance but it might also have been an expression of the Cuban people's own conception of the powerful significance of Mexican-Cuban relations.[12]

In the 1980s, Mexico and Cuba supported Central American resistance movements that opposed U.S.-backed military regimes and counterinsurgencies. Although not necessarily working in concert with Cuba, Mexican officials met with and financially assisted the guerrillas in El Salvador (the FMLN) and the Nicaraguan Sandinistas in the late 1970s and early 1980s, and "in August 1981 Mexico and France recognized the FMLN . . . as 'representative political forces.'"[13] The Reagan administration (1981–89) responded to this by helping convince ten other nations in the region to condemn "the Franco-Mexican declaration as 'interventionism.'"[14]

As López Portillo led the hemispheric drive to reincorporate Cuba into the inter-American system, and Carter favored extending diplomacy with Cuba, *Réplica*'s outrage was correspondingly hostile. Its headlines read "Mexico: Paladin of Political Asylum," "The People of Mexico Repudiate Marxism," and "Race against Time: Carter and the Communization of Mexico."[15] In "Race against Time," César Córdova Olmedo wrote that former president Echeverría had attempted to become a "life-time tyrant, like Fidel Castro, and [to put] the PRI in the role of the Communist Party."[16] This resembled the stance the Regional Anti-Communist Crusade (CRAC) took in the 1960s toward Lázaro Cárdenas, and *Réplica* also used nationalistic arguments that evoked the Mexican Revolution to oppose Castro's influence in Mexico. In a November 1973 article entitled "The Mexican Revolution was . . . Nationalist not Communist!" it stated that Mexican intellectuals had tried to represent the Mexican Revolution as a kind of precursor to the Cuban Revolution, as more leftist than it was.[17] Its evocation of the Mexican Revolution parallels CRAC's claim that Communism conflicted with the ideologies of Mexican nationalism, in effect equating Mexican anti-Communism with the Mexican Revolution. FEMACO also reacted harshly to Mexico's position on Central America. *Réplica* author Mario Valverde expressed his outrage over Mexico's assistance to the Sandinistas when he wrote, "Mexico and Cuba infiltrate the sister republic with Marxism, and this is done with our money."[18] He went on to implicate President López Portillo in the financial assistance initiative, claiming, "This cannot have been done behind the back of our president, whose inopportune approximation to Castro has been very visible lately."[19]

Yet, while Mexico's alignment with Cuba in Central America aggravated U.S. and Mexican anti-Communists, recently declassified documents reveal that the United States and Cuba called on Mexico's mediation services in 1981.[20] López Portillo and Jorge Castañeda arranged a meeting between U.S. Secretary of State Alexander Haig Jr. and Cuban Vice President Carlos Rafaél Rodríguez in Mexico City on November 23, 1981.[21] The conversation, from disputes over levels of Cuban involvement in Africa and Nicaragua to the Cuban embargo, was cordial and appeared productive. Of course, they both respectfully hurled accusations that the other would not admit to, but this was to be expected.[22] In the end, the Mexico-negotiated talks served to bridge the Cuban-U.S. divide only temporarily, as each side continued to support its chosen forces in the civil wars throughout the rest of the decade.

Mexican policy began to conflict with U.S. policy in Central America to the point that Mexico-Cuba connections reemerged as a point of discussion in anti-Communist circles in 1986 when the conservative, nonprofit organization CAUSA International, founded in 1980 by the Reverend Sun Myung Moon whose Unification Church had ties to WACL, sponsored a meeting of the International Security Council in San Diego, California. The meeting, entitled "Crisis and Response: A Roundtable on Mexico," was attended by American and Mexican business executives, politicians, authors, and professors.[23] According to the meeting's report, CAUSA's position was that "positive social change can only occur when God-accepting and conscientious people are united upon common goals."[24] CAUSA's Christian-based political philosophy thus echoed that of the Cuban exile group, the National Christian Movement (MNC), as well as CRAC and FEMACO of Mexico. Through the common cause against Communism, these organizations found an audience with power.

▼▼▼

The roundtable showed a strong concern over Mexican-Cuban relations. For instance, University of Pennsylvania professor and former U.S. ambassador to Thailand Dr. William Kintner quoted the pro-Cuba remarks of Jorge Díaz Serrano, director of PEMEX, Mexico's national petroleum company: "As an historian, I understand that what has happened during this century is imposing, but what has been done and is being done in Cuba will go down in human history as an example of dignity."[25] Kintner himself then commented that "Mexico faces many serious domestic problems. At issue is whether she can solve them best by increased flirtation with the Marxist-Leninist left or in collaboration with the United States."[26] The PRI is painted here with the same Communist-sympathizer brush favored by MNC, CRAC, and FEMACO, showing that there was a level of American anti-Communist concern as well over the Mexican-Cuban relationship in the mid-1980s.[27]

These worries were for nought; Mexico's 1982 debt default set the nation on a course away from state-sponsored capitalism toward free trade. The United States and the IMF played a central role in the effort to restructure the Mexican economy that had created the mess in the first place, and over the next twelve years, Mexico sold off large numbers of state-owned companies. And though, during the lead-up to the 1994 NAFTA agreement, armed conflict engulfed much of Central America, and the United States and Mexico supported opposite sides, Mexico's road to free trade signified yet another powerful incentive (economic) for the PRI to further align itself with the United States in general.

As the wars in Central America raged on, in January 1983 Panama hosted an effort to stop the bloodshed. Panamanian president Ricardo de la Espriella invited the foreign ministers from Venezuela, Colombia, and Mexico to meet on Contadora Island, off Panama's Pacific coast, with the hope that these nations could come up with a solution to the Central America crises. Fidel Castro welcomed Contadora, as did Mexico, since, even if the treaty arrived at opposed his wishes for El Salvador and Nicaragua, he hoped it would include nonintervention stipulations for the United States.[28] Cooperation yielded progress toward peace, but dialogue broke down permanently after Secretary of State George Shultz convinced the leaders of Costa Rica, Guatemala, Honduras, and El Salvador to demand adjustments to the treaty. Costa Rica's future president, Oscar Arias Sánchez, revived the peace process in 1987, for which he received the Nobel Peace Prize.[29]

As Mexico and the United States tested the resolve of their relationship over Central America, Cuba continued to vie for Mexico's friendship. In response to the September 19, 1985, earthquake that hit Mexico City, for example, which caused the deaths of thousands of people, $4 billion in damages, and left five hundred thousand people homeless, Castro called on all of Mexico's creditors to halt debt collection for one year, which he said would allow Mexico to accumulate $12 billion with which to rebuild Mexico City and offset the impending economic difficulties. The following year international oil prices fell, which increased Mexico's deficit as well as its never-ending high debt and rendered it unable to meet its debt obligations. Mexico soon came to an arrangement with international lending institutions whereby they would loan Mexico up to $13.7 billion over a period of two years, extending the due date for almost 50 percent of the debt.[30]

Meanwhile, the Cuban exile community in Miami remained vigilant in closely watching the Mexican-Cuban connection. Ronald Reagan's administration motivated the Floridian exiles to become more politically active as their anti-Communist sentiments paralleled his own. According to one Cuban exile author, in 1980, "record numbers became naturalized citizens and, on Election Day, a massive turnout gave Ronald Reagan an estimated 90 percent of the community's votes."[31] In addition, Cuban Americans began to occupy more political seats in the 1980s. By 1984, seven out of nineteen district seats in Dade County were held by Cuban-Americans.[32] President Reagan also brought Cuban-Americans into higher government offices, which in turn helped open up access to the president. In the words of one Cuban American scholar, "[b]y the mid-1980s, the Cuban-American National Foundation (CANF) had become one of the most sophisticated, and influential lobbying groups in Washington, and a powerful influence in Florida politics."[33]

In 1987, the Cuban exile community came head-to-head with Mexico over alleged human rights abuses in Cuba. The emergence of books and

▼▼▼

films produced by Cuban dissidents who had fled Cuba after having served long terms in Castro's infamous prisons, as well as the Cuban dissident group called the Cuban Committee for Human Rights (CCPDH), were exposing the regime's human rights violations. Eventually, the Reagan administration began to "support Cuban exile efforts to bring the attention of the UN Commission on Human Rights (UNCHR) on the violation of human rights in Cuba."[34] Led by U.S. Ambassador to the United Nations Vernon Walters and formerly imprisoned Cuban poet Armando Valladares, a delegation went to Geneva, Switzerland, to plead the case against Cuba for alleged human rights abuses.[35]

In the end, the Cuban exile/Reagan administration effort to discredit Castro failed to garner enough votes to pass at the United Nations, owing to a lack of support from Latin American countries and, according to UN Ambassador Jeane Kirkpatrick, "the overlapping Soviet and non-aligned blocs."[36] Mexico played no small part in the defense of Cuba at the UNCHR meeting in Geneva, reportedly lobbying the other Latin American delegates to defend Cuba and lavishing praise on Cuba for its achievements. According to Armando Valladares, Mexico also made Ambassador Walters's position out to be "politicizing the human rights issue."[37]

Mexico's defense of Cuba no doubt improved their bilateral friendship at least on the surface, if not fundamentally. This became evident quickly after the UNCHR meeting, as the two countries began discussing the issue of improved trade relations.[38] After the turbulent Mexican elections of 1988, ex-president De la Madrid traveled to Cuba where he received the order of José Martí and bestowed on Castro the Aztec Eagle, the highest honor given to a foreigner.[39] The next Mexican president was an economist just like Miguel de la Madrid and would break down free trade barriers under NAFTA. The Cuban exile community butted heads with Mexico over its desire to expand economically, and in this way, Cuba found its way into the middle of the free trade initiative.

MEXICO, 1988

The 1988 Mexican elections themselves provide a good example of how the idea, mainly cultivated by Castro and the PRI, that Cuba and Mexico share a historically rooted revolutionary connection informs the official relationship between the two countries. The nationalism rooted in revolution that was such a common thread in the political environment of Mexican-Cuban relations had been tested from 1959 to 1988. Castro's reaction to the Mexican elections of 1988 illustrate this point, as his behavior spoke of a past and foretold of a future in which the elder statesman had little choice but to accept Mexico for what it was: a U.S. ally but a U.S. ally whose appearance of friendship to Cuba could nevertheless support his own political legitimacy.

Lázaro Cárdenas' son, Cuauhtémoc, ran for president as an opposition candidate against Salinas in 1988. Castro no doubt felt torn between the historical depths of the Cárdenas-Castro family revolutionary allegiance and Castro's dependence on the PRI for legitimacy. Originally a member of the left-wing arm of the PRI, the party his father had helped form, Cuauhtémoc had served as a reformist governor in his home state of Michoacán and had hoped to be able to change the system from within. He soon found an ally within the party in Porfirio Muñoz Ledo, former PRI president and advisor to four presidential administrations, who was also distraught by the path that the PRI had taken. The two of them would organize "the 'Democratic Current' as a reform movement within the PRI in 1985."[40] In 1987, Cuauhtémoc collected 780,000 signatures petitioning primary elections in the hope of running as a PRI candidate. However, as Muñoz Ledo said, "All of this was denied, of course. No one paid any mind to us; they acted as if we didn't exist."[41]

Cuauhtémoc and his followers convinced the relatively weak Authentic Party of the Mexican Revolution (PARM) to let him run as its candidate, and they established the National Democratic Front (FDN) to bring together the small left-wing parties to his side. The groups brought to the FDN were the Socialist Workers Party (PST), the Movement to Socialism (MAS), as well as followers of Maoist and Castroist philosophies, to name a few.[42] The son of the deceased father of agrarian reform surely paralleled Castro much more at this point than Salinas, who served the interests of private power and had firmly aligned himself with the United States shortly into his term. Still, Cuauhtémoc's campaign was the closest contest against

▼▼▼

the PRI in history. "The public would never know the real results of those elections," according to historian Enrique Krauze, because the computer the government was using to count the votes crashed; when the system was restored, Salinas was declared president.[43] The surge of the left was renewed in Mexico under the leadership of the son of the leader who had helped revive the leftist movement when Castro came to power in 1959.

The Mexican left wing felt dejected when Cuauhtémoc lost to Salinas (1988–94). Castro, who attended his inauguration, mentioned that his presence signified his honorable support for President Salinas.[44] He was quoted as saying that he was "enjoying a great democracy in Mexico."[45] Furthermore, Castro must have upset Cuauhtémoc and his followers when he denounced Cuauhtémoc for protesting the results of the elections as fraudulent.[46] In Castro's defense, although Cuauhtémoc had supported Castro formerly as a member of the National Liberation Movement (MLN) in the 1960s, Castro was not in a position politically to side with him nor would he necessarily desire to, considering the cordial relations that had been enjoyed between Castro and the PRI over the years. Castro's willingness to accept the new president would matter a great deal to him the next year, when perestroika led to a cutoff of aid and trade to Cuba from the Soviet bloc. With the disappearance of the Soviet Union and the Council of Mutual Economic Assistance by 1991, Cubans lost their true political, economic, ideological, and military allies, and Mexico stepped in to help fill the void.[47]

FOUR REUNIONS ON CUBA

From 1991 to 1994, Latin American leaders held a series of four meetings in Madrid, during which time statesmen raised the subject of Cuba repeatedly. An Argentine suggestion of "explicit and implicit demands on the Cuban president to achieve a political opening and the democratization of the island" sparked particular interest.[48] Mexico opposed the demand because, if implemented, it would lead to a military or political intervention or both in Cuba. The Mexican government continued to cite international law for justification of its position on this matter, viewing the Argentine suggestion as an invitation to intervention. Furthermore, when asked if he had anything to recommend to Castro, Salinas responded that he did not make recommendations, for he would not appreciate suggestions made to him if the situation were reversed.[49]

Castro had a few words to say in Madrid as well. Declaring "that the attitudes of the Ibero-american leaders were frustrating except for Salinas," at a later meeting in Cartagena de Indias, Castro praised Mexico for its friendship and solidarity with Cuba when the rest had given up on it.[50] This coming from Castro alludes to the depth of Cuba's dependency on Mexico's friendship at this time, revealing the power Mexico now wielded over Cuba.

In 1992, twelve U.S. senators wrote to President Salinas expressing their concern over the Mexican-Cuban connection. Specifically, they alluded to a possible conflict of interest between Mexico's trade with Cuba and the impending NAFTA agreement. Again, Mexico was not in much of a position to oppose the United States, but it did so anyway, adhering to the long-standing Mexican foreign policy doctrine of the right to self-determination and nonintervention. Mexico's industrial promotion and commerce secretary responded that Mexico would not be pressured into altering its trade with Cuba, and the matter was dropped.[51]

The source of resistance in the United States to Mexico's trade with Cuba came from the Miami Cubans. That same year, President Salinas improved relations with the Miami Cubans by meeting with the most prominent members of the exile leadership. He met with figures such as Jorge Más Canosa of the Cuban American National Foundation (CANF) and Alberto Montaner, an exile living in Spain who was a member of the Madrid-based Cuban Liberal Union (CLU). The exiles assured Salinas that if Mexico would curtail its relations with Cuba, they would not stand in NAFTA's way. In response, Salinas "agreed to cancel low-interest credits to Cuba, such as guarantees to Mexican businessmen who might invest in Cuba; the Mexican government would refuse to negotiate the debt with Cuba[,] . . . and [Mexico would] maintain current levels of commerce with Cuba at international prices."[52] In reality, Salinas's concession to the Cuban exiles was not much more than a gesture, yet an incident involving exiles in Mexico soon put the Mexican president into a bind.

▼▼▼

In August 1993, a group of Cubans fleeing Cuba arrived at the Mexican state of Quintana Roo. Eighteen people were on board when the boat capsized, after which seven drowned, and three were presumed missing and dead. The Mexican government had the survivors deported, which angered the Cuban exile community in Miami because of the possibility that their original destination might have been Miami. A crowd of over five hundred Cuban exiles expressed its anger by protesting, chanting, and burning a Mexican flag in front of the Mexican embassy in Washington, D.C., as well as by urging people to boycott Mexico. The outcry pressured the Mexican government to grant visas for the eight survivors of the wreck, after which they traveled back to Mexico and flew to the United States. CANF's Jorge Más Canosa later expressed his gratitude to the Mexican president.[53]

President Salinas demonstrated he was capable of achieving what many Mexican leaders had before him: a deft balance in the realm of foreign relations between the practical and desirable. For example, according to one author, "The Mexican government structured its economic project in a unique initiative whose success depended a lot on the good disposition of the United States," which illustrates how Mexico's economic interests, on which its politics must rest considerably, parallel those of the United States, not Cuba.[54] Mexico wanted to become an industrialized, developed "First World" nation, not a state-centered totalitarian regime like Cuba. Furthermore, the exile community's pull within the United States meant that the Salinas administration would possibly benefit politically from the exile community's approval of NAFTA. Still, the next seven years would see a tremendous upsurge in trade between Mexico and Cuba.[55]

In acknowledging the political and economic concerns of the anti-Castro Cubans living in Miami as it related to Mexican economic interests, Mexico made a change in its official foreign policy. This change signified yet another dimension of the transnational nature of the triangular relations among Mexico, Cuba, and the United States, but at the same time, it was a manifestation of the PRI's true political ideology. That is, although the PRI government consistently defended Cuba's sovereignty in international institutions, it still sanctioned the secretive information

▼▼▼

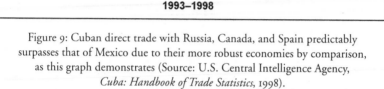

Figure 9: Cuban direct trade with Russia, Canada, and Spain predictably surpasses that of Mexico due to their more robust economies by comparison, as this graph demonstrates (Source: U.S. Central Intelligence Agency, *Cuba: Handbook of Trade Statistics*, 1998).

gathering on the part of U.S. officials in Mexico and its ambassadors in Cuba, cooperated extensively with the United States to thwart Cuban influence during the Cold War, and desired a robust economy that would bring Mexico into the "First World" while enabling it to project an image of independence from that very world through its simultaneous projection of friendship with Cuba.

TRADE ISSUES

Trade is yet another area in which Mexico demonstrated its agency in international relations. Although Mexican-Cuban trade gradually rose from 1985 to 1992, Cuba's loss of the Soviet Union's annual assistance pushed Cuba to diversify its economic connections throughout the world, and from 1993 to 1998, Mexico was its number one Latin American trade partner.[56] At the same time, Cuban-Russian trade far from evaporated. In fact, Russia was Cuba's principal trade partner from 1993–98 at least, importing $2.1 billion worth of Cuban goods in that period and exporting $1.3 billion worth of goods to Cuba from 1994 to 1998 ($3.4 billion combined).[57]

▼▼▼

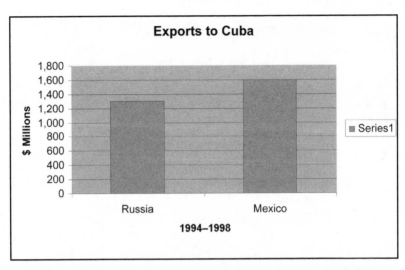

Figure 10: This graph demonstrates the importance of the Cuban market for Mexico, since it shows that Cuba's number one overall trading partner, Russia, exported less to Cuba than Mexico did from 1994 to 1998 (Source: U.S. Central Intelligence Agency, *Cuba: Handbook of Trade Statistics*, 1998).

Nevertheless, Canada and Spain are significantly more important direct trade partners for Cuba than Mexico. Canada's trade with Cuba reached $2.5 billion from 1993 to 1998, and Spain's trade with Cuba reached $3 billion.[58] Additionally, although Mexican-Cuban trade remains important for Mexico, Mexico's trade relationship with the United States surpasses it by a long shot. For example, in 1994 alone, on the inauguration of NAFTA, direct trade between the United States and Mexico surpassed $106 billion.[59]

Further, Mexico has exported considerably more goods to Cuba than Cuba has exported to Mexico. For example, Cuba exported $265 million worth of goods to Mexico from 1985 to 1998, whereas Mexico exported $2.5 billion worth of goods to Cuba.[60] Compare that with Cuba's second most important Latin American trade partner during the same period, Venezuela, a nation that imported $175 million worth of Cuban goods from 1985 to 1998 and exported $1.35 billion worth of goods to Cuba in that same period.[61] Cuba exports rum, steel sheets, sugar, cowhides, coffee, cigars, refrigerators, shirts, and other products to Mexico; Mexico

▼▼▼

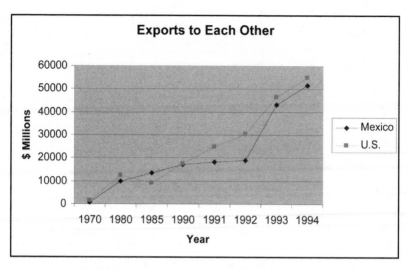

Figure 11: U.S.-Mexico exports to one another from 1970 to 1994 gradually increased almost in perfect balance (Source: U.S. Central Intelligence Agency, *Cuba: Handbook of Trade Statistics*, 1998).

exports furniture and equipment for hotels, cement, beer, cryogenic gases and equipment, soap, lubricants, kerosene, vehicles, automobiles, crude petroleum, propane-butane, escalators, and other products to Cuba.[62] In the 1980s, the average yearly trade between Mexico and Cuba was $60.8 million, but from 1995 through 2000, the average was $300 million.[63]

Specifically, Cuba does not have as much to offer Mexico in terms of goods as vice versa. Cuba's top exports to Mexico include goods that Mexico does not generally lack, such as sugar, molasses, and honey ($12 million worth from 1993 to 1998), fish ($1 million), tobacco ($13 million), and medicinal products ($21 million).[64] The major commodities Mexico exports, however, do tend to be goods Cuba lacks and range from industrial equipment to natural resources. For example, Cuba purchased $534 million worth of fuel, $132 million worth of foodstuffs, $137 million worth of machinery, $363 million worth of semifinished goods, $337 million worth of chemicals, $119 million worth of consumer goods, $59 million worth of transportation equipment, and $110 million worth of raw materials from Mexico from 1993 to 1998.[65] The U.S. embargo prevents Cuba from

▼▼▼

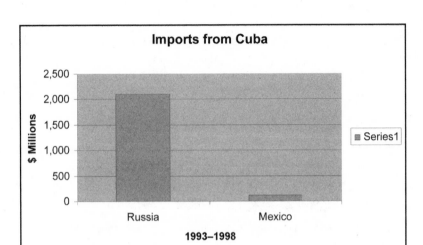

Figure 12: A comparison between Mexican and Russian importation of Cuban goods reveals the continuing importance of the commercial relationship established between Russia and Cuba during the Cold War, which remains strong in the post–Cold War era (Source: U.S. Central Intelligence Agency, *Cuba: Handbook of Trade Statistics*, 1998).

importing these types of goods directly from the U.S., but its access to Mexico, Canada, and Europe allows it to circumvent the U.S. restrictions to a certain degree, and as such, Cuba is able to import items that support its tourism industry.

While the trade figures represent an important indicator of Mexico's role in the Cuban economy, other factors, such as private investment and tourism, help reduce Cuba's trade gap with Mexico. Thousands of Mexican tourists visit the Communist island every year, and by 2004, Mexicans had invested $2.7 billion in Cuba. Cuba's debt to Mexico reached $425 million that same year.[66] However, Mexico's geopolitical proximity to Cuba has also facilitated Cuban trade through non-Mexican, foreign-based companies, making Mexico the conduit for over 70 percent of Cuban trade with the rest of the planet, according to one report.[67] In particular, petroleum sales from Mexico to Cuba have formed a source of solidarity between the two nations. Mexico became a major oil exporter in the 1970s but had not registered a sale to Cuba until 1985. The increase in oil sales to Cuba

▼▼▼

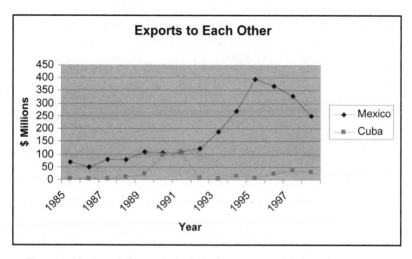

Figure 13: Mexican-Cuban trade statistics from 1985 to 1998 show the increasing diversification of Cuba's trade relations with capitalist countries in the wake of the end of the Cold War as well as the increased level of trade between these two nations even after NAFTA was enacted in 1994 (Source: U.S. Central Intelligence Agency, *Cuba: Handbook of Trade Statistics*, 1998).

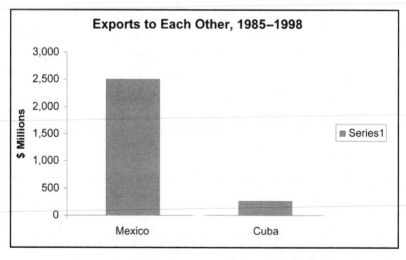

Figure 14: This graph shows the overall volume of trade between Mexico and Cuba from 1985 to 1998 and demonstrates the trade imbalance in favor of Mexico (Source: U.S. Central Intelligence Agency, *Cuba: Handbook of Trade Statistics*, 1998).

▼▼▼

throughout both the De la Madrid and Salinas administrations become a topic of consideration when discussing NAFTA.[68]

In 1994 the Cuban and Mexican petroleum industries carried out negotiations at a convention set on furthering economic integration between the two countries. Specifically, the meeting "formalized the establishment of a mixed corporation between Cupet and Mexpetrol to acquire and modernize the refinery at Cienfuegos," under which Mexpetrol would invest $100 million and, to alleviate Cuba's original $350 million debt, the Mexican government would sell pieces of Cuba's debt to Mexpetrol, which in turn would forgive that part of the debt for a share in the Cuban state-owned enterprise. Mexpetrol owned 49 percent and Cupet owned 51 percent.[69] Mexico came in at a crucial moment here, as did Canada, Spain, and Russia, each of whom accelerated trade with Cuba during the period following their 1989–93 trade drop of more than 70 percent. With the advent of NAFTA and the new joint ventures between Cuba and Mexico, along with Cuba's economic connections to Europe and Canada, exports from Cuba have risen.[70]

After the Soviet bloc dissolved, the United States strengthened sanctions against Cuba. Within three years of the collapse, the United States passed the Torricelli bill (Cuban Democracy Act [CDA]), which "further tightened the trade embargo and prohibited subsidiaries of U.S. corporations in Third World countries from trading with Cuba."[71] This included trade in food and medical supplies, which in 1992 represented 90 percent of all Cuban trade with U.S. subsidiaries.[72] Mexican Foreign Minister Fernando Solana, among others, denounced the law as "unacceptable."[73] In November 1992, the UN General Assembly noted its displeasure with the new law as well, passing a resolution expressing concern "over the promulgation and application by member states of laws and regulations whose extraterritorial effects affect the sovereignty of other states and the legitimate interests of entities or persons under their jurisdiction."[74]

Mexico no doubt felt itself in a conundrum with respect to its relations with its eastern and northern neighbor. Although it was headed toward a foreign policy in which free trade with the United States as well as Cuba figured largely, its response to the CDA was definitive: "Mexico would resist any extraterritorial intent to apply laws" against free trade.[75] In keeping with the line that past Mexican presidents had consistently espoused regarding foreign policy, on a visit to Havana, President Salinas called for the repeal of the blockade because, in his words, "it [did] not resolve anything."[76]

The Zapatista uprising of 1994 coincided with President Salinas's last year in office and still had not been quelled by the last year of the following presidency, six years later. The new president, Ernesto Zedillo Ponce de León (1994–2000), came into his candidacy only after the original PRI candidate, Luis Donaldo Colosio, had been assassinated while campaigning in Tijuana on March 6, 1994. During his *sexenio*, Cuban-Mexican relations would continue to be affected by pressures from the United States, setting the stage for the changes that would occur under Vicente Fox Quesada (2000–2006).

The United States' primary Cuban trade concern in the 1990s had to do with former American private-sector properties nationalized under Castro in the early 1960s. By 1994, Mexico had become Cuba's largest foreign investor, which created tension between the United States and Mexico, especially after the Mexican cement company, Cemex SA, negotiated a contract with Cuba to operate and own half of a facility that Castro seized from Lone Star, a formerly Connecticut-based company that had lost its business under Castro in 1960.[77] The issue of former American private properties came up again two years later, after the Helms-Burton act passed. The law was designed to deter foreign businesses from investing in Cuba and gave Americans the legal right "to bring suit in United States courts against anyone 'trafficking' in property belonging to them before it was confiscated by Castro."[78]

When the Helms-Burton bill passed into law in early March of 1996, it drew fierce opposition from the two other trading partners of NAFTA. Canada and Mexico both expressed outrage, but Mexico vowed to bring the matter before the World Trade Organization for arbitration. The bill came to the fore after two Cessnas, flown by the Cuban exile-funded and -staffed Brothers to the Rescue, were shot down by Cuban MiGs, killing

▼▼▼

four people.[79] On March 13, Canada said that it had lodged a trade protest with the Clinton administration over Helms-Burton, after which Mexico requested to be part of the investigation as to why the United States had passed this law and how it planned to implement it. Canada and Mexico both trade extensively with Cuba and had every intention of continuing to do.[80] Under Helms-Burton, the United States could punish Mexico for its cement deal with Cuba.

Mexico's response was calculated yet swift, using rhetoric akin to that used by U.S. nationalists. On June 14, the *Washington Post* quoted President Zedillo as saying, "Like Canada, Mexico considers inadmissible any measures which, instead of promoting freedom, hinders that of others [and] instead of tearing down barriers, raises them to the detriment of investment and international trade."[81] At this time, European nations also began condemning the Helms-Burton law. The attempts to block Helms-Burton brought Canada's ambassador Raymond Chretien and Mexico's Jesús Silva Herzog "very close" together, according to Ambassador Chretien.[82] The two devised a resolution later accepted by the OAS petitioning the Inter-American Justice Court to investigate whether Helms-Burton violated international law.[83] On August 29, the *New York Times* announced that the OAS had found Helms-Burton to be a violation "of the sovereign right of nations to govern companies in their territories."[84] It also reported that "Mexico intends on using this nonbinding ruling to conduct an international legal challenge to the law."[85]

The first two implementations of Helms-Burton came in mid-August 1996. The U.S. government announced that it would send letters to let Grupos Domos SA in Mexico and Sherritt International Corporation in Canada know that their executives would be denied visas for entry to the United States because of their business ties to Cuba. Grupo Domos SA owned 49 percent of the Cuban telephone company, Cuban Telecommunications Enterprise, which had been ITT before its 1960 expropriation by Castro. Sherritt International Corporation was a mining company that operated a nickel mine in Cuba that used to be the McMoran Company, a subsidiary of the New Orleans-based Freeport Company.[86] The executives from both countries lost their U.S. visas on August 29.[87]

In 1997, after standing up for Cuba time and again at the OAS and the United Nations, Mexico again pushed for Cuba's reincorporation into the international system. However, this initiative aimed to establish political reform in Cuba, and Mexican representative José Angel Gurria presented a proposal to the OAS that would put pressure on Cuba to lift its repression of dissidents and to create a more democratic atmosphere. Still, using anticapitalist rhetoric, he insisted that "no one [attempt] to dismantle the political structure" in order to open the island up to "neocapitalist penetration." In the end, the OAS did not readmit Cuba, but it would not be the last time Mexico tried to promote political pluralism in Cuba.[88]

An event in December 1998 strained Mexican-Cuban relations. At a SELA meeting on December 8, Mexican ambassador to Cuba Pedro Joaquín Coldwell was called back to Mexico from Havana after Castro allegedly insulted Mexico by saying that many Mexican children knew more about Mickey Mouse than about their own national heroes and that Mexico was less vocal about its noninterventionist foreign policy than it used to be. Upset by Castro's comments, Zedillo demanded an explanation to which the Cuban Foreign Ministry responded that the "media misinterpreted" Castro's remarks. The ambassador later returned to his post in Havana.[89]

Toward the end of Zedillo's administration, ties between Cuba and Mexico began to weaken as a series of decisions on Mexico's part signaled a shift from its long-standing foreign policy. In August of 1999, Mexico blocked Cuba's entry into the San José Pact, under which Mexico and Venezuela would sell oil to Central American and Caribbean nations under good terms, explaining that Cuba was excluded for "financial reasons."[90] On April 18, 2000, the *Wall Street Journal* announced that Mexico would abstain in the vote that would condemn Cuba of human rights abuses at Geneva's UN Human Rights Commission meeting. In 1999, Mexico had defended Cuba, voting in its favor; but in 2000, Mexico wanted Cuba to hold free elections and to allow freedom of expression, so it abstained.[91] The transition in power from the PRI to the National Action Party (PAN) in 2000 further affected the evolving relationship between Cuba and Mexico.

▼▼▼

Taken as a whole, the 1976–2000 period witnessed a deepening alignment between Mexico and the United States as well as the continuing
importance of the Mexican-Cuban relationship for political purposes. The
War on Drugs and economic factors drove the United States and Mexico
closer together while U.S. sanctions against Cuba, the Central American
crisis, the fall of the Soviet Union, and independent Mexican foreign policy combined provided many opportunities for increased Mexican-Cuban
relations. However, in the end, the relationship between the United States
and Mexico had become truly close, whereas the relationship between
Mexico and Cuba was more superficial, consisting in "friendly" interac-
tions intended to placate revolutionaries in both countries who sincerely
felt mutual affiliation with and affection toward one another.

EPILOGUE

THE SHIFT TO HONEST RELATIONS UNDER MEXICAN DEMOCRACY, 2000–2006

Mexico has radically changed its position at the international level.

Nobody pressures us, nor do we accept pressure from the United States or Cuba.

> —Mexican president Vicente Fox in April 2001 regarding National Action Party (PAN) foreign policy toward Cuba

In Mexico, a beloved, sister country to all Cubans, the National Congress asked their president to abstain from voting for the resolution, although President Bush had demanded that he do so. It is truly painful to see the great prestige and influence Mexico earned in the eyes of Latin America and the world with its unimpeachable international policy, which stemmed from a genuine, far-reaching revolution, turn to ashes.

> —Fidel Castro's 2004 May Day speech

▼▼▼

In July 2000, the Institutional Revolutionary Party (PRI) was defeated for the first time in a presidential election in seventy-one years. Vicente Fox Quesada of the PAN was inaugurated in December 2000, and soon Mexican-Cuban relations underwent a dramatic change. Castro had been used to dealing strictly with PRI presidents, who were committed to a foreign policy doctrine based on nonintervention, the right to self-determination, and, particularly, a revolutionary mutuality founded on similar nationalist ideals. The PRI used this doctrine with Cuba, and in maintaining relations with a revolutionary government, hoping to preserve its own revolutionary image. The PAN, on the other hand, never aspired to such an image and in fact founded itself as a party opposed to the so-called "revolutionaries" of the PRI. Therefore it never needed Cuban solidarity as part of its political platform.

The PAN president could not have chosen a more apt foreign policy advisor and representative than former Party of the Democratic Revolution (PRD) supporter and UNAM political science professor Jorge G. Castañeda. The two of them, along with other legislators of the PAN, did not advocate eliminating the old doctrine entirely but sought to supplement it: the PAN policy paralleled that of former U.S. president Jimmy Carter, who had instituted a human rights certification policy for dealing with foreign relations. Human rights and democracy in Cuba were more important issues in the Fox administration than in any other Mexican administration, and these concerns shaped its relations with Castro.

After Fox was elected, Carlos Salazar, PAN's director of international relations, said that the Fox administration would encourage democracy in Latin America, adding, "and evidently Cuba is not a democracy."[1] While the PAN administration remained opposed to the U.S. embargo against Cuba, President Fox claimed to reorient Mexican foreign policy to promote democracy, human rights, and free trade, all of which were required by U.S. policy makers and none of which had reached a level in Cuba that satisfied either Mexico or the United States. Castro, cognizant that Fox planned to maintain free trade with Cuba, told the Mexican government to worry about U.S. hegemony, saying that it was evident that the U.S. Republican Party wanted "economic annexation and political subordination" of Mexico.[2] PAN, however, dismissed Castro's overtures. Adolfo Aguilar Zinzer, coordinator of international affairs for the Fox transition team, said, "The era of annexations ended long ago."[3]

The PAN displayed its anti-Castro roots shortly after the January 2001 arrest and imprisonment of two Czech men in Cuba, who were detained for allegedly meeting with Cuban dissidents on the island. The Czech government responded by bringing a resolution to the UN Human Rights Commission (UNHRC) to condemn Cuba for human rights abuses. President Fox had asked Cuba for transparency on human rights before this incident, and so, after the Czechs decided to bring the resolution to the United Nations, Fox said that Mexico would only side with Cuba "if we confirm that there are no violations of human rights"; otherwise "we would denounce [Cuba]."[4] Pressure was on Fox to weigh the options between voting against Cuba, which would be counter to previous policy, or siding with Cuba to preserve their long-standing ties. This case demonstrated the PAN's own independence in shaping Mexico's image in opposition to the PRI-defined idea of it as a nation joined in revolutionary solidarity with other revolutionaries.

This was truly a test of Mexico's new president because despite its shortcomings, the PRI had at the very least established a strong record of relatively independent foreign policy, a legacy that had become ingrained in Mexican nationalism as a "sacred cow" of sorts, alongside the protection of Pemex as a nationalized business, for example. Therefore, Fox's decision concerning Cuba not only mattered in terms of Mexican-Cuban popular solidarity, nor was it solely a political party issue, but it also mattered in terms of pure nationalist pride. In addition, voting against Cuba at the UNHRC would have signified not just a break with tradition, but it would have been seen as an open alignment with U.S. interests, a stand that would have no doubt tarnished Fox's reputation at this early point in his presidency.

Of course, Fox would never have conceded that the United States pressured him. Concerning the vote for the resolution, Fox asserted, "Nobody pressures us, nor do we accept pressure from the United States or Cuba," even though both had in fact asked for his support.[5] In this area,

▼▼▼

Fox diverged from the past strict PRI adherence to anti-intervention in foreign affairs, stating that "we will be alert to any human rights violations in this part of the world" and that "Mexico has radically changed its position at the international level."[6] At the same time, Fox denied that the policy of nonintervention was null and void, asserting that "we will now express our opinion on what occurs in other countries, will let others express their opinion on what we are doing here, and will allow visits and supervision."[7]

In fact, as my account of Mexico's role in international affairs since the 1960s and particularly from 1970s to the present has shown, Mexico had been much more active than Fox gives it credit for. For example, referring to Mexico's candidacy to the UN Security Council, Fox said, "We are interested in Mexico leaving its political ostracism [behind], going out into the world and being part of the events and decisions," implying that the PRI was isolated, inactive, passive, and permissive in dealing with Communist Cuba in particular.[8] And yet, the PRI worked extensively to thwart pro-Castro movements within Mexico beginning in the early 1960s and continued to do so throughout the 1960s, the most profound instance of its anti-Castroism being the Tlatelolco Massacre of October 2, 1968. The PRI presidents Luis Echeverría and José López Portillo promoted tercermundismo policies, traveling the world to foster developing world pride, and they also moved against pro-Castro leftists throughout the 1970s especially. The Mexican government's opposition to anything resembling Cuban-style leftism can be seen in its and the U.S. government's response to the Zapatista rebellion of 1994, which grew out of pro-Castro as well as pro-Zapata ideals and was met with stiff resistance from the Mexican military with U.S. support. Were its involvement in stemming the tide of pro-Cuban leftism in Mexico the real extent of the PRI's proactive involvement, the PAN's criticism would perhaps contain a grain of truth; however, the steady improvement in relations with the United States beginning with the Kennedy and Johnson administrations and continuing through to the present-day NAFTA integration that the PRI effected as well as the tercermundismo initiative of Echeverría and López Portillo's follow-up belie the PAN's suggestion that the PRI was uninvolved in world affairs.

In fact, in a very real way, the PRI helped establish a peaceful way for the Third World to have a say in international affairs within the Cold War atmosphere that was rooted in superpower aspirations. They showed other countries, big and small, that the globalizing nature of the Cold War actually gave Third World actors the means to express their independence, nationalism, and other aspirations on a world stage and thereby the ability to shape events. The global conflict between the Soviets and the Americans created a widespread battlefield that they themselves could not wholly control, and as a result, the war pulled Third World actors onto the stage, sometimes against their will but also because there were internal real life concerns that compelled the Third World to assert itself. The Cold War was not as an East-West struggle but an international struggle over the future of all nations, which spelled tragedy as well as opportunity for the people of the Third World in particular.

This war is also the source of present-day dilemmas for Mexico, such as Cuba's human rights situation. On April 11, 2001 the majority of the Mexican Senate pleaded with President Fox to insist that the Mexican delegate to Geneva's fifty-seventh session of the UNHRC "vote in solidarity with the Cuban people and against any resolution that might infringe upon the sovereignty of the Republic of Cuba."⁹ Thirteen PAN members supported this request, while the rest supported a measure to have the delegate abstain in the vote. Arguing for abstention, PAN Senator Adame said, "We have a duty to put certain principles above our commitment to any system or to any government, and this is true of the unswerving respect that we must show for human rights."¹⁰ However much the PAN's desire to establish a change in Mexican foreign policy might be founded on principles of respect for human rights, its aim was too high at this point in time. Fox's foreign relations minister Castañeda said that Mexico will be in the forefront of the movement to defend fundamental freedoms, "a position it should always have occupied," and on April 12, in reference to the Mexican Senate's request, Foreign Minister Castañeda mentioned that "the Executive branch—as is clearly defined in Article 89 of the Constitution—will make the decision."¹¹ He then announced that Mexico would abstain on the vote because the Czech resolution lacked the "type of consensus" needed.¹²

▼▼▼

The Cuban foreign policy apparatus responded positively to Mexico's decision, highlighting its understanding of the level of solidarity it could expect from Fox. After the UNHRC vote, Cuban Foreign Minister Felipe Pérez Roque said that Mexico's abstention was what they expected, and he welcomed it. Out of fifty-three member nations, only twenty-two supported the Czech resolution, while twenty rejected it, and ten abstained.[13] Then, on June 29, after three days of talks in Veracruz, the Interparliamentary Meeting between Cuba and Mexico resolved that the two countries would maintain friendly ties. The PAN representatives helped pass a clause that stipulated Mexico would continue to conduct affairs with Cuba provided it respect human rights and democracy but that both countries would forbid outside authorities from using those conditions as a premise "for political intervention in the domestic affairs of the two countries."[14]

In an interview in *LASA Forum*, Castañeda explained why Mexico abstained at the UNHRC:

> We voted this way because public opinion in Mexico is not yet ready for a new, more critical position on Cuba. A change in policy on Cuba would take a lot more time. You have to remember that Cuba is not a foreign policy issue in Mexico or in the United States. It's not a foreign policy matter for any country. It is always a domestic issue around which domestic political forces face off against one another. Fidel is not going to be pushed from power with a blockade. And he will not be persuaded to change his policies through a program of "constructive engagement." In fact, internationally, you can't do anything to change what goes on in Cuba. There is no pressure to be exerted. This is why it's not a foreign policy issue for us or anyone else; there's simply nothing you can do one way or the other.[15]

Fox and Castañeda made it clear that Mexico's foreign policy would no longer be dictated by the doctrine of nonintervention-based tolerance of Castro's political intransigence. As a center-right party with antirevolutionary roots, the PAN, unlike the PRI, did not need to make revolutionary, leftist leaning overtures. Given that Fox was also representing the PAN as its first president of the republic, a shift to an ideology that embraced human rights might promote PAN's image abroad.

The need to project that image presented itself during the diplomatic crisis around events in March and April 2002. For instance, after Castro dropped the bombshell that Fox had asked him to leave early from the UN Summit on Financing for Development, held in Monterrey, Mexico, in March 2002, the Fox administration appears to have retaliated and in an unprecedented way. In mid-April 2002, "Mexico broke tradition and approved a UN resolution condemning Cuba's Human Rights record," aligning itself exactly with the U.S. position and causing Castro to come forth with evidence (a tape recording) proving that Fox had in fact asked the Cuban leader to leave early from the summit.[16] Also as mentioned in the introduction chapter, relations became strained to the point of near rupture again in May 2004, which also made international headlines.

The roots of the PAN-PRI divide go back to the roots of each party. The PAN/Sinarquista movements of the 1930s found common ground in their opposition to the PRI's "revolutionary" socialistic policies regarding business and Church interests. The PAN's set of interests ran parallel to that of the United States especially with the rise of pro-Castro Mexican leftism in the 1960s and still do, as demonstrated by the PAN's opposition to the PRI's tolerance toward Castro, which PAN supporters expressed in the pages of *Mensaje Quincenal.* In addition, one of the participants at the anti-Communist-oriented International Security Council meeting in San Diego in 1986 was the former president of the PAN, José Angel Conchello.[17]

The sectors inside and outside the governments of Mexico and Cuba, including the U.S. government as well as Mexican, American, and Cuban anti-Communists and pro-Castro Mexican leftists profoundly affected the character of relations between Cuba and Mexico, raising questions unasked by those Mexicans and Cubans who promote the concept of the historically rooted Mexican-Cuban friendship that "unite[s]" the two countries and is validated by the "special" era of relations, from 1964 to 1970. The poetry, speeches, letters, and books that laud this relationship speak of the Mexican-Cuban connection as if to blur the lines between

▼▼▼

civil society and government, as if the two nations were operating as individual human beings. Hence the name of the anthology: "Mexico and Cuba: Two Peoples United in History." We have to ask, how can history unite people? And if the people are in fact "united in history," then we have to ask, which people? The answers lie in the manner in which this history is appropriated by those with an interest in promoting an agenda linked to political legitimacy and power.

I contend that the relationship's complexities betray the logic of two nations simply "united" and that the meaning of such words is based on subjective degrees of reality. In other words, we can certainly acknowledge that many Mexicans and Cubans feel a historically based affinity for each other rooted in real events in history. Yet, we may simultaneously acknowledge the use of that sentiment as history by the interested political parties and interest groups who have constructed a reality that excludes "nonrevolutionary" voices as well as actions and discourse contrary to the constructed history. Never mind that the PRI's "revolutionary" credentials were in question during the very period, 1964–70, in which Mexico was the only Latin American nation not to sever relations with "revolutionary" Cuba.

My interviews and conversations with interested Mexicans and Cubans as well as comments by officials and political interest groups reveal countless expressions of solidarity between the two peoples but only from those who claim affinity with the left or "revolutionary" political wings.[18] This includes pro-Castroites and progressive leftists in Cuba and Mexico, such as members of the Worker's Party (PT), the PRI, and the PRD in Mexico. PAN officials, however, have expressed no friendship toward revolutionary Cuba, though they do acknowledge the long-standing friendship between Mexico and Cuba. They instead have consistently expressed disagreement with Castro's policies, even if they have recognized the necessity for stable Mexican-Cuban relations. In movements beyond the mainstream Mexican political parties (PRI and PAN), the rhetoric in favor of Castro's Cuba today parallels that of the National Liberation Movement (MLN) of the 1960s. Militants in the Worker's Party and the Frente Zapatista de Liberación Nacional (FZLN), the political front group for the Zapatistas, consistently portray Castro's government as Mexico's ideal.[19] Their

▼▼▼

solidarity with Cuba parallels that which Lázaro Cárdenas and his followers expressed four decades ago, and just like four decades ago, the promise of revolutionary rejuvenation in Mexico is not on the real agenda of those in power today.

Thus, like other successful political machines, the PRI and Castro deftly constructed a history of meaningful relations amid the inevitable contradictory evidence. The PRI projected itself as independent and revolutionary, an image the only outward sign of was its public official resistance to the U.S. position on Cuba on issues such as the embargo and maintaining relations. At the same time, as we have seen, it cooperated with the United States to thwart Castro's influence. And, as we have also seen, this made perfect sense, as the PRI was not Communist and in fact took pains to strengthen its economic and political relationship with the United States during and after the Cold War, the culmination of which was NAFTA. Thus I have contended, against prominent U.S.-Mexican relations scholars who argue that Mexico really began aligning itself with the U.S in the 1970s and 1980s owing to further bilateral economic integration, that in fact Mexico took up cause with the United States much earlier. The PAN, on the other hand, has always been against the PRI's friendship with Cuba, as have Mexican and Cuban anti-Communists, and instead of holding to the PRI's foreign policy of nonintervention and the right to self-determination, a rather broad standard in international affairs, the PAN adheres to the policy of human rights verification, of which the PAN sees little evidence. Indeed, the party has led efforts to lobby for the release of several political prisoners in Cuba today.[20] The struggle over human rights will no doubt play a role in shaping Mexican-Cuban relations into the future, inevitably with the shadow of the United States cast over them both, shaping to one degree or another the manner in which these two vibrant Latin American nations interact with one another on all levels, from the government to civil society.

The broader relevance of this study is the extent to which we can view historical appropriation as a commonly constructed political tool, not just within the context of Mexican-Cuban relations or even bilateral relations in general but in all aspects of persuasion related to power dynamics. In this

▼▼▼

case, we have a particularly poignant example of how a hegemonic entity such as the United States can influence the manner in which politically active groups and parties use historical appropriation for their own needs. The end result is reflected at all levels of discourse: all parties, from the most localized of groups to the international media, from the left all the way to the right wing, believe that Mexico and Cuba have had a special relationship under the Castro regime and that that relationship is in need of repair today.

I have attempted to fill in the scholarly gaps regarding the nature of the Mexican-Cuban relationship, but the implications of U.S. or perhaps European, Asian, or Soviet influence on the bilateral relations of other countries opens up untapped scholarly territory that could raise many questions as to the validity of traditional bilateral relations studies. Focusing on the U.S. role in shaping relations among Central American nations, among South American nations, and among the Caribbean nations and territories likely reveals more about the extended effects of economic, cultural, and political influence emanating from the greatest power structure the planet has ever seen than about the relationship between the United States and these nations or between these nations and other First World countries. This study, on the other hand, helps us to see how relatively weaker nations found their voices as a result of Cold War pressures. Thus, the extent of superpower influence on the foreign policies and activities of weaker nations is only one aspect of international relations; the other is the actions taken themselves by those weaker nations such as Mexico and Cuba.

And the documentary evidence of agency on the part of governments and groups in these nations is there: ephemera from various groups interested in transnational issues, newspapers, presidential archives, official and unofficial correspondence, announcements, reports, and studies all help paint a picture of an ever-globalizing world in which the actions of one group or state or ideology have had profound effects on all involved parties. These materials contain the germ out of which many future studies might grow, studies that would draw attention to the micro as well as the macro processes operating within the chaotic realm of international relations.

▼▼▼

That Mexico and Cuba found some level of autonomy in the international relations arena should reveal to all readers, whether from the developed or the developing world, that "weaker" nations indeed have agency and are not always mere victims. Precisely because they operated outside the demands of the superpowers, Cuba and Mexico were able to use their relationship to empower themselves and quite possibly give a bit of hope to future Third World actors with dreams of reversing the problems inherent to underdevelopment. At the same time, the solidarity of hope and the hope for solidarity has suffered a setback in recent years, as is evidenced by Fidel Castro's statements against the PAN at the May Day celebrations in Havana in 2004 and 2006, in which the Cuban leader portrayed the Mexican leader as a lackey of the Bush administration. Thus, the role of the Mexican-Cuban friendship is now under threat unlike at any other period in its history. Still, as Cuba and Mexico both become less "revolutionary," the significance of their relationship will no doubt change again in the very near future.

NOTES

INTRODUCTION

Epigraph source: Mexican Movement for Solidarity with Cuba (MMSC), "Es el gobierno de México quien nos ha puesto en esta situación," http://www.geocities. com/cubaymexico/document/pr5may.html.

1. Bruce Cumings, "The American Century in the Third World," in *The Ambiguous Legacy: U.S. Foreign Relations in the "American Century,"* ed. Michael J. Hogan (Cambridge: Cambridge University Press, 1999), 291.

2. Kevin Sullivan, "Castro Lashes out at Fox as Ties with Mexico Fray: Cuban Alleges Lies over UN Meeting," *Washington Post*, April 23, 2002, outlines this issue quite well, while other major newspapers, such as the *Wall Street Journal*, the *New York Times*, the *Los Angeles Times*, the *Guardian*, and the *Miami Herald* as well as the major Cuban and Mexican newspapers such as *Granma* and *La Jornada* and smaller leftist papers all covered the story.

3. Examples of this history abound, but Andres Oppenheimer, "Mexico to Abstain in UN Vote on Rights in Cuba," *Miami Herald*, April 13, 2001, usefully outlines the context of Mexico's historical position on this matter amid its internal debate concerning Cuban human rights.

4. Oppenheimer.

5. Harris Whitbeck, "Mexico, Peru Pull Envoys to Cuba," *CNN.com*, May 3, 2004, http://www.cnn.com/2004/WORLD/americas/05/03/mexico.cuba.

6. Jo Tuckman, "Mexico and Cuba Back in Harmony," *Guardian Unlimited*, July 20, 2004.

7. Nelson Notario Castro, "1988 Speech Castro Speaks in Tuxpan, Notes Event," December 5, 1988, *Castro Speech Database, UTLANIC*, http://lanic.utexas.edu/la/cb/cuba/castro.html.

8. The authors are Andrés Iduarte, Rodolfo Echeverría Ruiz, Victor Rico Galán, Vicente Lombardo Toledano, and the Mexican Workers and Campesinos, Communist, and Popular Socialist parties. See Centro de Investigación Científica Jorge L. Tamayo, ed., *México y Cuba: Dos pueblos unidos en la historia*, vol. 2 (Mexico City: Centro de Investigación Científica Jorge L. Tamayo, 1982).

▼▼▼

9. Authors such as Adolfo Leyva de Varona, Raymond Graves, Ana Covarrubias Velasco, Jorge Tamayo, and Mario Ojeda Gómez, among others, have written dissertations or articles that refer to this as proof of the uniqueness of the Mexican-Cuban relationship.

10. Peggy Fenn, "México, la no intervención y la autodeterminación en el caso de Cuba." *Foro Internacional* 4.1 (1963): 1–5; Senate Committee on Foreign Relations, *Inter-American Relations: A Collection of Documents, Legislation, Descriptions of Inter-American Organizations, and Other Material Pertaining to Inter-American Affairs*, 100th Cong., 2d sess., 1988, 1–9, 217–19.

11. Fidel Castro, "1980 Message Decoration of López Portillo," August 1, 1980, *Castro Speech Database, UTLANIC*, http://lanic.utexas.edu/la/cb/cuba/castro .html.

12. G. Pope Atkins covers the "realist-idealist dichotomy" in his *Latin America and the Caribbean in the International System*, 4th ed. (Boulder, CO: Westview Press, 1999), 60.

13. This understanding has been expressed in writing and in interviews and conversations with the author by many authorities both official and academic, such as in Alan Riding's *Distant Neighbors: A Portrait of the Mexicans* (New York: Vintage, 1985) and in conversations with Cuban-Mexican professor Carlos Bojorquez Urzaiz and Cuban professor Tomas Fernandez Robaina as well as in interviews with Mexican professor Enrique Camacho Navarro, Mexican political secretary Daniel Martinez, and several others.

14. Jorge Dominguez, *To Make the World Safe for Revolution: Cuba's Foreign Policy* (Cambridge: Harvard University Press, 1989), 113–14.

15. "Counterdependency" is used by Michael H. Erisman, *Cuba's Foreign Relations in a Post-Soviet World* (Gainesville: University of Florida Press), 20.

16. Eric Hobsbawm, "Introduction: Inventing Traditions," in *The Invention of Tradition*, ed. Eric Hobsbawm and Terence Ranger (Cambridge: Cambridge University, 1983), 1.

17. Hobsbawn, 1.

18. Maurice Halbwachs, *On Collective Memory*, ed. and trans. Lewis A. Coser (Chicago: University of Chicago Press, 1992), 39–40.

19. For more on the PAN's foreign policy, see Jorge Castañeda and Judith Adler Hellman, "Human Rights in Mexico: An Interview with Jorge Castaneda," *LASA Forum* 32.2 (2001): 5–71, and I gained a considerable amount of insight into this from a July 1, 2003, interview with PAN federal deputy Tarcicio Navarrete Montes de Oca, an outspoken figure in the anti-Castro wing of

Mexican politics. Leonardo Curzio and Tarcisio Navarrete Montes de Oca, "Entrevista con el Diputado Tarcisio Navarrete," *Grupo Parlamentario Federal,* Mexico, D.F., February 25, 2002, also reveals more insight into this matter.

20. Examples of Mexican groups include National Union of Civic Action (UNAC), the Regional Anti-Communist Crusade (CRAC), Mexican Anti-Communist Federation (FEMACO); examples of a Cuban American group would be the National Christian Movement (MNC); examples of American groups include the authors of *Free Cuba News* and *National Review.*

21. Telephone conversation between Secretary Rusk and President Johnson, November 12, 1964, in Kate Doyle, "Double Dealing: Mexico's Foreign Policy toward Cuba," National Security Archive, electronic briefing book, http://www.gwu.edu/~nsarchiv/NSAEBB/NSAEBB83/index.htm.

22. Quoted in Carl Migdail's chapter, "Mexico, Cuba, and the United States: Myth Versus Reality," in *Cuba's Ties to a Changing World,* ed. Donna Rich Kaplowitz (Boulder, CO: Lynne Rienner, 1993), 207.

23. See quote in Castro interview in chapter 2.

CHAPTER ONE

Epigraph source: Fulgencio Batista, "Letter to Ambassador Gilberto Bosques," December 16, 1953, Gilberto Bosques's file, II–26–14–29, no. 1115, Archivo de Concentraciones, Secretaría de Relaciones Exteriores (SRE), Mexico City.

1. See both Inga Clendinnen's *Ambivalent Conquests: Maya and Spaniard in Yucatan, 1517–1570,* 2nd ed. (Cambridge: Cambridge University Press, 2003) and Bernal Díaz del Castillo's *The Discovery and Conquest of Mexico, 1517–21,* trans. A. P. Maudslay, ed. Genaro García (Cambridge, MA: Da Capo, 2004).

2. A comprehensive discussion of this matter can be found in Charles Mann's historiographical book *1491: New Revelations on the Americas before Columbus* (New York: Knopf, 2005).

3. Louis A. Perez, *Cuba: Between Reform and Revolution* (Oxford: Oxford University Press, 1995), 31.

4. Peter Bakewell, *Silver Mining and Society in Colonial Mexico: Zacatecas, 1546–1700* (Cambridge: Cambridge University Press, 1971); Francois Chevalier, *Land and Society in Colonial Mexico: The Great Hacienda* (Berkeley: University of California Press, 1963); and D. A. Brading, *Haciendas and Ranchos in the Mexican Bajío: León, 1700–1860* (Cambridge: Cambridge University Press, 1978) detail the various aspects of mining and land tenure in colonial Mexico.

▼▼▼

5. See Bakewell, Chevalier, and Brading.

6. Julio Le Riverend, "Antecedentes: Siglos XVI–XVIII," in *México y Cuba: Dos pueblos unidos en la historia*, vol. 1, ed. Centro de Investigación Científica Jorge L. Tamayo (Mexico City: Centro de Investigación Científica Jorge L. Tamayo, 1982), 2; José L. Franco, *Relaciones de Cuba y México durante el período colonial* (Havana: Ministerio de Educación, 1961), 5–7.

7. Le Riverend, 4–8.

8. See John Lynch, *The Spanish American Revolutions, 1808–1826*, 2nd ed. (New York: W. W. Norton, 1986).

9. Rodolfo Ruz Menéndez, "Yucatán y Cuba: Dos pueblos hermanos," *Revista de la Biblioteca Nacional José Martí* 30.3 (1988): 100.

10. Antonio López de Santa Anna, "Antonio López de Santa Anna, comandante general del estado libre de Yucatán, ofrece sus servicios para luchar por la independencia de Cuba," in *México y Cuba: Dos pueblos unidos en la historia*, 1:24–26; Lucila Flamand, "La emancipación de México y la lucha independentista de Cuba," in *México y Cuba: Dos pueblos unidos en la historia*, 1:15.

11. Enrique Krauze, *Mexico: Biography of Power*, trans. Hank Heifetz (New York: HarperCollins, 1997), 119.

12. Lucás Alamán, "Instrucciones de Lucas Alamán, secretario de relaciones exteriores de México a José Mariano de Michelena, agente diplomático Mexicano en Inglaterra," in *México y Cuba: Dos pueblos unidos en la historia*, 1:27–28.

13. Flamand, 13–14.

14. Adrián del Valle, "La Gran Legión del Aguila Negra," in *México y Cuba: Dos pueblos unidos en la historia*, 1:110.

15. Flamand, 13–14.

16. Flamand, 15.

17. Joel Poinsett, "Joel R. Poinsett, comunicado al secretario de relaciones Mexicanos, el plan que propone su gobierno para lograr la paz entre España y sus colonias," in *México y Cuba: Dos pueblos unidos en la historia*, 1:72–78.

18. Flamand, 15. For Spanish attempts at reconquest, see Michael Meyer and William L. Sherman, *The Course of Mexican History*, 6th ed. (Oxford: Oxford University Press, 1995), 320–21.

19. In a letter to the Mexican secretary, Poinsett details a plan whereby Mexico would be able to defend its own shores much more effectively if it desisted from battling Spain further. See his letter in Poinsett, 72–78.

▼▼▼

20. Quoted in Lars Schoultz, *Beneath the United States: A History of U.S. Policy toward Latin America* (Cambridge: Harvard University Press, 1998), 19.

21. Manuel Gómez Pedraza, "Decreto de Guadalupe Victoria que autoriza la salida de tropas a Cuba, México y Cuba: Dos pueblos unidos en la historia," in *México y Cuba: Dos pueblos unidos en la historia*, 1:79–80.

22. Flamand, 16.

23. Enrique Rodriguez Sosa, *Proyectos de invasion a Yucatán desde Cuba, 1828–1829* (Mérida and Havana: Coedición de la Universidad Autónoma de Yucatán y la Universidad de La Habana, 1996), 19–20.

24. Meyer and Sherman, 320–21.

25. Rafael Rojas, "La política mexicana ante la guerra de independencia de Cuba," *Historia Mexicana* 45.4 (1996): 797; Flamand, 16.

26. Quoted in Schoultz, 4. Dozens of statements of this sort uttered by policy makers throughout the nineteenth century can be found in Schoultz's book.

27. Jorge Domínguez and Rafael Fernández de Castro, eds., *The United States and Mexico: Between Partnership and Conflict* (New York: Routledge, 2001), 9.

28. Louis A. Pérez, *Cuba and the United States: Ties of Singular Intimacy*, 2nd ed. (Athens: University of Georgia Press, 1997), 43.

29. Pérez, 44–46.

30. For a complete explanation of the Confederates in Mexico, see Andrew Rolle's *The Lost Cause: The Confederate Exodus to Mexico*, rev. ed. (Norman: University of Oklahoma Press, 1992).

31. Ramón de Armas, "Las guerras cubanas: Luchas y solidaridad," in *México y Cuba: Dos pueblos unidos en la historia*, 1:265.

32. Menéndez, 97–108.

33. Armas, 265.

34. Jorge L. Tamayo, "El Grito de Yara resonó en México," in *México y Cuba: Dos pueblos unidos en la historia*, 1:102–4.

35. Carlos Manuel de Céspedes, "Carta a José Inclán," in *México y Cuba: Dos pueblos unidos en la historia*, 1:176.

36. Tamayo, 106.

37. Tamayo, 104–5.

38. Tamayo, 104–5.

▼▼▼

39. Eligio Ancona and Manuel Peniche, "Los diputados M. Peniche y E. Ancona explican su posición," in *México y Cuba: Dos pueblos unidos en la historia*, 1:168–69; Tamayo, 105.

40. Rojas, 788 (translation mine); Céspedes quoted in Armas, 253–54.

41. Tamayo, 105–6.

42. See *El Universal*, Mexico City, vols. 1875 and 1876.

43. Armas, "Las guerras cubanas," 254.

44. Menéndez, 106.

45. Menéndez, 97–108; Menéndez, *La primera emigración cubana a Yucatán* (Mérida: Universidad de Yucatán, 1969), 7, 23–26.

46. Armas, 254.

47. Menéndez, *La primera emigración*, 30–31.

48. Menéndez, "Yucatán y Cuba," 106–7.

49. Pérez, 51, 53.

50. Quoted in Pérez, 51.

51. Pérez, 52.

52. Quoted in Pérez, 52.

53. Menéndez, "Yucatán y Cuba," 105; Menéndez, *La primera emigración*, 32–33.

54. Menéndez, "Yucatán y Cuba," 105. Stories of such experiences as playing chess and talking of politics and literature with these men are described in some detail in Alfonso Herrera Franyutti, *Martí en México: Recuerdos de una época* (Mexico City: A. Mijares, 1969), 76–78.

55. Menéndez, *La primera emigración*, 32–33.

56. Ramón de Armas, "José Martí: El apoyo desde México," *Universidad de la Habana* 219 (1983): 81.

57. Armas, "Las guerras cubanas," 268.

58. Armas, 273.

59. Armas, "José Martí," 88.

60. Alfonso Herrera Franyutti, "Cartas de José Marti," *Cuadernos Americanos* 3.27 (1991): 206.

▼▼▼

61. Quoted in Herrera Franyutti, "José Martí y Porfirio Díaz, 1894," *Cuadernos Americanos* 3.27 (1991): 215.

62. Herrera Franyutti, "José Martí y Porfirio Díaz, 1894," 214.

63. Armas, "Las guerras cubanas," 272.

64. Armas, "Las guerras cubanas," 272.

65. Herrera Franyutti, "José Martí y Porfirio Díaz, 1894," 217.

66. Rojas, 783.

67. Rojas, 783. From February 1895 to March 1896, Mexico was neutral. From March 1896 to June 1896, Mexico attempted mediation. For the duration of the war, Mexico was neutral, leaning more toward Spain.

68. Pérez, *Cuba and the United States*, 77, 78.

69. Pérez, *Cuba and the United States*, 79.

70. Rojas, 785.

71. Rojas, 787; Pérez, *Cuba: Between Reform and Revolution*, 165–67.

72. Rojas, 789–90.

73. Rojas, 791.

74. Rojas, 791–92.

75. Rojas, 799–803.

76. Aline Helg, "Race in Argentina and Cuba, 1880–1930: Theory, Policies, and Popular Reaction," *The Idea of Race in Latin America, 1870–1940*, ed. Richard Graham (Austin: University of Texas Press, 1990), 47–48; Rojas, 801–2.

77. Rojas, 801–4.

78. Pérez, *Cuba: Between Reform and Revolution*, 415.

79. Quote from Pérez, *Cuba and the United States*, 78.

80. The increase was from 196 per year to 441 per year. Luis Angel Argüelles Espinosa, "Los refugiados mexicanos en Cuba (1910–1927)," *Palabra y el Hombre* 70 (1983): 117–48.

81. Argüelles Espinosa, 118–19.

82. Argüelles Espinosa, 118–19, 124.

83. Argüelles Espinosa, 121–23.

84. Argüelles Espinosa, 126.

▼▼▼

85. Argüelles Espinosa, 126.

86. Argüelles Espinosa, 127.

87. Argüelles Espinosa, 128.

88. Argüelles Espinosa, 128.

89. Argüelles Espinosa, 134.

90. Argüelles Espinosa, 128–30, 132. Prominent among the Huertista generals residing in Cuba were Manuel Mondragón, Félix Díaz (Porfirio Díaz's nephew),
Rincón Gallardo, and Prisciliano Cortés.

91. Argüelles Espinosa, 131.

92. Argüelles Espinosa, 131.

93. Meyer and Sherman, 599.

94. Angel Gutiérrez, *Lázaro Cárdenas y Cuba* (Michoacán: Universidad Michoacana
de San Nicolás de Hidalgo, 1989), 12.

95. Gutiérrez, 13.

96. Fidel Castro, "A Cárdenas debo la libertad; a Mexico la inspiración, dice Fidel a
la Revista Siempre!" *Siempre!*, August 12, 1959, 32.

97. Pérez, *Cuba: Between Reform and Revolution*, 420.

98. Jon Lee Anderson, *Che Guevara: A Revolutionary Life* (New York: Grove, 1997),
184.

99. Anderson, 195–96.

100. Anderson, 196.

101. Grupo Ateneo IV Centenario, "Carta abierta dirigida al C. Adolfo Ruiz
Cortines, presidente de la república Mexicana," *Excelsior* (Mexico City),
June 29, 1956, 3–4.

102. Comité Ejecutivo del Movimiento Revolucionario Cubano "26 de Julio" en
el exilio, "Carta abierta dirigida al presidente de la república y al pueblo de
México," *Excelsior* (Mexico City), July 9, 1956.

103. Anderson, 200.

104. On Toledano, see Enrique Krauze's *Mexico*, 432–749.

105. House Committee on Un-American Activities, 85th Cong., 2nd sess., February 21,
1958, *Who Are They? Part 8: Vicente Lombardo Toledano and Luis Carlos Prestes
(Mexico-Brazil)*, 2.

▼▼▼

106. House Committee on Un-American Activities, 1.

107. Gilberto Bosques, "Letter to Fulgencio Batista," December 16, 1953, Gilberto Bosque's file folder II–26–14–29, no. 1115.

108. Bosques.

109. National Liberation Movement (MLN), *Programa y llamamiento* (Mexico City: República del Salvador, 1961), 19.

110. Bosques.

111. Batista.

CHAPTER TWO

Epigraph source: quoted in Krauze, *Mexico: Biography of Power*, trans. Hank Heifetz (New York: HarperCollins, 1997), 622.

1. "Béisbol Diplomacy with Cuba," National Security Archive, electronic briefing book, http://www.gwu.edu/~nsarchiv/NSAEBB/NSAEBB12/docs/index.html.

2. Louis A. Pérez, *Cuba: Between Reform and Revolution* (Oxford: Oxford University Press, 1995), 310.

3. Richard Weitz, "Insurgency and Counterinsurgency in Latin America, 1960–1980" *Political Science Quarterly* 101 (1986): 397.

4. Weitz, 398.

5. Weitz, 400–401.

6. Weitz, 400–401. A recent study on Che Guevara's Bolivian adventure can be found in Henry Butterfield Ryan's *The Fall of Che Guevara: A Story of Soldiers, Spies, and Diplomats* (Oxford: Oxford University Press, 1999). Ryan asserts that the average Bolivian citizen did not identify with Guevara's movement and even trusted the Bolivian and U.S. government troops in the country more at the time.

7. Weitz, 413.

8. For a comprehensive description of this, see Omar Cabezas, *Fire from the Mountain: The Making of a Sandinista*, trans. Kathleen Weaver (New York: Crown, 1985), 21–31.

9. Paco Ignacio Taibo II, *Guevara: Also Known as Che*, trans. Martin Roberts (New York: St. Martin's, 1997), 74.

10. Weitz, 413.

▼▼▼

11. Weitz, 413.

12. Weitz, 413.

13. Weitz, 413.

14. Quoted in Pérez, *Cuba*, 310.

15. Pérez, *Cuba*, 310–11.

16. Weitz, 411–12.

17. Cole Blasier, *The Hovering Giant: U.S. Responses to Revolutionary Change in Latin America, 1910–1985*, rev. ed. (Pittsburgh, University of Pittsburgh, 1985).

18. Enrique Krauze, *Mexico: Biography of Power*, trans. Hank Heifetz (New York: HarperCollins, 1997), 654–55.

19. John Dinges, *The Condor Years: How Pinochet and His Allies Brought Terrorism to Three Continents* (New York: New Press, 2005).

20. On Castro's kangaroo courts, curtailment of freedoms, executions, etc., see Hugh Thomas, *Cuba, or, The Pursuit of Freedom* (New York: Da Capo Press, 1998), book 9; for Argentina, see Marguerite Feitlowitz, *A Lexicon of Terror: Argentina and the Legacies of Torture* (Oxford: Oxford University Press, 1999); for Guatemala, see, among others, the report by the Archdiocese of Guatemala, *Guatemala: Never Again!* (New York: Orbis, 1999); and for El Salvador and Nicaragua, see William Leogrande's *Our Own Backyard: The United States in Central America, 1977–1992* (Chapel Hill: University of North Carolina Press, 1998).

21. Krauze, 649.

22. Krauze, 649.

23. Lázaro Cárdenas, "Carta a Miguel A. Duque de Estrada," January 5, 1960, in *Epistolario de Lázaro Cárdenas*, ed. Elena Vázquez Gómez, vol. 2 (Mexico City: Siglo 21, 1975), 96.

24. Of course, he was stopped at the Mexico City airport before he could board the plane to Havana. On activism, see Arthur K. Smith, "Mexico and the Cuban Revolution: Foreign Policy-Making under President Adolfo López Mateos" (Ph. D. diss., Cornell University, 1970), 61, and Nacional Liberation Movement (MLN), *Programa y llamamiento* (Mexico City: República del Salvador, 1961). For letters, see Cárdenas. For Bay of Pigs, see Smith, 93.

25. Fidel Castro, "A Cárdenas debo la libertad; a Mexico la inspiración, dice Fidel a la Revista Siempre!" *Siempre!* August 12, 1959, 32.

26. Castro, 32.

▼▼▼

27. For Zapata's agrarian reform program, see Alan Knight's two-volume study, *The Mexican Revolution* (Lincoln: University of Nebraska Press, 1990); and for explanation of its implementation by Obregon, Calles, and Cárdenas, see chapters 14–16 in Krauze.

28. Krauze, 242.

29. Krauze, 484.

30. Krauze, 473–75.

31. Pérez, *Cuba: Between Reform and Revolution*, 320.

32. Pérez, 320.

33. Pérez, 320.

34. Delegación Mexicana al Encuentro de la Solidaridad con Cuba, "Cuba es el Ejemplo Actual de América," *Política*, May 15, 1960, 17.

35. Delegación Mexicana, 17–20.

36. Smith, 83.

37. Smith, 65–70.

38. Quoted in Olga Pellicer de Brody, *México y la revolución cubana* (Guanajuato: Colegio de México, 1972), 99.

39. Pellicer de Brody, 96–99.

40. MLN, 5.

41. Quoted in MLN, 5.

42. MLN, 5.

43. Krauze, 650.

44. Smith, 61; Krauze, 652.

45. Krauze, 652.

46. Krauze, 650; Dan La Botz, *Democracy in Mexico: Peasant Rebellion and Political Reform* (Boston: South End Press, 1995), 87–89.

47. MLN, 13.

48. MLN, 14.

49. Angel Bracho's lasting influence in Mexico is evidenced by the fact that the bicentennial celebrations of the birth of Benito Juárez in March 2006 began with a guided official tour of a courtyard (across the street from the Benito

▼▼▼

Juárez monument in the Parque Alameda in Mexico City) full of Bracho's lithographs honoring the life of Benito Juárez. Bracho's militant leftist workshop, Taller de Gráfica Popular, which he headed from 1961–63, developed out of the Sindicato de Obreros, Técnicos, Pintores, Escultores y Grabadores Revolucionarios de México, a leftist group that included such famous leftist muralists as Diego Rivera, José Clemente Orozco, and David Alfaro Siqueiros (Consejo Nacional para la Cultura y las Artes, "60 Años del Taller de la Gráfica Popular, extensa revisión del papel del grabado en México," http://www.cnca .gob.mx/cnca/nuevo/diarias/310398/60anosde.html).

50. MLN, 20.

51. MLN, 20.

52. MLN, 20, 21.

53. MLN, 21.

54. MLN, 68–71.

55. Cárdenas, "Carta a Fidel Castro," December 14, 1961, 130.

56. Popular Socialist Party (PPS), *Al pueblo mexicano: Defender a Cuba es defender a Mexico y América Latina* (Mexico City: Ediciones del Partido Popular Socialista, 1961).

57. PPS, 7, 8.

58. PPS, 9.

59. This proposal failed. See Smith, 92–96.

60. Pellicer de Brody, 108–10.

61. Smith, 94–96. Although Mexico generally adhered to these policies, it violated them on three occasions: when it refused to recognize Francisco Franco's regime in Spain in the 1930s, Anastasio Somoza Debayle's regime in Nicaragua in 1979, and the belligerency status of the Farabundo Martí National Liberation Front (FMLN) and other guerrilla factions of El Salvador in the 1980s.

62. Smith, 93.

63. "Independencia de México," *Independencia* (Havana), September 16, 1961, in Gilberto Bosques's file, III 26–14–29, Archivo de Concentraciones, Secretaría de Relaciones Exteriores (SRE), Mexico City.

64. "Independencia de México."

65. Pellicer de Brody, 101.

66. Krauze, 655.

▼▼▼

67. Author unspecified, special to the *New York Times*, "A Warning on Cuba Stirs Mexico City," *New York Times*, May 26, 1961.

68. Author unspecified, special to the *New York Times*, "A Warning on Cuba Stirs Mexico City," *New York Times*, May 26, 1961.

69. Paul P. Kennedy, "Mexican Rightists Ask Inquiry on Cárdenas' Pro-Cuba Action," *New York Times*, May 29, 1961, 6.

70. No author, special to the *New York Times*, "A Warning on Cuba Stirs Mexico City," *New York Times*, May 26, 1961.

71. Kennedy.

72. Kennedy.

73. Kennedy.

74. Kennedy.

75. The MHN is cited in Smith but without explanation of the acronym.

76. Pellicer de Brody, 70; Andres Oppenheimer, *Bordering on Chaos: Mexico's Roller-Coaster Journey toward Prosperity* (Boston: Little, Brown, 1998), 93.

77. Smith, 100.

78. CRAC, "Otra disposición tiránica contra el pueblo cubano," *Mensaje Quincenal* (Monterrey, Mexico), November 10, 1961, 1, 4.

79. CRAC, "Un padre de 10 hijos explica cómo escapó de las garras de Fidel Castro," *Mensaje Quincenal*, March 20, 1962, 4.

80. CRAC, "Congreso comunista en Monterrey," *Mensaje Quincenal*, May 31, 1962, 1.

81. CRAC, "Congreso comunista en Monterrey."

82. CRAC, "Intensificación de la 'Guerra Fría' entre pueblo y gobierno de México," *Mensaje Quincenal*, May 31, 1962, 7.

83. CRAC, "La Gestapo Cubana en México?" *Mensaje Quincenal*, May 8, 1962, 3.

84. CRAC, "La Gestapo Cubana."

CHAPTER THREE

Epigraph source: Senate Committee on the Judiciary, "Documents of the Latin-American Conference for National Sovereignty, Economic Emancipation and Peace," in *Cuban Aftermath—Red Seeds Blow South: Implications for the United States of the Latin American Conference for National Sovereignty and Economic Emancipation and Peace*, 87th Cong., 1st sess., 1961, 52.

▼▼▼

1. Robert A. Pastor, *Exiting the Whirlpool: U.S. Foreign Policy toward Latin America and the Caribbean*, 2nd ed. (Boulder, CO: Westview, 2001), 207. For examples and theoretical analyses of Cold War Third World solidarity movements, such as the Non-Aligned Movement, see Robert Young's *Postcolonialism: An Historical Introduction* (Malden, MA: Blackwell, 2001), 192 and chapter 16. For specifics about Cuba's Africa campaigns, namely in Zaire, Guinnea-Bissau, and Angola, see Piero Gleijeses's *Conflicting Missions: Havana, Washington, and Africa, 1959–1976* (Chapel Hill: University of North Carolina Press, 2002), and for details about Cuban involvement in Latin American revolutionary movements, namely in Chile, Nicaragua, and Bolivia, see Jorge G. Castañeda, *Utopia Unarmed: the Latin American Left after the Cold War* (New York: Knopf, 1993), 57–59, 60, 63–67, 74, 81–89, 97–98.

2. Jorge I. Domínguez, *To Make the World Safe for Revolution: Cuba's Foreign Policy* (Cambridge: Harvard University Press, 1989), 20. For the roots of the Cuban Revolution and the road to Cuban Communism in the aftermath of the revolution, see Hugh Thomas's *Cuba, or, The Pursuit of Freedom* (New York: Da Capo, 1998), books 8 and 11.

3. U.S. Department of State, briefing paper, biographic data, "Antonio Carrillo Flores, Ambassador to the United States," February 1959, records of President Dwight D. Eisenhower, White House central files, confidential file, 1953–61, box 35.

4. Antonio Carrillo Flores, oral history files, Lyndon Baines Johnson Presidential Library, Austin, TX.

5. U.S. Department of State, briefing paper, biographic data, "Adolfo López Mateos, President of Mexico," February 1959, records of President Dwight D. Eisenhower, White House central files, confidential file, 1953–61, box 35.

6. Examples abound in the CIA's intelligence reports, such as the following: director of the CIA, "Security Conditions in Mexico," special national intelligence estimate, #81–62, June 13, 1962, national security file, country file, Mexico, box 60, 1, Lyndon Baines Johnson Presidential Library, Austin, TX; director of the CIA, "Developments Relative to President Johnson's Trip to Mexico," intelligence memorandum, national security file, country file, Mexico, background cables and joint communiqué file, 10/26–28/67, box 62, 1, Lyndon Baines Johnson Presidential Library, Austin, TX.

7. U.S. Department of State, position paper, "Communism in Mexico," February 1959, records of President Dwight D. Eisenhower, White House central files, confidential file, 1953–61, box 369.

8. U.S. Department of State, "Communism in Mexico."

▼▼▼

9. Pérez, *Cuba: Between Reform and Revolution* (Oxford: Oxford University Press, 1995), 421; Alexandr Fursenko and Timothy Naftali, *One Hell of a Gamble: Khrushchev, Castro, and Kennedy, 1958–1964* (New York: W. W. Norton, 1997).

10. Angel Gutiérrez, *Lázaro Cárdenas y Cuba* (Michoacán: Universidad Michoacana de San Nicolás de Hidalgo, 1989), delves deeply into Cárdenas's significance in Castro's Cuba.

11. Senate Committee on the Judiciary, 4, 9; Senate, Committee on the Judiciary, appendix 1, 25, 26.

12. The actual wording of the official purpose follows: "To establish a common policy which will enable the people of Latin America to play the part, for themselves and for all mankind, which devolves on them at this historical moment." See Senate Committee on the Judiciary, appendix 1, 22.

13. Joseph F. Thorning, "Castro: The Brute Facts," *National Review* 9.26, December 1960, 412–13; Senate Committee on the Judiciary, 3.

14. Senate Committee on the Judiciary, 5.

15. Senate Committee on the Judiciary, 5.

16. Senate Committee on the Judiciary, 13.

17. Senate Committee on the Judiciary, appendix 1, 25, 26.

18. Senate Committee on the Judiciary, appendix 1, 25, 26.

19. Thorning, 413.

20. Thorning, 413.

21. Philip Burnham, "No Communism in Mexico," *National Review* 9.26, December 1960, 335–37.

22. Burnham, 335–37.

23. Burnham, 335–37.

24. Burnham, 335–37.

25. This connection is mentioned in Paul P. Kennedy, "Mexican Rightists Ask Inquiry on Cárdenas' Pro-Cuba Action," *New York Times*, May 29, 1961, and the roots of the Sinarquist and PAN movements can be found in Enrique Krauze, *Mexico Biography of Power*, trans. Hank Heifetz (New York: HarperCollins, 1997), 504–7.

26. See full-text articles in Senate Committee on the Judiciary, appendix 1, 26–31.

▼▼▼

27. Sergio Aguayo, *Myths and [Mis]perceptions: Changing U.S. Elite Visions of Mexico*, trans. Julián Brody (La Jolla: Center for U.S.-Mexican Studies, University of California, San Diego, 1998), 263.

28. Aguayo, appendix A, figures 20, 33.

29. Senate Committee on Judiciary, *Communist Threat to the United States through the Caribbean*, part 13, 87th Cong., 1st sess., March 1961, 858.

30. This discussion is based on the findings in Senate Committee on Judiciary, *Communist Threat to the United States through the Caribbean*, parts 12 and 13.

31. Senate Committee on Judiciary, *Communist Threat to the United States through the Caribbean*, parts 12 and 13.

32. Senate Committee on Judiciary, *Communist Threat to the United States through the Caribbean*, part 13, 831–37.

33. House Committee on Un-American Activities, *Who are They? Part 8: Vicente Lombardo Toledano and Luis Carlos Prestes (Mexico-Brazil)*, 85th Cong., 1st sess., February 21, 1958.

34. The end of chapter 1 details this subject using House Committee on Un-American Activities, *Who are They? Vicente Lombardo Toledano and Luis Carlos Prestes.*

35. Senate, Committee on Judiciary, *Communist Threat to the United States through the Caribbean*, part 13, 833.

36. Senate Committee on Judiciary, *Communist Threat to the United States through the Caribbean*, part 13, 834.

37. Hill testified that Wieland was in fact his superior. Senate Committee on Judiciary, *Communist Threat to the United States through the Caribbean*, part 13, 832.

38. Senate Committee on Judiciary, *Communist Threat to the United States through the Caribbean*, part 13, 847.

39. Senate Committee on Judiciary, *Communist Threat to the United States through the Caribbean*, part 13, 848.

40. Senate Committee on Judiciary, *Communist Threat to the United States through the Caribbean*, part 13, 844–45.

41. Senate Committee on Judiciary, *Communist Threat to the United States through the Caribbean*, part 13, 845.

42. Senate Committee on Judiciary, *Communist Threat to the United States through the Caribbean*, part 13, 849.

▼▼▼

43. Senate Committee on Judiciary, *Communist Threat to the United States through the Caribbean*, part 13, 855.

44. Senate Committee on Judiciary, *Communist Threat to the United States through the Caribbean*, part 13, 855.

45. Senate Committee on Judiciary, *Communist Threat to the United States through the Caribbean*, part 13, 856.

46. Senate Committee on Judiciary, *Communist Threat to the United States through the Caribbean*, 856.

47. Senate Committee on Judiciary, *Communist Threat to the United States through the Caribbean*, part 13, 858.

48. Senate Committee on Judiciary, *Communist Threat to the United States through the Caribbean*, part 13, 859.

49. Senate Committee on Judiciary, *Communist Threat to the United States through the Caribbean*, part 13, 860.

50. Senate Committee on Judiciary, *Communist Threat to the United States through the Caribbean*, part 13, 860.

51. Senate Committee on Judiciary, *Communist Threat to the United States through the Caribbean*, part 12, 794.

52. Senate Committee on Judiciary, *Communist Threat to the United States through the Caribbean*, part 12, 794.

53. Senate Committee on Judiciary, *Communist Threat to the United States through the Caribbean*, part 12, 795.

54. Senate Committee on Judiciary, *Communist Threat to the United States through the Caribbean*, part 12, 796.

55. Senate Committee on Judiciary, *Communist Threat to the United States through the Caribbean*, part 12, 799.

56. Senate Committee on Judiciary, *Communist Threat to the United States through the Caribbean*, part 12, 802–4.

57. Senate Committee on Judiciary, *Communist Threat to the United States through the Caribbean*, part 12, 813.

58. Senate Committee on Judiciary, *Communist Threat to the United States through the Caribbean*, part 12, 813.

▼▼▼

Chapter Four

Epigraph source: Dean Rusk, "Memorandum for the President," Department of State, February 18, 1964, in Kate Doyle, "Double Dealing: Mexico's Foreign Policy toward Cuba," National Security Archive, electronic briefing book, http://www.gwu.edu/~nsarchiv/NSAEBB/NSAEBB83/index.htm.

1. Senate Committee on Foreign Relations, *Inter-American Relations: A Collection of Documents, Legislation, Descriptions of Inter-American Organizations, and Other Material Pertaining to Inter-American Affairs*, 100th Cong, 2d sess., 1988, 224. For 1967 Protocol, see "Third Special Inter-American Conference, Buenos Aires, Argentina, approved the Protocol of Amendments to the Charter of the OAS," in Senate Committee on Foreign Relations, 221.

2. Senate Committee on Foreign Relations, 224.

3. CRAC, "La 'CRAC' se dirige al presidente en Carta Abierta," *Mensaje Quincenal* (Monterrey, Mexico), January 20, 1962, 1.

4. CRAC, "El régimen comunista de Castro expulsado del seno de la O.E.A.," *Mensaje Quincenal*, February 5, 1962, 3.

5. Dean Rusk, "American Republics Unite to Halt the Spread of Communism in Western Hemisphere," *U.S. State Department Bulletin* 46.1182, February 19, 1962, 270.

6. Delegation of Mexico, in *U.S. State Department Bulletin*, 283.

7. Adolfo Leyva de Varona, "Cuban-Mexican Relations During the Castro Era" (Ph.D. diss., University of Miami, 1994), 138–40.

8. Enrique Krauze, *Mexico: Biography of Power*, trans. Hank Heifetz (New York: HarperCollins, 1997), 656.

9. Leyva de Varona, 139–40.

10. Arthur K. Smith, "Mexico and the Cuban Revolution: Foreign Policy-Making under President Adolfo López Mateos" (Ph.D. diss. Cornell University, 1970), 161–63.

11. CRAC, "El régimen comunista de Castro expulsado del seno de la O.E.A.," 3.

12. CRAC, "El socialismo, municipal y estatal, factor para explotar, el trabajo por medio del jornal," *Mensaje Quincenal*, March 20, 1962, 2.

13. CRAC, "Dividir al campo es dividir al pais," *Mensaje Quincenal*, October 1, 1962, 3.

14. CRAC, "La 'CRAC' se Dirige al Presidente en Carta Abierta," 2.

▼▼▼

15. Adolfo López Mateos, *Tres informes de gobierno* (Mexico City: Editorial La Justicia, 1961), 261.

16. Adolfo López Mateos, *Cinco informes de gobierno* (Juárez, Mexico: Novaro Editores, 1964), 233.

17. Smith, 177–81.

18. Gilberto Bosques, "Letter from Bosques to Rosenweig Díaz, Jr.," March 23, 1963, Gilberto Bosques's file, III 26–14–29, Archivo de Concentraciones de la Secretaría de Relaciones Exteriores (SRE), Mexico City.

19. "Juárez," *El Mundo*, March 21, 1963, in Gilberto Bosques's file, III 26–14–29, Archivo de Concentraciones, SRE, Mexico City.

20. Olga Pellicer de Brody, *México y la revolución cubana* (Guanajuato: Colegio de México, 1972), 32.

21. Michael Meyer and William S. Sherman, *The Course of Mexican History*, 6th ed. (Oxford: Oxford University Press, 1995), 652.

22. Smith, 134.

23. Quoted in Smith, 92.

24. Leyva de Varona, 143.

25. Smith, 194.

26. Leyva de Varona, 144.

27. Pellicer de Brody, 108–10.

28. Pellicer de Brody, 36.

29. Leyva de Varona, 140–41.

30. Krauze, 656.

31. Smith, 194.

32. Pellicer de Brody, 37.

33. Quoted in Pellicer de Brody, 37.

34. Mario Ojeda Gómez, "Las relaciones de México con el régimen revolucionario cubano," *Foro Internacional* 56 (1974): 482.

35. Raymond Graves, "Mexican Foreign Policy toward Cuba and its Impact on U.S.-Mexican Relations, 1970–1982" (Ph.D. diss., University of Miami, 1985), 29.

36. Pellicer de Brody, 118.

▼▼▼

37. Graves, 29.

38. Osvaldo Dorticós Torrado, *Cuba in the Second Conference of Non-Aligned Nations* (Republic of Cuba: Foreign Ministry, Information Department, 1964), 48. Chilean President Salvador Allende resumed relations with Cuba after his electoral victory in 1970. See Michael Erisman, *Cuba's Foreign Relations in a Post-Soviet World* (Gainesville: University of Florida Press, 2000), 83; the Non-Aligned Movement, January 2002, http://www.nam.gov.za/background/members.htm.

39. Cited in Dorticós, 67.

40. Dorticós, 16. At this time, Castro was officially the prime minister and later became the president.

41. In December 1970, Socialist Chilean President Salvador Allende resumed relations with Cuba. Over the next decade, Peru, Barbados, Guyana, Jamaica, Trinidad and Tabago, Argentina, Panama, Venezuela, Colombia, Costa Rica, Ecuador, St. Lucia, and Suriname established relations with Cuba (Erisman).

42. Dean Rusk, "Memorandum for the President."

43. Dean Rusk, "Memorandum for the President."

44. Telephone conversation between Secretary Rusk and President Johnson, November 12, 1964, in Kate Doyle, "Double Dealing."

45. Gustavo Díaz Ordaz, Lyndon B. Johnson, Antonio Carrillo Flores, and Thomas Mann, "Memorandum of Conversation," November 12, 1964, U.S. Department of State, in Kate Doyle, "Double Dealing."

46. Gustavo Díaz Ordaz et al.

47. Gustavo Díaz Ordaz et al.

48. Attachment, "Memorandum of Conversation," "Double Dealing."

49. Gilberto Bosques, "Acervo histórico diplomático," Gilberto Bosques's file, III 26–14–29, no. 1115, Archivo de Concentraciones, SRE, Mexico City.

50. Paul D. Bethel, ed., "The Organization of American States, and U.S. Policy (Interpretive)," *Free Cuba News*, Washington, D.C., July 17, 1964, 8.

51. Bethel, 7.

52. Bethel, 7.

CHAPTER FIVE

Epigraph source: John H. Crimmins, "Meeting of Presidents Johnson and López Mateos in California, February 20–22, 1964: Talking Points: U.S.-Mexican Cooperation on Cuba," national security file, country file, Mexico, Mexico briefing book–Mateos visit, 2/20–22/64, box 61, 2, 3, Lyndon Baines Johnson Presidential Library, Austin, TX.

1. Robert Jones Shafer and Donald Mabry, *Neighbors—Mexico and the United States: Wetbacks and Oil* (Chicago: Nelson Hall, 1981), 1.

2. Jorge I. Domínguez and Rafael Fernández de Castro, eds., *The United States and Mexico: Between Partnership and Conflict* (New York: Routledge, 2001), 36–37.

3. Domínguez and de Castro, 36–37.

4. American Embassy, Mexico City, "Exposure of Mexican Passport Fraud May Affect Training of Subversives in Cuba," U.S State Department airgram, January 22, 1964, national security file, country file, Mexico, box 60, vol. 1, Lyndon Baines Johnson Presidential Library, Austin, TX.

5. Crimmins, 2.

6. Crimmins, 2.

7. Crimmins, 3.

8. Robert W. Adam, counselor of embassy, Mexico City, U.S. State Department airgram, "Mexican Second Secretary Causes Dispute at Airport," February 17, 1964, national security file, country file, Cuba, box 54, vol. 1, Lyndon Baines Johnson Presidential Library, Austin, TX.

9. Adam.

10. Adam.

11. American Embassy, Mexico City, U.S. State Department airgram, "Authorities Seize Cuban Propaganda at Airport," October 30, 1964, national security file, country file, Cuba, box 54, vol. 1, Lyndon Baines Johnson Presidential Library, Austin, TX.

12. American Embassy, Mexico City, U.S. State Department airgram, "Authorities Seize Cuban Propaganda at Airport."

13. American Embassy, Mexico City, U.S. State Department airgram, "Authorities Seize Cuban Propaganda at Airport."

14. Bob Sayre, "Letter from Bob Sayre to National Security Advisor, McGeorge Bundy," July 7, 1964, national security file, country file, Mexico, box 54, vol. 1, Lyndon Baines Johnson Presidential Library, Austin, TX.

▼▼▼

15. Sayre.

16. Paul S. Dwyer, American consul, Mérida, Yucatán, U.S. State Department airgram, "Cuban Involvement in Recent Civil Disturbance in Yucatan," February 10, 1965, national security file, country file, Cuba, box 54, 1:2, Lyndon Baines Johnson Presidential Library, Austin, TX.

17. Dwyer, 2.

18. Dwyer, 2.

19. Dwyer, 2.

20. American Consulate, Mérida, Yucatán, U.S. State Department airgram, "Indications of New Attitude of Mexican Military Authorities with Respect to Cuban Fishing Vessels," April 12, 1965, national security file, country file, Cuba, box 53, vol. 4, Lyndon Baines Johnson Presidential Library, Austin, TX.

21. American Consulate, Mérida, Yucatán, U.S. State Department airgram, "Indications of New Attitude of Mexican Military Authorities with Respect to Cuban Fishing Vessels."

22. American Consulate, Mérida, Yucatán, U.S. State Department airgram, "Indications of New Attitude of Mexican Military Authorities with Respect to Cuban Fishing Vessels."

23. American Consulate, Mérida, Yucatán, U.S. State Department airgram, "Indications of New Attitude of Mexican Military Authorities with Respect to Cuban Fishing Vessels."

24. American Consulate, Mérida, Yucatán, U.S. State Department airgram, "Indications of New Attitude of Mexican Military Authorities with Respect to Cuban Fishing Vessels."

25. Secretary's delegation to the twentieth session of United Nations General Assembly, New York, September–October 1965, Memorandum of Conversation, "LA Nuclear Free Zone and Cuba," national security file, country file, Mexico, box 59, 1:2, Lyndon Baines Johnson Presidential Library, Austin, TX.

26. Secretary's delegation, 2.

27. Secretary's delegation, 2.

28. Director of the CIA, "Security Conditions in Mexico," Special National Intelligence Estimate, Number 81–66, 07 April 1966, national security file, country file, Mexico, box 60, 2, 3, Lyndon Baines Johnson Presidential Library, Austin, TX.

▼▼▼

29. Director of the CIA, "Developments Relative to President Johnson's Trip to Mexico," intelligence memorandum, national security file, country file, Mexico, background cables and joint communiqué file, 10/26–28/67, box 62, 1, Lyndon Baines Johnson Presidential Library, Austin, TX.

30. American Embassy, Mexico City, secret airgram, "Guerrilla Problem in Latin America," June 10, 1967, in Kate Doyle, "Double Dealing: Mexico's Foreign Policy toward Cuba," National Security Archive, electronic briefing book, http://www.gwu.edu/~nsarchiv/NSAEBB/NSAEBB83/index.htm; on Mexican guerrillas, see "Confidential Report on Ambassador Pamanes," September 1971, Fernando Pamanes Escobedo's files, III 2940–2, no. 281, 10, Archivo de Concentraciones de la Secretaría de Relaciones Exteriores (SRE), Mexico City.

31. American Embassy, Mexico City, secret airgram, "Conversation between Embassy Officer and Mexican Ambassador to Cuba" June 10, 1967, in Doyle.

32. Secretaría de Relaciones Exteriores, "Memorandum para información del Presidente," February 24, 1966, Fernando Pamanes Escobedo's files, file III 2822–9, Archivo de Concentraciones, SRE, Mexico City.

33. Alfonso Herrera Salcedo, Secretaría de Relaciones Exteriores, "Letter to Fernando Pamanes Escobedo," February 14, 1967, and "Memorandum para información del Señor Presidente," February 10, 1967, Fernando Pamanes Escobedo's files, III 3056–1, Archivo de Concentraciones, SRE, Mexico City.

34. Pamanes, "Letter to the Secretaría de Relaciones Exteriores," January 26, 1967, Fernando Pamanes Escobedo's files, III 3056–1, no. 108, Archivo de Concentraciones, SRE, Mexico City.

35. Salcedo, "Letter to Pamanes" and "Memorandum para información del Señor Presidente."

36. Pamanes, "Letter to Secretaría de Relaciones Exteriores," February 28, 1967, Fernando Pamanes Escobedo's files, III 3056–1, nos. 221, 231, Archivo de Concentraciones, SRE, Mexico City.

37. Salcedo, "Letter to Pamanes," March 5, 1967, Fernando Pamanes Escobedo's files, III 3056–1, no. 222, Archivo de Concentraciones, SRE, Mexico City.

38. Pamanes, *Llamamiento a la juventud,* "Letter to the Mexican Foreign Secretariat," April 12, 1967, in Doyle.

39. Henry Dearborn, "Memorandum: Conversation between Embassy Officer and Mexican Ambassador to Cuba," U.S. State Department, June 10, 1967, in Doyle.

▼▼▼

40. Pamanes, "Letter to Secretaría de Relaciones Exteriores," April 17, 1967, Fernando Pamanes Escobedo's files, III 3056–1, no. 414:1, Archivo de Concentraciones, SRE, Mexico City.

41. Pamanes, "Letter to Secretaría de Relaciones Exteriores," April 17, 1967, 2.

42. Pamanes, "Letter to Secretaría de Relaciones Exteriores," April 17, 1967, 2.

43. Pamanes, "Letter to Secretaría de Relaciones Exteriores," April 21, 1967, Fernando Pamanes Escobedo's files, III 3056–1, no. 426, Archivo de Concentraciones, SRE, Mexico City.

44. Pamanes, "Letter to Secretaría de Relaciones Exteriores," May 9, 1967, Fernando Pamanes Escobedo's files, III 3056–1, no. 459-B15, Archivo de Concentraciones, SRE, Mexico City.

45. Pamanes, "Letter to Secretaría de Relaciones Exteriores," *Semana de Solidaridad con los Pueblos Latinoamericanos*, May 10, 1967, Fernando Pamanes Escobedo's files, III 3056–1, no. 469, Archivo de Concentraciones, SRE, Mexico City.

46. Dearborn.

47. Dearborn.

48. Dearborn.

49. Dearborn.

50. Dearborn.

51. Dearborn.

52. Dearborn.

53. Dearborn.

54. Pamanes, "Letter to Secretaría de Relaciones Exteriores," July 4, 1967, Fernando Pamanes Escobedo's files, III 3056–1, Archivo de Concentraciones, SRE, Mexico City.

55. Secretaría de Relaciones Exteriores, "Confidential Report on Ambassador Pamanes," 2.

56. Secretaría de Relaciones Exteriores, "Confidential Report on Ambassador Pamanes," 3.

57. Secretaría de Relaciones Exteriores, "Confidential Report on Ambassador Pamanes," 3.

58. Secretaría de Relaciones Exteriores, "Confidential Report on Ambassador Pamanes," 4.

59. Secretaría de Relaciones Exteriores, "Confidential Report on Ambassador Pamanes," 4.

60. Secretaría de Relaciones Exteriores, "Confidential Report on Ambassador Pamanes," 4.

61. Secretaría de Relaciones Exteriores, "Confidential Report on Ambassador Pamanes," 4.

62. Secretaría de Relaciones Exteriores, "Confidential Report on Ambassador Pamanes," 6.

63. Secretaría de Relaciones Exteriores, "Confidential Report on Ambassador Pamanes," 6.

64. Secretaría de Relaciones Exteriores, "Confidential Report on Ambassador Pamanes," 6.

65. Secretaría de Relaciones Exteriores, "Confidential Report on Ambassador Pamanes," 6–7.

66. Secretaría de Relaciones Exteriores, "Confidential Report on Ambassador Pamanes," 7.

67. Victor Alfonso Maldonado, "Letter to Secretaría de Relaciones Exteriores," April 14, 1970, Fernando Pamanes Escobedo's files, III 2940–2, no. 369–70, Archivo de Concentraciones, SRE, Mexico City.

68. *Granma, El insólito caso del espía de la CIA bajo el manto de funcionario de la embajada de México en Cuba* (Havana: Instituto del Libro, 1969), 19. Ana Covarrubias Velasco has covered some aspects of Colón's situation in "A Case for Mutual Nonintervention," *Cuban Studies* 26 (1996): 134–35.

69. *Granma,* 4–6.

70. *Granma,* 5.

71. Dearborn.

72. Covián, "Confidential Letter to Secretario de Relaciones Exteriores Antonio Carrillo Flores," March 21, 1968, Fernando Pamanes Escobedo's files, III 3075–3, no. 244, 1, Archivo de Concentraciones, SRE, Mexico City.

73. Covián, 2.

74. Covián, 3.

75. Covián, 3.

76. Covián, 3.

▼▼▼

77. Covián, 3.

78. Covián, 3.

79. "Vengo de un pais libre y llego a un pais libre," *El Mundo* (Havana), September 12, 1967.

80. American Embassy, Mexico City, confidential telegram, "Change of Mexican Ambassadors in Havana," September 7, 1967, 2, in Doyle.

81. American Embassy, Mexico City, confidential telegram, "Change of Mexican Ambassadors in Havana," 3.

82. American Embassy, Mexico City, confidential telegram, "Change of Mexican Ambassadors in Havana," 3.

83. Dearborn, incoming telegram, June 26, 1967, in Doyle.

84. National Christian Movement (MNC), June 1968, 5.28.

85. MNC, June 1968, 5.28.

86. MNC, June 1968, 5.28.

87. MNC, July 1969, 6.39.

88. MNC, May 1969, 6.37.

89. Fourth anniversary of attack issue, MNC, October 1969, 6.42.

90. MNC, July 1968, 5.29.

91. Don Bohning, "Cubans Here Push Anti-Red Terror," *Miami Herald*, August 1, 1965.

92. Bohning.

93. Bohning.

94. Bohning.

95. Bohning.

96. MNC, July 1968, 5.29.

97. MNC, Sept. 1969, 6.41.

98. MNC, Sept. 1969, 6.41.

99. MNC, Sept. 1969, 6.41.

100. MNC, Sept. 1969, 6.41.

101. Centro de Investigación Científica Jorge L. Tamayo, ed, *México y Cuba: Dos pueblos unidos en la historia*, 2 vols. (Mexico City: Centro de Investigación Científica Jorge L. Tamayo, 1982).

102. Mexican Anti-Communist Federation (FEMACO), *Federacion Mexicana Anticomunista de Occidente: Su fundacion, sus actividades iniciales* (Mexico City: Editorial Luz, 1967).

103. FEMACO, 21.

104. FEMACO, 23.

105. Scott Anderson, and Jon Lee Anderson, *Inside the League* (New York: Dodd, Mead, 1986), 77, 79.

106. FEMACO, 58.

107. Anderson and Anderson, 12.

108. FEMACO, 23.

109. Many other expressions of support for the PRI's Cuba policy can be found in letters, poetry, and speeches; see Alberto Bremauntz's *México y la revolución socialista Cubana* (Morelia, Mexico: Fímax Publicistas, 1966), for an in-depth look at Mexico's solidarity with Cuba's socialist experiment.

110. Bremauntz, 82.

111. Bremauntz, 88.

Chapter Six

Epigraph source: Fidel Castro and Luís Suárez, "1974 Mexican Magazine Interview," February 15, 1974, in *Castro Speech Database, UTLANIC,* http://lanic.utexas.edu/la/cb/cuba/castro.html, abridged version of interview published in the February 15, 1974, edition of *Siempre!*

1. Raymond Graves, "Mexican Foreign Policy toward Cuba and its Impact on U.S.-Mexican Relations, 1970–1982" (Ph.D. diss., University of Miami, 1985), 87; Manuel Tello, *Gira de trabajo del presidente Luís Echeverría Alvarez a catorce paises de America, Africa y Asia, 8 de julio a 22 de agosto, 1975* (Mexico City: Secretaria de Relaciones Exteriores, 1975).

2. Enrique Krauze, *Mexico: Biography of Power*, trans. Hank Heifetz (New York: HarperCollins, 1997), 728.

3. Krauze, 741.

4. For Corpus Cristi, see Krauze, 752; for the most detailed account of the disappearances, see Sergio Aguayo, *La charola: Una historia de los servicios de inteligencia en México* (Mexico City: Grijalbo Mondadori, 2001).

5. Graves, 108.

6. Alan Riding, *Distant Neighbors: A Portrait of the Mexicans* (New York: Vintage, 1985), 347.

7. Riding, 347.

8. Graves, 108.

9. Luís Echeverría Alvarez, *Informe de gobierno IV* (Mexico City: Cultura y Ciencia Política, 1974).

10. Henry A. Kissinger, "The United States and Latin America: the New Opportunity," in *Secretary Henry A. Kissinger before the Combined Service Club*, March 1, 1975, Houston, TX (Washington, D.C.: Government Printing Office, 1975), 3.

11. Graves, 115.

12. Senate, Committee on Foreign Relations, *Inter-American Relations: A Collection of Documents, Legislation, Descriptions of Inter-American Organizations, and Other Material Pertaining to Inter-American Affairs*, 100th Cong., 2nd sess., 1988, 234; Graves, 288.

13. Graves, 288. For the nations who resumed relations with Cuba, see H. Michael Erisman, *Cuba's Foreign Relations in a Post-Soviet World* (Gainesville: University of Florida Press, 2000), 83–225. Chile resumed relations in 1970; Peru, Barbados, Guyana, Jamaica, Trinidad and Tobago in 1972; Argentina in 1973; Panama and Venezuela in 1974; Colombia in 1975; Costa Rica in 1977; Ecuador, St. Lucia, and Suriname in 1979; Bolivia in 1983; Uruguay in 1985; Brazil in 1986.

14. Graves, 116.

15. Graves, 36. SELA stands for Sistema Económico Latinoamericano.

16. Secretaría de Relaciones Exteriores, *Informe de labores, 1974–75: Memoria de la secretaría de relaciones exteriores por el periodo comprendido del 1 de Septiembre de 1974 al 31 de agosto de 1975* (Mexico City, 1975).

17. Henry Kissinger, *Years of Renewal* (New York: Simon and Schuster, 1999), 718.

18. Kissinger, 719.

19. "The Nixon Tapes," June 15, 1972, 10:31 a.m.–12:10 p.m., conversation no. 735–1, cassette nos. 2246–48, Oval Office, National Security Archive.

▼▼▼

20. "The Nixon Tapes."

21. "The Nixon Tapes."

22. "The Nixon Tapes."

23. "Datos biográficos del Señor Licenciado Victor Alfonso Maldonado," January 8, 1970, Victor Maldonado's files, XI 127–1 no. 443, Archivo de Concentraciones de la Secretaría de Relaciones Exteriores (SRE), Mexico City.

24. Victor Alfonso Maldonado, "Letter to Carrillo Flores," April 22, 1970, Victor Maldonado's files, XI 127–1 no. 456, Archivo de Concentraciones, SRE, Mexico City.

25. Maldonado, "Letter to Carrillo Flores."

26. Maldonado, informe político, "Desvío de avión," October 30, 1971, Victor Maldonado's files, III 3154–2, no. 1260, 2, Archivo de Concentraciones, SRE, Mexico City.

27. Maldonado, informe político, "Importancia internacional del Segundo Congreso de la Unión de Jovenes Comunistas, verificando en la Habana del 28 de marzo al 4 de abril del corriente año," April 3, 1972, Victor Maldonado's files, III 3188–7, no. 361, 1, Archivo de Concentraciones, SRE, Mexico City.

28. Maldonado, informe político, "Importancia internacional del Segundo Congreso de la Unión de Jovenes Comunistas, verificando en la Habana del 28 de marzo al 4 de abril del corriente año," 1.

29. Maldonado, informe político, "Importancia internacional del Segundo Congreso de la Unión de Jovenes Comunistas, verificando en la Habana del 28 de marzo al 4 de abril del corriente año," 3.

30. Maldonado, informe político, "Desfile del 10 de mayo y discurso de Fidel Castro," May 2, 1972, Victor Maldonado's files, III 3188–7, no. 479, 6, Archivo de Concentraciones, SRE, Mexico City.

31. Maldonado, informe político, "Notaria actividad diplomática de la cancillería cubana en Africa y en América Latina," September 2, 1972, Victor Maldonado's files, III 3188–7, no. 1039, 1, Archivo de Concentraciones, SRE, Mexico City.

32. Maldonado, informe político, "Notaria actividad diplomática de la cancillería cubana en Africa y en América Latina," 1.

33. Maldonado, informe político, "Notaria actividad diplomática de la cancillería cubana en Africa y en América Latina," 1.

34. Maldonado, informe político, "Notaria actividad diplomática de la cancillería cubana en Africa y en América Latina," 1, 3.

▼▼▼

35. Maldonado, informe político, "Notaria actividad diplomática de la cancillería cubana en Africa y en América Latina," 2.

36. Maldonado, informe político, "Notaria actividad diplomática de la cancillería cubana en Africa y en América Latina," 7–8.

37. Maldonado, informe político, 2, "Baja y grosera campaña de prensa cubana en contra de los Estados Unidos de América," October 30, 1972, Victor Maldonado's files, III 3188–7, no. 1232, p. 1.

38. Maldonado, informe político, 2, "Unidades navales extraordinarias de la URSS visitan con frecuencia el Puerto de la Havana," Victor Maldonado's files, III 3188–7, no. 361, 1, Archivo de Concentraciones, SRE, Mexico City.

39. Maldonado, informe político, 2.

40. Maldonado, informe político, 2.

41. Maldonado, informe político, "Llega a Cuba una delegación del partido comunista de Colombia," June 7, 1973, Victor Maldonado's files, III 3213–1, no. 661, Archivo de Concentraciones, SRE, Mexico City.

42. Maldonado, informe político, "Llega a Cuba una delegación del partido comunista de Colombia."

43. Maldonado, informe político, 2, "El señor presidente Dorticós presidio la delegacion cubana que asistió a la toma de posesion del presidente Argentina Doctor Hector J. Cámpora, aprovechando de este viaje para motivos de propaganda política," June 7, 1973, Victor Maldonado's files, III 3213–1, no. 661, 1, Archivo de Concentraciones, SRE, Mexico City.

44. Maldonado, informe político, 2, "El señor presidente Dorticós presidio la delegacion cubana que asistió a la toma de posesion del presidente Argentina Doctor Hector J. Cámpora, aprovechando de este viaje para motivos de propaganda política,"1.

45. Maldonado, informe político, 2, "El señor presidente Dorticós presidio la delegacion cubana que asistió a la toma de posesion del presidente Argentina Doctor Hector J. Cámpora, aprovechando de este viaje para motivos de propaganda política," 1.

46. Maldonado, informe político, 2, "El señor presidente Dorticós presidio la delegacion cubana que asistió a la toma de posesion del presidente Argentina Doctor Hector J. Cámpora, aprovechando de este viaje para motivos de propaganda política," 1.

47. Maldonado, informe político, 2, "El señor presidente Dorticós presidio la delegacion cubana que asistió a la toma de posesion del presidente Argentina Doctor

Hector J. Cámpora, aprovechando de este viaje para motivos de propaganda política," 2.

48. Maldonado, informe político, 1, "Decepción en los circulos oficiales del gobierno cubano con respecto a la situación política del gobierno argentino," July 4, 1973, Victor Maldonado's files, III 3213–1, no. 777, 1, Archivo de Concentraciones, SRE, Mexico City.

49. Maldonado, informe político, 1, "Decepción en los circulos oficiales del gobierno cubano con respecto a la situación política del gobierno argentino," 1.

50. Quoted in Luis Echeverría, *Presidente Echeverria: Siete Conferencias de Prensa*, 3.

CHAPTER SEVEN

Epigraph source: Nelson Notario Castro, "1988 Speech Castro Speaks in Tuxpan, Notes Event," December 5, 1988, *Castro Speech Database, UTLANIC*, http://lanic .utexas.edu/la/cb/cuba/castro.html.

1. Agustín Velasco García, secretary of foreign relations, FEMACO, "Rockefeller, Kissinger and Others Pretend that the Cuban Bankruptcy be Paid with the Money of the Taxpayers of the United States," Guadalajara, letter, April 12, 1975. For an extensive elaboration on FEMACO's activities and goals, see Mexican Anti-Communist Federation, *Su fundación, sus actividades iniciales*, (Mexico City: Editorial Luz, 1967).

2. Rafael Rodríguez, secretary general, CAL, "Letter to the U.S. Government," Guadalajara, August 16, 1975; Rodríguez, secretary general, CAL, "Letter to the U.S. Government," Guadalajara, August 23, 1975. Neither letter specifies to whom they are addressed, but the contents reveal a desire to appeal to the U.S. government in general.

3. Quote from Walter Lafeber, *Inevitable Revolutions: The United States in Central America* (New York: W. W. Norton, 1993), 336. The following is a list of just a few of WACL's members and participants: General John Singlaub (chair of WACL until 1986, exposed for involvement in the Iran/Contra scandal), Roberto D'Aubuisson (Salvadoran colonel, presidential candidate and alleged death squad leader in the 1980s), North Carolina Senator Jesse Helms, South Carolina Senator Strom Thurman, Lewis Tambs (Reagan's ambassador to Colombia and Costa Rica), and Alberto Piedra (Reagan's ambassador to Guatemala). In addition, presidents Ronald Reagan and George Bush publicly commended the WACL in 1985 and 1989, respectively (Interhemispheric Resource Center, "World Anti-Communist League," October 1990, http://rightweb.irc-online.org/gw/2815).

▼▼▼

4. A thorough search of *Ulrich's International Periodicals Directory* found no citation to *Réplica*, and therefore I cannot report its circulation at this time. However, the magazine cites several affiliated international press services, such as Asian Outlook and WACL Bulletin, whose circulations were forty-five hundred and two thousand, respectively.

5. *Réplica* 109–13, January–May 1979.

6. *Réplica* 109–13, January–May 1979. One example is in César Córdova Olmedo, "Race against Time: Carter and the Communization of Mexico," *Réplica* 109, January 1979, 26.

7. Raymond Graves, "Mexican Foreign Policy toward Cuba and Its Impact on U.S.-Mexican Relations, 1970–1982" (Ph.D. diss., University of Miami, 1985), 160–61.

8. Graves, 191.

9. Graves, 176.

10. Graves, 170.

11. Castro, "Speech Friendship Rally for Mexican President Portillo," August 2, 1980, *Castro Speech Database, UTLANIC*, http://lanic.utexas.edu/la/cb/cuba/castro.html.

12. Castro, "Speech Friendship Rally."

13. Alan Riding, *Distant Neighbors: A Portrait of the Mexicans* (New York: Vintage, 1985), 351–54.

14. Riding, 355.

15. Pablo Huerta G., "Mexico: Paladin of Political Asylum for Communist Guerrillas," *Réplica* 110, February 1979, 22–24; "The People of Mexico Repudiate Marxism," *Réplica* 113, May 1979.

16. Olmedo, 26.

17. FEMACO, *Réplica* 53, November 1973.

18. Mario Valverde, "Why is Mexico Financing Nicaragua's Marxist Literacy Texts?" *Réplica* 135, April 1981, 2.

19. Valverde, 2, 39.

20. Although some politicians claimed that the Sandinistas were running a Communist totalitarian state, some U.S.–Latin American academics have debunked this as propaganda. For example, Cole Blasier, the foremost specialist on USSR policy in Latin America, claims that "By 1985, Soviet relations

▼▼▼

with Nicaragua were closer than with most other non-socialist countries" (*The Giant's Rival: The U.S.S.R. and Latin America*, rev. ed. [Pittsburgh: University of Pittsburgh, 1987], 145); Rodríguez's claims regarding the level of Cuban assistance to Nicaragua are detailed in a transcript of a meeting between U.S. Secretary of State Alexander M. Haig Jr., and Cuban Vice Premier Carlos Rafaél Rodríguez, November 23, 1981, Mexico City, in *Cold War International History Project* 8–9, 9, http://www.wilsoncenter.org/index.cfm?topic_id=1409 &fuseaction=va2.document&identifier=5034EF21-96B6-175C-9C45700AE8493 D87&sort=Collection&item=US-Cuban%20Relations.

21. Transcript, 1.

22. Transcript, 1–18.

23. International Security Council, *Crisis and Response: A Roundtable on Mexico* (New York: International Security Council, 1986), 96.

24. *Crisis and Response*, 96.

25. William Kintner, "Mexico in United States Strategy," in *Crisis and Response*, 19.

26. Kintner, 20.

27. The following is a list of the roundtable's participants (see page 5 of *Crisis and Response*): conference chairman Richard Cavazos (general, U.S. Army, retired), Worth H. Bagley (former vice chief of Naval Operations [admiral, U.S. Navy, retired]), Joseph Churba (president, International Security Council), José Angel Conchello (former president, PAN), Luis Farias (mayor of Monterrey, Nuevo León, Mexico), George W. Grayson (delegate, member of the Virginia General Assembly), Alejandro Gurza (business executive, Mexico), Daniel James (author and lecturer, United States), William R. Kintner (former U.S. ambassador to Thailand, professor, University of Pennsylvania), Richard C. Lawrence (rapporteur, colonel, U.S. Air Force, retired), Margarita Michelena (journalist and commentator, Mexico), Luis Pazos (professor, Escuela Libre de Derecho, Mexico), Phillip V. Sánchez (former U.S. ambassador to Honduras and Colombia), Rafaél Segovia (director for international studies, El Colegio de México), Donald C. Shufstall (international banking executive, United States), Martin Sicker (senior vice president, International Security Council), Gordon Sumner Jr. (lieutenant general, U.S. Army, retired, former chairman of the Inter-American Defense Board), and Jacobo Zaidenweber (president, American Textile S.A., Mexico).

28. Leyva de Varona, "Cuban-Mexican Relations during the Castro Era" (Ph.D. diss., University of Miami, 1994), 329–30.

29. For the Central America crisis, see William Leogrande's *Our Own Backyard: The United States in Central America, 1977–1992* (Chapel Hill: University of North Carolina Press, 1998).

30. Leyva de Varona, 343–51.

31. Leyva de Varona, 357–58.

32. Leyva de Varona, 357–58.

33. Leyva de Varona, 357–58; for an in-depth study of Cuban exile influence out of Miami, see Ann Louise Bardach's *Cuba Confidential: Love and Vengeance in Miami and Havana* (New York: Vintage, 2002).

34. Leyva de Varona, 365–69.

35. Leyva de Varona, 365–69.

36. Leyva de Varona, 370–71.

37. Leyva de Varona, 370.

38. Leyva de Varona, 372–73.

39. Jorge Chabat and Luz María Villasana, "La política mexicana hacia Cuba durante el sexenio de Salinas de Gortari: mas allá de la ideología," *Foro Internacional* 34 (1994): 688.

40. Dan La Botz, *Democracy in Mexico: Peasant Rebellion and Political Reform* (Boston: South End Press, 1995), 87–89.

41. Quoted in La Botz, 91.

42. La Botz, 92–93.

43. Enrique Krauze, *Mexico: Biography of Power*, trans. Hank Heifetz (New York: HarperCollins, 1997), 770. An inclusive look at the 1988 elections can be found in Julia Preston and Samuel Dillon, *Opening Mexico: The Making of a Democracy* (New York: Farrar, Straus and Giroux, 2004), 149–80.

44. Ana Covarrubias Velasco, "La política mexicana hacia Cuba durante el gobierno de Salinas de Gortari," *Foro Internacional* 34 (1994): 664.

45. Quoted in Velasco, 664.

46. Chabat and Villasana, 689.

47. Velasco, 661.

48. Velasco, 667.

49. Velasco, 667.

50. Velasco, 668.

51. Velasco, 670.

52. Velasco, 671–72.

53. "Cuban Exiles Criticize Mexico," *Washington Post*, August 21, 1993, A2.

54. Velasco, 681.

55. Velasco, 681.

56. U.S. Central Intelligence Agency, *Cuba: Handbook of Trade Statistics*, 1998.

57. U.S. Central Intelligence Agency.

58. U.S. Central Intelligence Agency.

59. Jorge I. Domínguez and Rafael Fernández de Castro, eds., *The United States and Mexico: Between Partnership and Conflict* (New York: Routledge, 2001), 68, 69.

60. U.S. Central Intelligence Agency.

61. U.S. Central Intelligence Agency.

62. Ruberto Flores y Fernández, "México, Cuba y el tratado de libre comercio," *Caribbean Studies* 29 (1996): 160–64.

63. "Cuba-Mexico Relations Undergoing a Shift," *NotiCen*, August 31, 2000, http://www.allbusiness.com/central-america/623740-1.html.

64. U.S. Central Intelligence Agency.

65. U.S. Central Intelligence Agency.

66. Louis Nevaer, "In Rift with Mexico, Cuba is the Loser," *Pacific News Service*, May 24, 2004, 2.

67. Nevaer, 3. To elaborate, foreign-based, non-Mexican companies can trade with Cuba through Mexico, as has been the case for several U.S. subsidiaries, including companies like ALCOA and Worthington Pump, which own foreign-based companies licensed to trade with Cuba. For further information, see Michael D. Kaplowitz and Donna Rich Kaplowitz, "Cuba and the United States: Opportunities Lost and Future Potential," in *Cuba's Ties to a Changing World*, ed. Donna Rich Kaplowitz (Boulder: Lynne Rienner, 1993), 223–44.

68. Velasco, 677–78.

69. Velasco, 677–79.

70. Paul B. Carroll, "Mexico Plays Growing Role in Helping Cuba withstand U.S. Trade Embargo," *Wall Street Journal*, August 3, 1994, A7.

▼▼▼

71. Louis A. Pérez Jr., *Cuba and the United States: Ties of Singular Intimacy*, 2nd ed. (Athens: University of Georgia Press, 1997), 263.

72. Pérez, 384.

73. Quoted in Pérez, 402.

74. Pérez, 402.

75. Velasco, 665.

76. Velasco, 666.

77. Carroll, A7.

78. Therese Rapael, "U.S. and Europe Clash over Cuba," *Wall Street Journal*, March 31, 1997, A14.

79. Michael M. Phillips, "Senate Passes Bill to Tighten Cuba Embargo," *Wall Street Journal*, March 6, 1996, A22.

80. Richard W. Stevenson, "Canada, Backed by Mexico, Protests to U.S. on Cuba Sanctions," *New York Times*, March 14, 1996, A7.

81. Nora Boustany, "What the U.S. Separates, Helms-Burton Unites," *Washington Post*, July 19, 1996, A35.

82. Boustany, A35.

83. Boustany, A35.

84. Julia Preston, "U.S. Finds Mexico is Adamant on Cuba Trade," *New York Times*, August 29, 1996, A5.

85. Preston, A5.

86. José de Córdoba, "Mexico's Domos Catches U.S.-Cuba Heat; Telecom Firm's Officials are to be Denied Visas for Links to Havana," *Wall Street Journal*, August 19, 1996, A9.

87. Preston, A5.

88. "Cuba: Pluralismo y diálogo," *Excelsior*, June 3, 1997, editorial.

89. "Cuba: Cuba-Mexico Incident Said Turning 'Delicate,'" Agence-Press France, December 8, 1998.

90. "Cuba-Mexico Relations Undergoing a Shift."

91. "Mexico to Abstain in Vote to Censure Cuba on Human Rights," *Wall Street Journal*, April 18, 2000, A15.

▼▼▼

Epilogue

Epigraph sources: quoted in "Mexico's Fox Asks Cuba for Transparency on Human Rights," *Mexico City Notimex*, April 1, 2001; Fidel Castro Ruz, "Speech Given by Commander in Chief Fidel Castro Ruz, President of the Republic of Cuba, at the Labour Day Celebration in Revolution Square on May 1, 2004, including the Additional Remarks Made During the Delivery of the Speech and Added Comments," Partido Comunista Cubano, http://www.cuba.cu/gobierno/discursos/2004/ing/f010504i.html.

1. Quoted in "Cuba-Mexico Relations Undergoing a Shift," *NotiCen*, August 31, 2000, http://www.allbusiness.com/central-america/623740-1.html.

2. "Cuba-Mexico Relations Undergoing a Shift."

3. "Cuba-Mexico Relations Undergoing a Shift."

4. Quoted in "Mexico's Fox Asks Cuba for Transparency on Human Rights."

5. "Mexico's Fox Asks Cuba for Transparency on Human Rights."

6. "Mexico's Fox Asks Cuba for Transparency on Human Rights."

7. "Mexico's Fox Asks Cuba for Transparency on Human Rights."

8. "Mexico's Fox Asks Cuba for Transparency on Human Rights."

9. "Mexico's Fox Asks Cuba for Transparency on Human Rights."

10. Quoted in Esperanza Barajas, "Mexico: Senate Seeks Cuba-Solidarity Vote," *Mexico City Reforma*, April 11, 2001.

11. "Mexican Foreign Secretariat to Define Vote on Cuba in Geneva Based on Resolution," *Mexico City Notimex*, April 11, 2001; "Castañeda Says Human Rights Situation in Cuba 'Worrisome,'" *Mexico City Reforma*, April 12, 2001.

12. "Castañeda Says Human Rights Situation in Cuba 'Worrisome.'"

13. "Cuba Welcomes Mexico's Abstention Vote on UN Human Rights Resolution," *Mexico City Notimex*, April 18, 2001.

14. "Cuba-Mexico Interparliamentary Resolution Rejects Using Human Rights as Leverage," *Mexico City Reforma*, June 30, 2001.

15. Quoted in Jorge G. Castañeda and Judith Adler Hellman, "Human Rights in Mexico: An Interview with Jorge Castaneda," *LASA Forum* 32.2 (2001): 6–7.

16. Nick Miroff, "Fox Outfoxed: Cuba-Mexico Relations Hit New Low," *World Press Review* 26, April 2002.

17. International Security Council, "The San Diego Declaration," *Crisis and Response: A Roundtable on Mexico* (New York: International Security Council, 1986), 5.

18. See list of interviews and conversations in bibliography for dates of interviews with the following: Miguel Díaz, Elías Gonzalez, Daniel Martínez, Tarsicio Navarrete, Enrique Camacho Navarro, Jonas Sandoval Orosco, José Antonio Ramírez, José Róa, Tomas Fernández Robaina, and Carlos Bojórquez Urzaiz.

19. Miguel Díaz, Zapatista National Liberation Front (FZLN), interview with author, May 21, 2003; José Antonio Ramírez, FZLN, interview with author, July 8, 2003; Elías Gonzalez, FZLN, interview with author, June 10, 2003; José Roa, Workers Revolutionary Party (PRT), general manager, interview with author, June 27, 2003.

20. Interview with Tarcisio Navarrete, Mexican Congressional Commission of Foreign Relations secretary, July 1, 2003.

BIBLIOGRAPHY

ARCHIVES AND LIBRARIES CONSULTED

Archivo de Concentraciones de la Secretaría de Relaciones Exteriores (SRE), Mexico City.

Correspondence files of Ambassador Gilberto Bosques, 1953–64.

Correspondence files of Ambassador Fernando Pamanes Escobedo, 1965–67.

Correspondence files of Ambassador Miguel Covian Pérez, 1967–70.

Correspondence files of Ambassador Victor Alfonso Maldonado, 1970–74.

Correspondence files of Ambassador Edmundo Flores, 1975.

Correspondence files of Ambassador Celso H. Delgado Ramírez, 1975–77.

Correspondence files of Ambassador Ernesto Madero Vasquez, 1977–80.

Correspondence files of Ambassador Gonzalo Martinez Corbalá, 1980–81.

Correspondence files of Ambassador Rodolfo Echeverría Ruíz, 1982–85.

Correspondence files of Ambassador Enrique Olivares Santano, 1985–87.

Correspondence files of Ambassador Raúl Castellano Jiménez, 1989–90.

Archivo General de la Nación, Mexico City.

Collección de Lázaro Cárdenas.

Archivo Histórico de Orizaba, Veracruz, Mexico.

El Archivo del Ministerio de Relaciones Exteriores, Lima, Peru.

Dwight D. Eisenhower Presidential Library, Abilene, KS.

Dulles-Herter series.

National Security Council series.

White House central files.

Jimmy Carter Presidential Library, Atlanta, GA.

Bourne collection.

▼▼▼

Brzezinski files.

White House central files.

Lyndon Baines Johnson Presidential Library, Austin, TX.

Antonio Carrillo Flores.

Dean Rusk.

Walt Rostow.

Oral history files.

National security files.

Senatorial files, 1946–61.

White House central files.

National Security Archive. Electronic briefing books (online), Washington, D.C.

"After the Revolution."

"Béisbol Diplomacy with Cuba."

"Double Dealing Mexico's Foreign Policy toward Cuba."

"The Nixon Tapes."

"The Tlatelolco Massacre."

Richard M. Nixon Project. National Archives 2, College Park, MD.

Henry Kissinger State Department telecommunications transcripts.

National Security Council files.

United States Department of State. National Archives 2, College Park, MD.

Record group 59, general records, subject numeric files, 1970–73, political and defense files.

LIBRARIES CONSULTED

Anschutz Research Library, University of Kansas.

Benson Latin American Collection, University of Texas.

Biblioteca del Acervo Histórico de la Secretaría de Relaciones Exteriores, Mexico City.

Biblioteca de la Cámara de Diputados H. Congreso de la Union, Mexico City.

Biblioteca de Estudios Latinoamericanos, UNAM, Mexico City.

Biblioteca Miguel Lerdo de Tejada, Mexico City.

Biblioteca Nacional de Jose Marti, Havana, Cuba.

La Casa de las Americas, Havana, Cuba.

Spencer Research Library, University of Kansas.

Watson Library, University of Kansas.

INTERVIEWS AND CONVERSATIONS

Díaz, Miguel. Zapatista National Liberation Front (FZLN). Interview with author. May 21, 2003.

Gonzalez, Elías. FZLN. Interview with author. June 10, 2003.

Lara, Enrique Condés. Former Mexican guerrilla leader. Interview with author. July 5, 2003.

Martinez, Daniel. Foreign Relations Commission technical secretary. Interview with author. June 20, 2003.

Navarrete, Tarsicio. Mexican Congressional Commission of Foreign Relations secretary. Interview with author. July 1, 2003.

Navarro, Enrique Camacho. Professor of history, UNAM. Interview with author. June 20, 2003.

Orosco, Jonás Sandoval. Special Commission of Public Security technical secretary. Interview with author. June 3, 2003.

Pastor, Robert. Former director of Latin American and Caribbean Affairs, National Security Council. Interview with author. June 1, 2004.

Ramírez, José Antonio. FZLN. Interview with author. July 8, 2003.

Roa, José. Workers Revolutionary Party (PRT), general manager. Interview with author. June 27, 2003.

Robaina, Tomás Fernández. Cuban cultural historian, Universidad de Havana, and bibliographer, Biblioteca Nacional de José Martí. Conversation with author. December 30, 2003.

Urzaiz, Carlos Bojórquez. Anthropologist, Universidad Autónoma de Yucatán. Conversation with author. September 9, 2004.

▼▼▼

PERIODICALS

Cuba

  Bohemia   *Juventud Rebelde*

  Granma   *Verde Olivo*

Mexico

  Agencia Informativa Latinoamericana Prensa Latina

  Excelsior   *Noticen*

  Financiero   *Reforma*

  La Jornada   *Réplica*

  Mensaje Quincenal   *Siempre!*

  Mexico City Notimex   *Sourcemex*

  Mexico City Reforma   *El Universal*

  Milenio

United States

  Acción   *National Review*

  Diario de las Americas   *New York Times*

  Free Cuba News   *Wall Street Journal*

  Los Angeles Times   *Washington Post*

  Miami Herald   *World Press Review*

▼▼▼

NONARCHIVAL PRIMARY SOURCES

IV Reunión Interparlamentaria México-Cuba. "Declaración conjunta," June 27–29, 2001, Veracruz, Mexico.

———. "Historia de las Reuniones Interparlamentarias," June 27–29, 2001, Veracruz, Mexico.

———. "Relación bilateral México-Cuba," June 27–29, 2001, Veracruz, Mexico.

———. "Temas de trabajo en la IV Reunión Interparlamentaria México-Cuba," June 27–29, 2001, Veracruz, Mexico.

Cárdenas, Lázaro. *Epistolario de Lázaro Cárdenas*. Ed. Elena Vázquez Gómez. Vols. 1 and 2. Mexico City: Siglo 21, 1974, 1975.

———. "Mensaje al pueblo de Cuba, 12 junio de 1938." Mexico City: D.A.P.P., 1938.

Castañeda, Jorge G., and Judith Adler Hellman. "Human Rights in Mexico: An Interview with Jorge Castaneda." *LASA Forum* 32.2 (2001): 5–7.

Castro Ruz, Fidel. "1980 Message Decoration of López Portillo," August 1, 1980. *Castro Speech Database, UTLANIC.* http://lanic.utexas.edu/la/cb/cuba/castro.html.

———. "XXX Aniversario de del asalto al Cuartel Moncada." Havana: Editora Politica, 1983.

———. "Address by Fidel Castro at the General Assembly of the United Nations." September 26, 1960.

———. "De Cuba a Ecuador y a Mexico." Mexico City: Editorial Mestiza, 1988.

———. "Speech Friendship Rally for Mexican President Portillo," August 2, 1980. *Castro Speech Database, UTLANIC.* http://lanic.utexas.edu/la/cb/cuba/castro .html.

———. "Speech given by Commander in Chief Fidel Castro Ruz, President of the Republic of Cuba, at the Labour Day Celebration in Revolution Square on May 1, 2004, including the Additional Remarks Made During the Delivery of the Speech and Added Comments." Partido Comunista Cubano. http://www. cuba.cu/gobierno/discursos/2004/ing/f010504i.html.

Castro, Fidel Ruz, and Luis Suárez. "1974 Interview Mexican Magazine Interview," February 15, 1974. *Castro Speech Database, UTLANIC.* http://lanic.utexas.edu/ la/cb/cuba/castro.html. Abridged version of interview published in the February 15, 1974, edition of *Siempre!*

Castro, Hugo, and Antonio Pujul. *Unidos detengamos la agresion! A la juventud mexicana!: Una amenaza sombria se cierna contra la revolución cubana.* Mexico City: Taller de Grafica Popular, 1961.

▼▼▼

Castro, Nelson Notario. "1988 Speech Castro Speaks in Tuxpan, Notes Event," December 5, 1988. *Castro Speech Database, UTLANIC.* http://lanic.utexas.edu/la/cb/cuba/castro.html.

Centro de Investigación Científica Jorge L. Tamayo, ed. *México y Cuba: Dos pueblos unidos en la historia.* 2 vols. Mexico City: Centro de Investigación Científica Jorge L. Tamayo, 1982.

Commission I. *Cultural Congress of Havana.* Havana: Instituto de Libro, 1968.

Commission de Relaciones Exteriores. *Informe annual.* 1970–2002.

Curzio, Leonardo, and Tarcisio Navarrete Montes de Oca. "Entrevista con el Diputado Tarcisio Navarrete." Grupo Parlamentario Federal. Mexico, D.F. 25 Feb 2002.

Dix, John A. *Speeches and Occasional Addresses.* Vol. 1. New York: D. Appleton, 1864.

Dorticós Torrado, Osvaldo. *Cuba in the Second Conference of Non-Aligned Nations.* Republic of Cuba: Foreign Ministry, Information Department, 1964.

Echeverría, Luís. *Ideario: Reflexiones sobre temas sociales de México.* Vol. 1–7. Mexico City: PRI, 1970.

———. *Informe de gobierno.* Vol. IV–VI. Mexico City: Cultura y Ciencia Política, 1974.

———. *Presidente Echeverria: Siete conferencias de prensa.*

Granma. El insólito caso del espía de la CIA bajo el manto de funcionario de la embajada de México en Cuba. Havana: Instituto del Libro, 1969.

Herrera Franyutti, Alfonso. "Cartas de José Martí." *Cuadernos Americanos* 3.27 (1991): 205–7.

Ibarra, Rosario. "Desgarrada Soledad," April 6, 2002. *Comité Eureka.* http://www.eureka.org.mx/opinion/040602.html (accessed 2003; site now discontinued).

International Security Council. *Crisis and Response: A Roundtable on Mexico.* New York: International Security Council, 1986.

Kissinger, Henry A. "The United States and Latin America: the New Opportunity." Secretary Henry A. Kissinger before the Combined Service Club, March 1, 1975, Houston, TX. Washington, D.C.: Government Printing Office, 1975.

———. *Years of Renewal.* New York: Simon and Schuster, 1999.

López Mateos, Adolfo. *Cinco informes de gobierno.* Juárez, Mexico: Novaro Editores, 1964.

———. *Tres informes de gobierno.* Mexico City: Editorial La Justicia, 1961.

▼▼▼

Lopéz Portillo, José. *En Costa Rica, Brasil y Cuba.* Mexico City: Secretaría de Relaciones Exteriores, 1980.

Mena, Luis Felipe Bravo. Press Conference by the president of National Executive Committee (CEN) of the National Action Party (PAN), April 12, 2002, Cancún, Mexico.

Mexican Anti-Communist Foundation (FEMACO). *Su fundación, sus actividades iniciales.* Mexico City: Editorial Luz, 1967.

Mexico. Comisión Nacional de los Derechos Humanos de Mexico, 2001. http://www.cndh.org.mx.

National Liberation Movement (MLN). *Programa y llamamiento.* Mexico City: República del Salvador, 1961.

———, and Alonso Aguilar M., eds. "El MLN en Marcha: Realizaciones, Problemas, Perspectivas." Mexico City: MLN, 1962.

Non-Aligned Movement, January 2002. http://www.nam.gov.za/background/members.htm.

Oca, Tarcisio Navarrete Montes de. Mexican Congressional Foreign Relations Commission Secretary. "Asunto Cuba: Osvaldo Payá." Position paper, September 23, 2002, Grupo Parlamentario Federal, Mexico.

———. "Declaración de solidaridad del Congreso Mexicano." Position paper, June 1, 2003, Grupo Parlamentario Federal, Mexico.

———. "Posicionamiento con punto de acuerdo respecto al voto de México durante el 59 Período de Sesiones de la Comisión de Derechos Humanos de la ONU, en Ginebra, Suiza, en el caso de la situación que guardan los derechos humanos de Cuba." Address to the Mexican Camara de Diputados, n.d., Grupo Parlamentario Federal, Mexico.

———. "Relaciones México-Cuba." Position paper, n.d., Grupo Parlamentario Federal, Mexico.

Oca, Tarcisio Navarrete Montes de, Omar López Montenegro, and Pedro Rodríguez. "El PAN no tiene aún una posición respecto a si condenará o no en Ginebra la situación de los DH en Cuba." Press Conference transcript, February 19, 2002, Grupo Parlamentario Federal, Mexico.

O'Reilly, Justo Sierra. *Diario de nuestro viaje a los Estados Unidos: La pretendida anexión de Yucatán.* Mexico City: Antigua Librería Robredo, de José Porrúa e Hijos, 1938.

▼▼▼

Popular Socialist Party (PPS). *Al pueblo mexicano: Defender a Cuba es defender a Mexico y América Latina.* Mexico City: Ediciones del Partido Popular Socialista, 1961.

Rodríguez, Rafael. Secretary General of the CAL (Latin America Anti-Communist Confederation). "Letter to the U.S. Government," August 16, 1975, Confederación Anticomunista Latinoamericana, Guadalajara, Mexico.

———. Secretary General of the CAL. "Letter to the U.S. Government," August 23, 1975, Confederación Anticomunista Latinoamericana, Guadalajara, Mexico.

Rusk, Dean. "American Republics Unite to Halt the Spread of Communism in Western Hemisphere." *U.S. State Department Bulletin* 46.1182, February 19, 1962, 270–88.

Secretaría de Relaciones Exteriores. *La embajada especial de Mexico en Cuba con motivo de la transmisión de pol poder ejecutivo de la república cubana, efectuada el 20 de mayo 1925.* Mexico City: Secretaría de Relaciones Exteriores, 1925.

———. *Memorias e Informes,* 1971–2002. Mexico, 2002.

Sociedad Cubano-Mexicana de Relaciones Culturales. *Memoria: Semana de Amistad Cubano-Mexicana.* Havana, 1965.

Tello, Manuel. *Gira de trabajo del presidente Luis Echeverria Alvarez a catorce paises de America, Africa y Asia, 8 de julio a 22 de agosto, 1975.* Mexico City: Secretaria de Relaciones Exteriores, 1975.

Transcript of meeting between U.S. Secretary of State Alexander M. Haig Jr., and Cuban Vice Premier Carlos Rafaél Rodríguez, November 23, 1981, Mexico City. *Cold War International History Project* 8–9. http://www.wilsoncenter.org/index .cfm?topic_id=1409&fuseaction=va2.document&identifier=5034EF21-96B6 -175C-9C45700AE8493D87&sort=Collection&item=US-Cuban%20Relations.

United Nations. General Assembly. "Voting Records," 1983–2002.

———. Security Council. "Voting Records," 1946–2002. http://unbisnet.un.org/ webpac-bin/wgbroker?new+-access+top.vote.

U.S. Congress. House Committee on Un-American Activities. *Who are They? Part 8: Vicente Lombardo Toledano and Luis Carlos Prestes (Mexico-Brazil).* 85th Cong., 1st sess., February 21, 1958.

U.S. Congress. Senate. Committee on Foreign Relations. *Inter-American Relations: A Collection of Documents, Legislation, Descriptions of Inter-American Organizations, and Other Material Pertaining to Inter-American Affairs.* 100th Cong., 2d sess., 1988.

———. Committee on Foreign Relations. *Legislation on Foreign Relations.* 93rd Cong., 2d sess., 1974.

———. Senate. Committee on the Judiciary. *Communist Threat to the United States through the Caribbean.* Parts 12 and 13. 87th Cong., 1st sess., 1961.

———. Committee on the Judiciary. *Cuban Aftermath-Red Seeds Blow South: Implications for the United States of the Latin American Conference for National Sovereignty and Economic Emancipation and Peace.* 87th Cong., 1st sess., 1961.

Velasco García, Agustín. Secretary of Foreign Relations. Federación Mexicana Anticomunista de Occidente. Letter, April 12, 1975. "Rockefeller, Kissinger and Others Pretend that the Cuban Bankruptcy be Paid with the Money of the Taxpayers of the United States."

SECONDARY SOURCES

Agee, Philip. *Inside the Company: CIA Diary.* New York: Bantam Books, 1984.

Aguayo, Sergio. *La charola: Una historia de los servicios de inteligencia en México.* Mexico City: Grijalbo Mondadori, 2001.

———. *Myths and [Mis]perceptions: Changing U.S. Elite Visions of Mexico.* Trans. Julián Brody. La Jolla: Center for U.S.-Mexican Studies, University of California, San Diego, 1998.

Anderson, Benedict. *Imagined Communities: Reflections on the Origin and Spread of Nationalism.* New York: Verso, 1991.

Anderson, Jon Lee. *Che Guevara: A Revolutionary Life.* New York: Grove, 1997.

Anderson, Scott, and Jon Lee Anderson. *Inside the League.* New York: Dodd, Mead, 1986.

Archdiocese of Guatemala, *Guatemala: Never Again!* New York: Orbis, 1999.

Argüelles Espinosa, Luis Angel. "Los refugiados mexicanos en Cuba (1910–1927)." *Palabra y el Hombre* 70 (1983): 117–48.

———. *Temas cubano mexicanos.* Mexico City: Universidad Nacional Autónoma de México, 1989.

Armas, Ramón de. "Apuntes sobre la presencia en Martí del México de Benito Juárez." *Casa de Las Américas* 20.115 (1979): 10–19.

———. "José Martí: El apoyo desde México." *Universidad de la Habana* 219 (1983): 80–103.

▼▼▼

Atkins, G. Pope. *Latin America and the Caribbean in the International System.* 4th ed. Boulder, CO: Westview Press, 1999.

Baeza Flores, Alberto. "México en Martí." *El Libro y el Pueblo* 24 (1967): 23–27.

Bakewell, Peter J. *Silver Mining and Society in Colonial Mexico: Zacatecas, 1546–1700.* Cambridge: Cambridge University Press, 1971.

Bardach, Ann Louise. *Cuba Confidential: Love and Vengeance in Miami and Havana.* New York: Vintage, 2002.

Basdeo, Sahadeo, and Heather N. Nicol, eds. *Canada, the United States, and Cuba: An Evolving Relationship.* Coral Gables, FL: North-South Center Press, 2002.

Bethell, Leslie, and Ian Roxborough, eds. *Latin America between the Second World War and the Cold War, 1944–1948.* Cambridge: Cambridge University Press, 1992.

Blachman, Morris J., William M. Leogrande, Kenneth Sharpe, eds. *Confronting Revolution: Security through Diplomacy in Central America.* New York: Pantheon, 1986.

Blasier, Cole. *The Giant's Rival: The USSR and Latin America.* Rev. ed. Pittsburgh: University of Pittsburgh Press, 1987.

———. *The Hovering Giant: U.S. Responses to Revolutionary Change in Latin America, 1910–1985.* Rev. ed. Pittsburgh: University of Pittsburgh Press, 1985.

Bohning, Don. *The Castro Obsession: U.S. Covert Operations against Cuba, 1959–1965.* Washington, D.C.: Potomac, 2005.

Bojórquez Urzaiz, Carlos. *Cubanos patriotas en Yucatán.* Mérida: Universidad Autónoma de Yucatán, 1988.

Borah, Woodrow. *New Spain's Century of Depression.* Berkeley: University of California Press, 1951.

Brading, D. A. *Haciendas and Ranchos in the Mexican Bajío: León, 1700–1860.* Cambridge: Cambridge University Press, 1978.

Bremauntz, Alberto. *México y la revolución socialista Cubana.* Morelia, Mexico: Fímax Publicistas, 1966.

Brenner, Anita and George R. Leighton. *The Wind that Swept Mexico: The History of the Mexican Revolution, 1910–1942.* Austin: University of Texas Press, 1971. First published in 1943 by Harper and Brothers.

Cabezas, Omas. *Fire from the Mountain: The Making of a Sandinista.* Trans. Kathleen Weaver. New York: Crown, 1985.

Cabrera, Olga. *El Antimperialismo en la historia de Cuba.* Havana: Editorial de Ciencias Sociales, 1985.

Casas, Bartolomé de las. *The Devastation of the Indies: A Brief Account.* Trans. Herma Briffault. Baltimore: Johns Hopkins University Press, 1994.

Castañeda, Jorge G. *Perpetuating Power: How Mexican Presidents Were Chosen.* Trans. Padraic Arthur Smithies. New York: New Press, 2000.

———. *Utopia Unarmed: The Latin American Left After the Cold War.* New York: Knopf, 1993.

Chabat, Jorge, and Luz María Villasana. "La política mexicana hacia Cuba durante el sexenio de Salinas de Gortari: Más allá de la ideología." *Foro Internacional* 34 (1994): 683–99.

Chávez Orozco, Luis. *Un esfuerzo de Mexico por la independencia de Cuba.* Mexico City: Secretaria de Relaciones Exteriores, 1930.

Chevalier, François. *Land and Society in Colonial Mexico: The Great Hacienda.* Trans. Alvin Eustis. Ed. Lesley Byrd Simpson. Berkeley: University of California Press, 1963.

Clayton, Lawrence, and Michael L. Conniff. *A History of Modern Latin America.* 1st ed. Belmont, CA: Wadsworth/Thomson Learning, 1999.

Clendinnen, Inga. *Ambivalent Conquests: Maya and Spaniard in Yucatan, 1517–1570.* 2nd ed. Cambridge: Cambridge University Press, 2003.

Coatsworth, John. *Central America and the United States: The Clients and the Colossus.* New York: Twayne, 1997.

Cockcroft, James. *Latin America: History, Politics, and U.S. Policy.* 2nd ed. Chicago: Nelson-Hall, 1996. First published in 1989 as *Neighbors in Turmoil: Latin America* by Harper and Row.

Cohen, Warren I., ed. *The Cambridge History of American Foreign Relations.* Vol. 4, *America in the Age of Soviet Power, 1945–1991.* Cambridge: Cambridge University Press, 1995.

Colegio Nacional. "Antonio Carrillo Flores." http://www.colegionacional.org.mx/ Carrillo.htm.

Connell-Smith, Gordon. "Latin America in the Foreign Relations of the United States." *Journal of Latin American Studies* 8.1 (May 1976): 137–50.

Cornelius, Wayne A. "The Political Economy of Mexico under De la Madrid: Austerity, Routinized Crisis, and Nascent Recovery." *Mexican Studies* 1.1. (Winter 1985): 83–124.

▼▼▼

Courtois, Stéphane, et al. *The Black Book of Communism: Crimes, Terror, Repression.* Translated by Jonathan Murphy and Mark Kramer. Cambridge: Harvard University Press, 1999.

Covantes, Hugo. *El Grabado Mexicano del Siglo XX, 1900–1999.* Colima, Mexico: CENEDIC/Universidad de Colima, 2000.

Crosby, Alfred W., Jr. *The Columbian Exchange: Biological and Cultural Consequences of 1492.* Westport, CT: Greenwood, 1972.

Dent, David W. *The Legacy of the Monroe Doctrine: A Reference Guide to U.S. Involvement in Latin America and the Caribbean.* Westport, CT: Greenwood, 1999.

Desch, Michael C. *When the Third World Matters: Latin America and the United States Grand Strategy.* Baltimore: Johns Hopkins University Press, 1993.

Díaz del Castillo, Bernal. *The Discovery and Conquest of Mexico, 1517–1521.* Trans. A. P. Maudslay. Ed. Genaro García. Cambridge, MA: Da Capo, 2004.

Díaz, Bernardo García, and Sergio Guerra Vilaboy, eds. *La Habana/Veracruz, Veracruz/La Habana: Las dos orillas.* Veracruz, Mexico: Universidad Veracruzana, 2002.

Dinges, John. *The Condor Years: How Pinochet and His Allies Brought Terrorism to Three Continents.* New York: New Press, 2005.

Domínguez, Jorge I. "Consensus and Divergence: The State of the Literature on Inter-American Relations in the 1970s." *Latin American Research Review* 3.1 (1978): 87–126.

———. *To Make the World Safe for Revolution.* Cambridge: Harvard University Press, 1989.

———. "U.S.-Cuban Relations in the 1980s: Issues and Policies." *Journal of Interamerican Studies and World Affairs* 27.1 (Feb. 1985): 17–34.

———. "U.S.-Cuban Relations from the Cold War to the Colder War." *Journal of Interamerican Studies and World Affairs* 39.3 (Autumn 1997): 49–75.

Domínguez, Jorge I., and Rafael Fernández de Castro, eds. *The United States and Mexico: Between Partnership and Conflict.* New York: Routledge, 2001.

Domínguez, Jorge I., and Rafael Hernandez, eds. *U.S.-Cuban Relations in the 1990s.* Boulder, CO: Westview, 1989.

Dozer, Donald Marquand. "Recognition in Contemporary Inter-American Relations." *Journal of Inter-American Studies* 8.2 (April 1966): 318–35.

Dumond, Don E. *The Machete and the Cross: Campesino Rebellion in Yucatan.* Lincoln: University of Nebraska Press, 1997.

Dunn, Timothy J. *The Militarization of the U.S.-Mexico Border, 1978–1992: Low-Intensity Conflict Doctrine Comes Home.* Austin: University of Texas Press, 1996.

Engel, James Franklin. "Mexican Reaction to United States Cuban Policy, 1959–63." Ph.D. diss., University of Virginia, 1964.

———. "The Revolution and Mexican Foreign Policy." *Journal of Inter-American Studies* 11.4 (October 1969): 518–32.

Erisman, H. Michael. *Cuba's Foreign Relations in a Post-Soviet World.* Gainesville: University of Florida Press, 2000.

Fehrenbach, T. R. *Fire and Blood: A History of Mexico.* New York: Da Capo Press, 1995. First published in 1973 by Macmillan.

Feitlowitz, Marguerite. *A Lexicon of Terror: Argentina and the Legacies of Torture.* Oxford: Oxford University Press, 1999.

Fenn, Peggy. "México, la no intervención y la autodeterminación en el caso de Cuba." *Foro Internacional* 4.1 (1963): 1–19.

Fernández, Frank. *Cuban Anarchism: The History of a Movement.* Trans. Charles Bufe. Tucson, AZ: See Sharpe, 2001.

Ferris, Elizabeth G., and Jennie K. Lincoln, eds. *Latin American Foreign Policies: Global and Regional Dimensions.* Boulder, CO: Westview, 1981.

Flores y Fernández, Ruberto. "México, Cuba y el tratado de libre comercio." *Caribbean Studies* 29 (1996): 160–64.

Foucault, Michel. *The Archaeology of Knowledge and the Discourse of Language.* Trans. A. M. Sheridan Smith. New York: Pantheon, 1972.

Franco, José L. *La batalla por el dominio del Caribe y el Golfo de Mexico.* Havana: Instituto de Historia, 1964.

———. *Relaciones de Cuba y México durante el período colonial.* Havana: Ministerio de Educación, 1961.

Friedberg, Aaron L. *In the Shadow of the Garrison State: America's Anti-Statism and Its Cold War Grand Strategy.* Princeton: Princeton University Press, 2000.

Fursenko, Aleksandr, and Timothy Naftali. *One Hell of a Gamble: Khrushchev, Castro, and Kennedy 1958–1964.* New York: W. W. Norton, 1997.

Gaddis, John Lewis. *We Now Know: Rethinking Cold War History.* Oxford: Oxford University Press, 1997.

▼▼▼

Gilderhus, Mark T. *The Second Century: U.S.-Latin American Relations since 1889.* Wilmington, DE: Scholarly Resources, 1999.

Gleijeses, Piero. *Conflicting Missions: Havana, Washington, and Africa, 1959–1976.* Chapel Hill: University of North Carolina Press, 2002.

Gómez, Mario Ojeda. "Las relaciones de México con el régimen revolucionario cubano." *Foro Internacional* 14 (1974): 474–506.

González Navarro, Moisés. "La guerra de castas en Yucatán y la venta de mayas a Cuba." *Historia Mexicana* 18.1 (1968): 11–34.

———. "El trabajo forzoso en México 1821–1917." *Revista de la Universidad Autónoma de Yucatán* 26.149 (January 1984): 13–38.

Gott, Richard. *Cuba: A New History.* New Haven: Yale University Press, 2004.

Grabendorff, Wolf. "European Community Relations with Latin America." *Journal of Interamerican Studies and World Affairs* 29.4 (Winter 1987): 69–87.

Graves, Raymond. "Mexican Foreign Policy toward Cuba and Its Impact on U.S.-Mexican Relations, 1970–1982." Ph.D. diss., University of Miami, 1985.

Grayson, George W. *Oil and Mexican Foreign Policy.* Pittsburgh: University of Pittsburgh Press, 1988.

———. *The United States and Mexico: Patterns of Influence.* New York: Praeger, 1984.

Guerra, Lillian. *The Myth of Jose Marti: Conflicting Nationalisms in Early Twentieth-Century Cuba.* Chapel Hill: University of North Carolina Press, 2005.

Gutiérrez, Angel. *Lázaro Cárdenas y Cuba.* Michoacán, Mexico: Universidad Michoacana de San Nicolás de Hidalgo, 1989.

Halbwachs, Maurice. *On Collective Memory.* Ed. and trans. Lewis A. Coser. Chicago: University of Chicago Press, 1992.

Harvey, Robert. *Liberators: Latin America's Struggle for Independence, 1810–1830.* New York: Overlook Press, 2000.

Herman, Donald L. *The Communist Tide in Latin America: A Selected Treatment.* Austin: University of Texas Press, 1973.

Herrera Franyutti, Alfonso. "José Martí y Porfirio Díaz, 1894." *Cuadernos Americanos* 3.27 (1991): 208–21.

———. *Martí en México: Recuerdos de una época.* Mexico City: A. Mijares, 1969.

Hixson, Walter L. *Parting the Curtain: Propaganda, Culture, and the Cold War, 1945–1961.* New York: St. Martin's, 1998.

Hobsbawm, Eric, and Terence Ranger, eds. *The Invention of Tradition*. Cambridge: Cambridge University Press, 1983.

Hogan, Michael J., ed. *The Ambiguous Legacy: U.S. Foreign Relations in the "American Century."* Cambridge: Cambridge University Press, 1999.

————, ed. *The End of the Cold War: Its Meaning and Its Implications*. Cambridge: Cambridge University Press, 1992.

Hogan, Michael J., and Thomas G. Paterson, eds. *Explaining the History of American Foreign Relations*. Cambridge: Cambridge University Press, 1991.

Interhemispheric Resource Center. "World Anti-Communist League" (October 1990). http://rightweb.irc-online.org/gw/2815.

Johnson, Carlos. "Dependency Theory and the Processes of Capitalism and Socialism." *Latin American Perspectives* 8.3–4 (Summer 1981): 55–81.

Joseph, Gilbert M., and Timothy J. Henderson, eds. *The Mexico Reader: History, Culture, Politics*. Durham, NC: Duke University Press, 2002.

Kaplowitz, Donna Rich, ed. *Cuba's Ties to a Changing World*. Boulder, CO: Lynne Rienner, 1993.

Kline, Michael. "Castro and 'New Thinking' in Latin America." *Journal of Interamerican Studies and World Affairs* 32.1 (Spring 1990): 83–118.

Knight, Alan. *Mexico*. 3 vols. Cambridge: Cambridge University Press, 2002–2005.

————. *The Mexican Revolution*. 2 vols. Lincoln: University of Nebraska Press, 1990. First published in 1986 by Cambridge University Press.

Kornbluh, Peter, ed. *Bay of Pigs Declassified: The Secret CIA Report on the Invasion of Cuba*. New York: New Press, 1998.

————, ed. *The Pinochet File: A Declassified Dossier on Atrocity and Accountability*. New York: New Press, 2004.

Korngold, Ralph. *Citizen Toussaint*. New York: Little, Brown, 1944.

Krauze, Enrique. *Mexico: Biography of Power*. Trans. Hank Heifetz. New York: HarperCollins, 1997.

Kunz, Diane B. *Butter and Guns: America's Cold War Economic Diplomacy*. New York: Free Press, 1997.

La Botz, Dan. *Democracy in Mexico: Peasant Rebellion and Political Reform*. Boston: South End Press, 1995.

▼▼▼

LaFeber, Walter. *The American Age: U.S. Foreign Policy at Home and Abroad 1750 to the Present.* 2nd ed. New York: W. W. Norton, 1994.

———. *Inevitable Revolutions: The United States in Central America.* New York: W. W. Norton, 1993.

Lajous, Alejandra. *Dónde se perdió el cambio?: Tres episodios emblemáticos del gobierno de Fox.* Mexico City: Planeta, 2003.

Langley, Lester D. *The Banana Wars: United States Intervention in the Caribbean, 1898–1934.* Rev. ed. Lexington: University Press of Kentucky, 1985.

Langston, Joy. "Breaking Out is Hard to Do: Exit, Voice, and Loyalty in Mexico's One Party Hegemonic Regime." *Latin American Politics and Society* 44.3 (Autumn 2002): 61–88.

Leogrande, William M. *Our Own Backyard: The United States in Central America, 1977–1992.* Chapel Hill: University of North Carolina Press, 1998.

Leonard, Thomas, ed. *United States-Latin American Relations, 1850–1903: Establishing a Relationship.* Tuscaloosa: University of Alabama Press, 1999.

Leyva de Varona, Adolfo. "Cuban-Mexican Relations during the Castro Era." Ph.D. diss., University of Miami, 1994.

Lynch, John. *The Spanish American Revolutions, 1808–1826.* 2nd ed. New York: W. W. Norton, 1986.

Mann, Charles C. *1491: New Revelations on the Americas before Columbus.* New York: Knopf, 2005.

May, Ernest R., ed. *American Cold War Strategy: Interpreting NSC 68.* Boston: Bedford, 1993.

Mclintock, Cynthia. "Why Peasants Rebel: The Case of Peru's Sendero Luminoso." *World Politics* 37 (1984): 48–84.

Mella, Julio Antonio. *Escritos revolucionarios.* Mexico: Siglo Veintiuno, 1978.

Mendez, Alberto Diaz. *Lázaro Cárdenas: Ideas politicas y acción antiimperialista.* Havana: Editorial de Ciencias Sociales, 1984.

Menéndez, Carlos R. *Historia del infame y vergonzoso comercio de indios vendidos a los esclavistas de cuba por los políticos yucatecos, desde 1848 hasta 1861.* Mérida: La Revista de Yucatán, 1923.

Meyer, Michael, and William L. Sherman. *The Course of Mexican History.* 5th ed. Oxford: Oxford University Press, 1995.

Mora, Frank O, and Jeanne A. K. Hey, eds. *Latin American and Caribbean Foreign Policy.* Lanham, MD: Rowman and Littlefield, 2003.

Morales, Josefina. *México y Cuba: Dos experiencias frente a la reinserción internacional.* Mexico City: Universidad Nacional Autónoma de México, 1997.

Muñoz, Heraldo, and Joseph S. Tulchin, ed. *Latin American Nations in World Politics.* Boulder: Westview, 1996.

Navarro, Enrique Camacho, ed. *Siete Vistas de Cuba: Interpretaciones de su Independencia.* Mexico, D.F.: UNAM, 2002.

Nieto, Clara. *Masters of War: Latin America and U.S. Aggression from the Cuban Revolution through the Clinton Years.* New York: Seven Stories, 2003.

Nunez, Gerardo Gonzalez, and Ericka Kim Verba. "International Relations between Cuba and the Caribbean in the 1990s: Challenges and Perspectives." *Latin American Perspectives.* 24, no. 5 (Sept. 1997): 81–95.

O'Brien, Thomas. *The Century of U.S. Capitalism in Latin America.* Albuquerque: University of New Mexico Press, 1999.

O'Brien, Thomas, and Alan Knight. *The Revolutionary Mission: American Enterprise in Latin America, 1900–1945.* Cambridge: Cambridge University Press, 1999.

Oppenheimer, Andres. *Bordering on Chaos: Mexico's Roller-Coaster Journey toward Prosperity.* Boston: Little, Brown, 1998.

Pastor, Robert A. *Exiting the Whirlpool: U.S. Foreign Policy toward Latin America and the Caribbean.* 2nd ed. Boulder, CO: Westview, 2001.

Pastor, Robert A, and Jorge G. Castañeda. *Limits to Friendship: The United States and Mexico.* New York: Knopf, 1988.

Paterson, Thomas G. *Contesting Castro: The United Status and the Triumph of the Cuban Revolution.* New York: Oxford University Press, 1994.

Pellicer de Brody, Olga. *México y la revolución cubana.* Guanajuato: Colegio de México, 1972.

Perez-Lopez, Jorge F. "Swimming against the Tide: Implications for Cuba of Soviet and Eastern European Reforms in Economic Relations." *Journal of Interamerican Studies and World Affairs* 33.2 (Summer 1991): 81–139.

Pérez, Louis A., Jr. *Cuba: Between Reform and Revolution.* Oxford: Oxford University Press, 1995.

———. *Cuba and the United States: Ties of Singular Intimacy.* 2nd ed. Athens: University of Georgia Press, 1997.

▼▼▼

Perez, Salvador E. Morales, and Laura del Alizal. *Dictadura, exilio e insurrección: Cuba en la perspective mexicana, 1952–1958.* Mexico City: Secretaría de Relaciones Exteriores, 1999.

Perry, Richard J. *From Time Immemorial: Indigenous Peoples and State Systems.* Austin: University of Texas Press, 1996.

Pichardo, Hortensia, ed. *Documentos para la historia de Cuba.* 4 vols. Havana: Instituto Cubano del Libro, 1969–1980.

Piña, Javier Rodríguez. *Guerra de castas: La venta de indios mayas a Cuba, 1848–1861.* Mexico City: Consejo Nacional para la Cultura y las Artes, 1990.

Preston, Julia, and Samuel Dillon. *Opening Mexico: The Making of a Democracy.* New York: Farrar, Straus and Giroux, 2004.

Pulido Llano, Gabriela. *Desde Cuba: Escenas de la diplomacia porfirista, 1887–1901.* Mexico City: Instituto Mora, 2000.

Purcell, Susan Kaufman. "The Changing Nature of U.S.-Mexican Relations." *Journal of Interamerican Studies and World Affairs* 39.1 (Spring 1997): 137–52.

Rabe, Stephen G. *The Most Dangerous Area in the World: John F. Kennedy Confronts Communist Revolution in Latin America.* Chapel Hill: University of North Carolina Press, 1999.

Ramírez, Blanca Torres. *Las relaciones cubano-sovieticas (1959–68).* Mexico City: Colegio de Mexico, 1970.

Reed, Nelson A. *The Caste War of Yucatán.* Revised edition. Stanford: Stanford University Press, 2001.

———. "Liderazgo de blancos y mestizos entre los Cruzoob." *Saastun: revista de cultura maya* 1 (April 1997): 63–88.

Riding, Alan. *Distant Neighbors: A Portrait of the Mexicans.* New York: Vintage, 1985.

Rojas, Rafael. "La política mexicana ante la guerra de independencia de Cuba." *Historia Mexicana* 45.4 (1996): 783–805.

Rolle, Andrew. *The Lost Cause: The Confederate Exodus to Mexico.* Norman: University of Oklahoma Press, 1992.

Ronning, C. Neale. "Intervention, International Law, and the Inter-American System." *Journal of Inter-American Studies* 3.2 (April 1961): 249–71.

Rugeley, Terry. "Tihosuco, 1800–1847: La sociedad Municipal y la genesis de la Guerra de Castas." *Saastun: Revista de Cultura Maya* 1 (April 1997): 19–62.

————. *Yucatán's Maya Peasantry and the Origins of the Caste War.* Austin: University of Texas Press, 1996.

Ruz Menéndez, Rodolfo. *La primera emigración cubana a Yucatán.* Mérida: Universidad Autónoma de Yucatán, 1969.

————. "Yucatán y Cuba: Dos pueblos hermanos." *Revista de la Biblioteca Nacional José Martí* 30.3 (1988): 97–108.

Ryan, Henry Butterfield. *The Fall of Che Guevara: A Store of Spies, Soldiers, and Diplomats.* Oxford: Oxford University Press, 1999.

Schmidt, Henry C. "The Mexican Foreign Debt and the Sexennial Transition from Lopez Portillo to de la Madrid." *Mexican Studies* 1.2 (Summer 1985): 227–54.

Schoultz, Lars. *Beneath the United States: A History of U.S. Policy toward Latin America.* Cambridge: Harvard University Press, 1998.

Schuler, Friedrich Engelbert. *Mexico between Hitler and Roosevelt: Mexican Foreign Relations in the Age of Lázaro Cárdenas, 1934–1940.* Albuquerque: University of New Mexico Press, 2000.

Seligson, Mitchell. "Agrarian Inequality and the Theory of Peasant Rebellion." *Latin American Research Review* 31.2. (1996): 140–57.

Shafer, Robert Jones, and Donald Mabry. *Neighbors—Mexico and the United States: Wetbacks and Oil.* Chicago: Nelson-Hall, 1981.

Smith, Arthur K. "Mexico and the Cuban Revolution: Foreign Policy-Making under President Adolfo López Mateos." Ph.D. diss. Cornell University, 1970.

Smith, Peter H. *Talons of the Eagle: Dynamics of U.S.-Latin American Relations.* Oxford: Oxford University Press, 1996.

Smith, Wayne S. *The Closest of Enemies: A Personal and Diplomatic Account of U.S.-Cuban Relations since 1957.* New York: W. W. Norton, 1987.

Sosa, Enrique Rodríguez. *Proyectos de invasion a Yucatán desde Cuba, 1828–1829.* Mérida and Havana: Coedición de la Universidad Autónoma de Yucatán y la Universidad de la Habana, 1996.

Sosa Rodríguez, Enrique, Carlos E. Bojórquez Urzaiz, and Luis Millet Cámara. *Habanero campechano.* Mérida: Univ autónoma de Yucatán, 1991.

Spencer, Daniela. *The Impossible Triangle: Mexico, Soviet Russia, and the United States in the 1920s.* Durham, NC: Duke University Press, 1999.

Sunshine, Catherine A. *The Caribbean: Survival, Struggle and Sovereignty.* 4th ed. Washington, D.C.: Ecumenical Program on Central America and the Caribbean, 1996.

Szumski, Bonnie, ed. *Latin America and U.S. Foreign Policy: Opposing Viewpoints.* St. Paul, MN: Greenwood Press, 1988.

Taibo, Paco Ignacio, II. *Guevara: Also Known as Che.* Trans. Martin Roberts. New York: St. Martin's, 1997.

Teichert, Pedro C. M. "Latin America and the Socio-Economic Impact of the Cuban Revolution." *Journal of Inter-American Studies* 4.1 (January 1962): 105–20.

Thomas, Alfred. "Latin American Nationalism and the United States." *Journal of Inter-American Studies* 7.1 (January 1965): 5–13.

Thomas, Hugh. *Cuba, or, The Pursuit of Freedom.* New York: Da Capo, 1998.

Velasco, Ana Covarrubias. "A Case for Mutual Nonintervention." *Cuban Studies* 26 (1996): 121–41.

———. "La política mexicana hacia Cuba durante el gobierno de Salinas de Gortari." *Foro Internacional* 34 (1994): 652–82.

Weitz, Richard. "Insurgency and Counterinsurgency in Latin America, 1960–1980." *Political Science Quarterly* 101 (1986): 397–413.

Wesson, Robert G. *U.S. Influence in Latin America in the 1980s.* New York: Praeger, 1982.

Westad, Odd Arne. *The Global Cold War: Third World Interventions and the Making of Our Times.* Cambridge: Cambridge University Press, 2005.

Wiarda, Howard. *American Foreign Policy toward Latin America in the 80s and 90s: Issues and Controversies from Reagan to Bush.* New York: New York University Press, 1992.

Whitfield, Stephen J. *The Culture of the Cold War.* Baltimore: Johns Hopkins University Press, 1996.

Young, Robert J. C. *Postcolonialism: An Historical Introduction.* Malden, MA: Blackwell, 2001.

REFERENCE

Atkins, G. Pope. *Handbook of Research on the International Relations of Latin America and the Caribbean.* Boulder, CO: Westview, 2001.

Microsoft Encarta Encyclopedia Standard. CD-ROM. Redmond, WA: Microsoft, 2001.

Ulrich's International Periodicals Directory. 18th ed. (1979–80) New York: R. R. Bowker, 1979.

United Nations. Statistical Office. *Statistical Yearbook.* 46th issue. New York: United Nations, 1999. 37–90.

USAID. "Latin America and the Caribbean Selected Economic and Social Data: Freedom Ratings." *UTLANIC,* 1998. http://lanic.utexas.edu/la/region/aid/aid98/democracy/tab1.html.

USAID. "Latin America and the Caribbean Selected Economic and Social Data: Total Fertility Rate." *UTLANIC,* 1998. http://lanic.utexas.edu/la/region/aid/aid98/health/tab4.html.

U.S. Central Intelligence Agency. *Cuba: Handbook of Trade Statistics.* Washington, D.C.: Directorate of the Central Intelligence Agency, 1998.

INDEX

Page numbers in italics indicate illustrations.

▼▼▼

▼▼▼

▼▼▼

▼▼▼

▼▼▼

▼▼▼